A Brand of Its Own

Since the Calgary Exhibition and Stampede has been the Stampede, this has been its trademark. Edward Borein, the famous American artist, gave the sketch to Guy Weadick, who added "I see U" and used it widely in early Stampede advertising and promotional material.

A Brand of Its Own

THE 100 YEAR HISTORY
OF THE CALGARY EXHIBITION
AND STAMPEDE

James H Gray

Western Producer Prairie Books
Saskatoon, Saskatchewan

Copyright © 1985 James H. Gray
Western Producer Prairie Books
Saskatoon, Saskatchewan

Book Design by Warren Clark, GDL
Cover photograph courtesy of the
Calgary Exhibition and Stampede – Morrison Photo

Printed and bound in Canada by
Modern Press
Saskatoon, Saskatchewan

The publisher acknowledges the support received
for this publication from the Canada Council.

Western Producer Prairie Books publications
are produced and manufactured in the middle of
western Canada by a unique publishing venture owned
by a group of prairie farmers who are members of Saskatchewan
Wheat Pool. From the first book in 1954, a reprint of a serial
originally carried in the weekly newspaper, *The Western Producer*,
to the book before you now, the tradition of
providing enjoyable and informative reading
for all Canadians is continued.

Canadian Cataloguing in Publication Data

Gray, James H., 1906–
    A brand of its own

Includes index.
ISBN 0-88833-163-0

1. Calgary Stampede – History. I. Title.
GV1834.56.C32C3 1985   791'.8   C85-091292–X

The basic purpose of the Calgary Exhibition and Stampede is to preserve and enhance the agricultural and historical legacy of Alberta and to fulfill appropriate aspects of the agricultural, trade, entertainment, sports, recreational, and educational needs of Calgary and southern Alberta, in particular, and where appropriate, those of Alberta and western Canada.

Contents

Foreword

Originally the Big Four—George Lane, A. E. Cross, Pat Burns, and Archie McLean—thought one of the best reasons for having the stampede would be to teach the younger generation the history of ranching, which they were afraid would be forgotten and disappear from Alberta. Of course, as we all know, ranching certainly has not disappeared or been forgotten, but has been a major factor in the development of agriculture in Alberta. It would have greatly pleased the Big Four to know one of their goals has been accomplished.

This book, which was written by James Gray with the assistance of a great many people, including the members of the Historical Committee of the Calgary Exhibition and Stampede, and the support of the Historical Resources Grant Program of Alberta Culture, would also make the Big Four very happy because it provides a true historical account of the Stampede's important role in the development of Alberta. The Calgary Exhibition and Stampede has provided a show place for every aspect of farming-ranching activity. In the process it has seen, and actively promoted, substantial improvements in the quality of everything the farms and ranches produce. The hundred years of the Calgary Exhibition and Stampede have seen momentous changes take place in the province of Alberta as well as within the ranching and farming community. I can personally recommend this book to anyone who is interested in the history of Alberta and the preservation of our cultural heritage.

J. B. CROSS

CHAPTER 1

"Westward the course of empire..."

I t began life, this Calgary Exhibition and Stampede, as a gleam in the eye of a newspaper editor in a tent-village on the banks of the Bow River on August 6, 1884. But, alas, it would not reach fruition for another two years. Yet that gleam reflected the almost ecstatic enthusiasm of the editor, Thomas Broden, for the quality of the grain crop then beginning to ripen in the fields around Calgary. The oat crop in Major James Walker's field reached a height of five feet, three inches. John Glenn had been in town showing around handfuls of grain which he claimed were the finest he had ever seen. Sam Livingstone had a head of wheat with two hundred grains on it.

What Calgary needed most, the Calgary *Herald* said, was to get busy and organize an exhibition which would demonstrate to all those eastern doubters that this was, indeed, superb agricultural country. By the summer of 1884 the consensus east of Manitoba was that the Northwest was a false dawn that had burned but briefly and was best filed and forgotten. The collapse of the Manitoba land boom of 1883 cost the Ontario and Quebec land speculators dearly. At its peak in 1882 Portage Avenue lots in Winnipeg were selling above the asking price for lots in the Chicago loop. But when the Red River flood of 1883 buried the real estate boom under three feet of Red River silt, no easterner wanted western property as a gift. That was particularly true of many Ontario home-steaders who had come west during the previous decade and experienced crop failure after crop failure before returning to Ontario to bad-mouth the new country.

But the crop then ripening in the Calgary area, the Calgary *Herald* contended, could be turned into the tinder which would reignite the flame of eastern interest in the true potential of western agriculture. The thing to do, the *Herald* suggested, was first to get an exhibition organized. That would give the farmers of the area a chance to compare their own production with the best their neighbors had grown. Then the prize exhibits of grain and vegetables could be loaded into an express car and sent on a tour of the farming districts of Ontario. Once the easterners saw what was possible

The special car the CPR sent through eastern Canada to publicize prairie agriculture in the fall of 1884. *Courtesy of CPR.*

in Alberta, there would be renewed interest in moving to the West.

The ironic twist was that this was happening in the crudest kind of tent-town, a shack village of perhaps four to five hundred people, in the midst of a farming community that might have contained a hundred homesteading farmers between the Red Deer and the Highwood rivers. In May 1884 Lieutenant-Governor Dewdney had written to Major James Walker in Calgary to suggest he conduct a census of the area to see if a thousand adults with a year's residence could be located. If so, the area would be allowed to elect a member to the Territorial Council.

At a public meeting called to discuss the letter, James Lougheed urged that the census be postponed because he was convinced it would not yet be possible to locate a thousand adults with a year's residence. However, he was overruled, the count was done, the thousand were found, and a member, J. D. Geddes, was elected to represent the Calgary area on the council.

It was a pretty skimpy population to underpin a full-fledged agricultural exhibition. Nevertheless, the Calgary and District Agricultural Society was established and steps were taken to organize a fall fair.

A preliminary survey, however, convinced the executive of the new association that a fair was not practical in 1884. But the members did come up with an idea that was. Why not, they asked, get the Canadian Pacific Railway to provide them with an express car in which they could set up an exhibit of the best grain and produce grown between the Red Deer and Highwood and send it on a tour of eastern Canada? The CPR not only bought the idea, but used part of the car for an exhibit of its own of the coal, timber, and other resources found adjacent to its right of way. To fill the balance of the car it used produce from other areas of the West.

The Calgarians formed themselves into a committee to prepare some leaflets for the junket extolling the virtues of the country.

Their secretary, J. G. Fitzgerald, who accompanied the car, could distribute the pamphlets en route to prospective settlers. There was scarcely a market town between London and Halifax that did not become a one-day host to that exhibition car during the fall and winter of 1884–85. The eastern farmers were certainly impressed by the massive sheaves of wheat and oats and the king-sized vegetables in infinite variety. Indeed, there were eastern farmers who were unwilling to believe their eyes when their eyes rested on stalks of wheat six feet long. They embarked on minute examinations to try to locate where the wily westerners had spliced the two stalks together to fool the gullible easterners. Even when no such splices could be located, they still doubted that the stalks were real.

As a result of the western promotion tour, there is little doubt that the spring and summer of 1885 would have seen a renewal of interest in western settlement, except for the Northwest Rebellion. Yet the southern Albertans were able to turn even that unfortunate event to their advantage. The farmers between the Bow and Oldman Rivers got their crops in very early that year following a mild and open winter. So their crops were growing while the farmers were making money hauling supplies to the forces fighting the rebellion. Then the rebellion was over in time for them to get back to their farms, get their crops off and their grain threshed. The crop was again good in 1885 and again the exhibition car was sent on its tour of eastern Canada. Indeed from 1884 onward such exhibits were made an integral part of the Canadian Pacific Railway's promotional campaigns in the United Kingdom and the United States, as well as for eastern Canada in the 1890s.

During the gestation period of 1884–85, when frontier Calgary was pregnant with the exhibition idea, an accident happened which practically assured the success of the project in its neonatal period. A federal deputy minister fell off a horse and broke his collarbone.

The deputy minister was A. M. Burgess. The Federal Department of Agriculture had established several experimental farms in the West and in 1884 Mr. Burgess came west on an inspection tour of the farms. On one located on Fish Creek southwest of the Calgary settlement, Mr. Burgess's accident happened. Fortunately for Mr. Burgess, and for Calgary, it happened just before Major Walker happened by driving a farm wagon. A former Mounted Police inspector and Cochrane ranch manager, Walker had been one of the moving spirits in the exhibition movement. He moved Burgess into his home where the deputy minister passed his recuperative period. In that interval Walker plied Burgess with arguments for Ottawa to support the Calgary Exhibition idea. When Burgess was again mobile, Walker took him on an inspection tour of the ninety-four-acre parcel of Crown land that hugged the Elbow River south of the town and which he said would make ideal exhibition grounds. Burgess was impressed, so much so that when he left Calgary to return to Ottawa he promised to support the sale of the land to the Calgary Exhibition once that organization had achieved a viable existence.

If ever there was an organization that was hell-bent on running before it had learned to crawl, it must surely have been the exhibition project of the Calgary Agricultural Society. And yet, unbeknownst to any of its zealous supporters, the ground was already prepared, the seeds planted for the creation of just the kind of special environment in which the Calgary Stampede idea could later put down permanent roots and bloom triumphantly. That process arose from the chance coming together of economic and social tides flowing through and out of the United Kingdom, eastern Canada, and the United States in the 1880s.

As the flow of settlement westward across the United States resumed after the Civil War, and the buffalo and the Indians were cleared from the Great Plains, the movement of the vast herds of cattle off the Texas ranges was accelerated. While hundreds of thousands of range cattle were herded to the railheads in Kansas and Missouri, tens of thousands of other cattle were driven northward to the still open ranges of the Dakotas, Montana, and Wyoming and up to and across the forty-ninth parallel.

The British Empire, the empire on which

the sun never set, was then at its zenith. The enterprising British were searching the world for opportunities of profitable investment, found them in the gold fields of South Africa, the steel mills of Pennsylvania, in railways and coal mines in Canada, and in the cattle ranches of Texas, Australia, and the Northwest Territories.

While the attitudes toward settlement of the West might have fluctuated between enthusiasm and aversion on the part of the eastern Canadian farmers, the attitude of eastern Canadian financial interests toward investment possibilities in the West remained fairly consistently favorable.

Within five years of the arrival of the North West Mounted Police at what would become Fort Calgary, all these influences, the British, the Canadian, and the American, came together on the Alberta frontier. The catalyst that brought them together was the decision of the federal government in 1881 to open the West to cattle ranching as well as homesteading. It enacted regulations which would enable cattle ranchers to lease up to 100,000 acres of land for a rental of one cent per acre per year. The term of the lease was twenty-one years and it required that within three years the lessees would stock their leases with one animal per ten acres. This was later changed to twenty acres when it was discovered that the original rule led to serious overgrazing in the shortgrass country.

Whether the Canadians or the Americans were first to recognize the cattle-ranching potential of the foothills can be argued either way. Certainly, it was the cattle drive by the American herders in 1876, when the stock for the Indians was imported, that brought ranching as a possible way of life to the attention of the Mounties. The Indian agency cattle were driven from the Missouri River to Fort Macleod by a platoon of American cowboys whose cattle herding experiences dated back to the great drives that began at the Rio Grande. They were but the vanguard of a small army of Americans who would drive tens of thousands of other cattle across the forty-ninth parallel over the next decade. Many of them would so like what they saw of the country that they would return to the States to bring back

cattle with which to start their own ranching enterprises.

As soon as their term of enlistment was complete many of the Mounties left the force to get started in the cattle business. Some did not wait for their discharge and bought their way out or hired a substitute to replace them so they could get back to civilian life. One such Mountie, Sergeant Robert Whitney, lacking either winter feed or barns, was forced to turn his herd loose on the Prairies for the winter while he was occupied with police work. The consensus of his friends was that if the Indians did not butcher his cattle for food they would wander away with the buffalo and be lost forever. But when the spring came and Whitney went looking for his cattle he found them alive and thriving within two days' ride of where he left them.

Inadvertently Whitney had proved that, given food and water, cattle tended to stay put and not wander very far afield. The need to confine cattle, taken as axiomatic by eastern farmers, was demonstrably unnecessary. After Whitney's cattle had survived the Indians, the buffalo, and the storms of winter without human assistance, branding the cattle and turning them loose on the open range became standard practice in the ranching country.

Perhaps the biggest plus of all for the Canadian Northwest was the visit in 1881 of the Marquis of Lorne, Queen Victoria's son-in-law, the current governor-general and the highest placed aristocrat Canada would ever have as a tub-thumping propagandist. Annoyed by the unfavorable publicity Canada was getting in the British press, Lorne invited a bevy of British journalists to accompany him on a trip through the West in the summer of 1881.

It was the West at its best, the West Palliser had never seen in his famous journey, hence his thumbs-down report. The winter snows and spring rains had covered the area in an ocean of grass. The country surpassed even Lord Lorne's expectations and that was all reflected in the enthusiastic copy that the British journalists sent back to their papers. When he returned to England, Lord Lorne became a peripatetic cheering section for Canada, and particularly for the western plains and foothills. After the reports of the British journalists and Lord Lorne's enthusiastic endorsements, it was small wonder that the interest of the British aristocracy and landed gentry was aroused in the hinterlands of Alberta to a point where they took an eager hand in the settlement of the region.

The interest-clincher for the British, and for wealthy Canadians, was the generosity of the new Canadian Government leasing regulations. It was a license to print money! Gazetteers were cracked open and pored over and passages booked and bank drafts arranged.

This great and sudden awakening of interest came at a time when developments in the United States were particularly propitious for the birth of a ranching industry in Alberta. The reign of the cowboy on the great plains of the United States was coming to a close. The influx of the wheat farmers had closed off the range and the demand for cowboying skills shrank with the open range. Thus, when agents for Canadian ranches turned up in the neighboring state of Montana to buy their foundation herds, they found reservoirs of skilled labor able and willing to join their enterprises.

More important however was another development that had been paralleling the Texas cattle boom on the other side of the mountains. The Texas longhorn had two things going for it: it could survive the worst weather nature could provide and it could live with any dietary deficiency. It was the easiest keeper known to man and it was the sorriest near-nothing excuse for a beef animal extant. But the cattle being raised in eastern Oregon, Washington, and Idaho were mainly developed from crossbreeding imported Hereford, Shorthorn, and Durham stock. These hybrids combined ruggedness with close conformity to the best British beef standards. By the 1880s these so-called "western" cattle were being driven eastward through the mountain passes to supplant the longhorns. These were the cattle which the pioneer ranchers of Alberta used to stock their new spreads, a factor which would ultimately enhance Alberta beef's acceptance in the eastern Canadian and British markets.

Among the first British investors to make the Canadian commitment was Walter F. C. Gordon-Cummings who es-

tablished a huge horse ranch west of Okotoks with the idea of raising hunters for the famous Quorn fox hunt in Leicestershire. Naturally he named his spread the Quorn Ranch. Major General T. B. Strange set up the Military Colonization Company to locate horse ranches along the Bow River with the objective of furnishing remounts for the British army. Sir John Pepys Lister-Kaye was responsible for a whole string of ranching ventures in Saskatchewan and Alberta. Lord Lathom and A. Stavely Hall, MP, joined forces to build, west of Stavely, the Oxley Ranch, named for Hall's estate in England. Lord Walrond-Walrond, Lord Boyle, the Marquis of Queensbury, Lord Castletown, and Sir Francis de Winton all played major parts in ranching enterprises in southern Alberta.

There were also hundreds of British public school graduates who would migrate singly and in groups to the Prairies to serve apprenticeships on the farms and ranches preparatory to embarking on

Sir John Lister-Kaye (pictured on his Namaka ranch in 1884) established a whole string of ranches between Regina and the Rockies in the 1880s. *Courtesy of Glenbow Archives, Calgary, Alberta.*

farming and ranching careers of their own. Some came directly to the West after completion of the CPR. Some were conned into signing on as "apprentice farming students" with sharp-witted Ontario farmers who were interested only in exploiting this cheap labor.

Not many duplicated the itinerary of Alfred E. Cross. Like the sons of many other affluent Canadians he was sent off to England to one of its public schools for his education. On his return he enrolled at the Ontario Agricultural College at Guelph before taking a post-graduate course at the Montreal Veterinary College and venturing onto the Alberta frontier. There he wrote one of the most successful chapters in Alberta business history.

By no means prepared to be outdone or elbowed aside on their own turf, eastern Canadians were even faster off the mark than the British in the race to acquire western ranching leases. One of the fastest was Senator M. H. Cochrane, of Compton, Quebec, who combined politics with purebred cattle raising. He made it to the Northwest almost before the ink was dry on the new regulations and selected a 100,000-acre spread in the big hill country west of Calgary. He got Inspector James Walker released from the Mounted Police to run the ranch and ordered three thousand head of cattle from Montana to stock the place.

The Cochrane-Walker operation turned into the kind of disaster that might have set the whole ranching industry back a couple of decades. The herd was driven north at so fast a pace that the animals lost weight and arrived at the ranch in very poor condition. As a result, heavy losses were suffered during their first winter in Canada. When the second winter was also climatically severe, Cochrane moved most of his herd to Fort Macleod and hired a new ranch manager. He ran into weather trouble there too while the winter at Cochrane was the mildest in years. It was not until Cochrane turned the original ranch into a sheep operation that his investments began to pay dividends.

Sir Hugh Allan had better luck. He sent Fred Stimson, his ranch manager, into the Idaho-Columbia basin country where he located a herd of Durham and Hereford crossbreeds. When the weather turned sour these whitefaces from Idaho-Oregon outrustled and outtoughed everything in sight.

But whether British or Canadian, the original ranching pioneers committed themselves to the improvement of the breed, to the upgrading of their herds once they had their ranches in operation. Indeed, Sir Hugh Allan demonstrated such a desire even before he had the Bar U in operation. On his way west to get started, Fred Stimson stopped off in Chicago and bought a carload of purebred Aberdeen Angus heifers and bulls as the foundation of his breeding stock. And while the Quorn Ranch herd was still being built up with American imports, Gordon-Cummings was scouring the farms of the English-Scottish borderland for the best polled Angus he could find for his Alberta ranch. On one occasion he wound up with a shipment of ninety-four heifers and six bulls for the Quorn.

Complementing the dedication to the improvement of the quality of livestock—cattle, horses, dogs, swine, sheep, and poultry—which the British and Canadians brought to the Alberta frontier, the Americans brought unmatched endurance and special skills in animal management. And they shared with the Canadians from Ontario and Quebec an acquired characteristic, an indomitable will not only to survive but to survive and prosper in what was frequently an insufferably capricious environment—climatically, economically, and socially.

The American drovers like Tom Lynch, John Ware, George Lane, Herb Miller, and the hundreds of others who followed them brought special skills of open range cattle herding to Alberta, skills which enabled them to rope, bridle, saddle, and ride their quick and sure-footed but fractious, stubborn, and almost intractable horses. It was not uncommon for them to have to win a bucking horse contest at dawn before they could begin their day's work. And to do it again midway through the day when they changed to fresh horses. Theirs was a way of life that entailed sleeping in the clothes they wore, with the cattle they herded and the horses they rode. With taken-for-granted physical strength and endurance,

they accommodated themselves to the sudden climatic changes of the country as easily as did their cows and horses.

Frequently illiterate, often uncouth, given to riotous behavior away from their animals, they nevertheless brought vitally needed skills to the ranching industry. They brought, as well, pride in their skills, and eyes which recognized and appreciated skills that exceeded their own when they encountered them. Ten years after Calgary's incorporation as a town in 1884, with its electric lights, water and sewer systems, and plank sidewalks, Calgary was still frequently discombobulated by the exuberance of cowboys on the loose.

The qualities which the British settlers brought to the frontier were frequently the opposite of the qualities of the Americans. The British were educated, cultured, dif-fident, restrained in their enthusiasms. They were so dedicated to games that they seemed prepared always to drop whatever they were doing for fun or a frolic. If their families had maintained hunting boxes on the moors of Yorkshire, they brought their guns and hunting dogs to the sloughs of Alberta and wrote glowing reports home of the abundance of wild game. Cricket was their sport and they kept it at the top of Alberta pastime popularity until well into the twentieth century. They thought nothing of taking a week off, in the summer of 1884, for example, to stage a cricket match between Calgary and Fort Macleod teams. That meant a three-day journey from

As an outpost of empire, southern Alberta beckoned just as strongly to British aristocracy as did South Africa, the Australian outback, or the road to Mandalay. And they mounted coyote hunts with English hounds (top) and played polo (left column, from left: Montague Baker, Stanley Pinhorn, E. Wilmot, A. E. Browning) with equal enthusiasm. The group in the right column includes Lady Adele and Sir Thomas Cochrane (back row) and Lord Norbury and the Duke and Duchess of Somerset. The Duchess, under the pen-name of Susan Margaret St. Maur, became the author of the widely read, in England, *Impressions of a Tenderfoot* in the 1890s. *Courtesy of Glenbow Archives, Calgary, Alberta.*

The fanciest ranch house in the Calgary area was undoubtedly Gilbert Goddard's architect-designed home on the Bow River Horse Ranch in 1892 (top). It contrasts with the Fred Stimson home on the Bar U. *Courtesy of Glenbow Archives, Calgary, Alberta.*

Calgary to the southern settlement, two days for the match, and three days for the return journey.

Significantly, when the Calgary and District Agricultural Society acquired title to its Victoria Park property, one of its first priorities was to develop the centerfield of the racetrack as a cricket pitch. It was here that the "English" frequently challenged "the rest" or the "all-comers" to matches which the English always won.

Like the British settlers who carried the white man's burden to darkest Africa, the British who came to Alberta did so with a determination to remake it into replicas of rural England. Out on the open plains the homesteaders would soon be making do with sod houses, but from the beginning the ranch homes of Alberta were bastions of gracious living in which the inhabitants frequently dressed for dinner, turned up at community dances in formal attire, and surveyed their world through beribboned monacles. They brought libraries of British books to their ranch homes, imported pianos and hand crafted furniture, along with the finest English china tea things. Accoutred in English jodhpurs, with English saddles on hunters imported from England, they rode to English hounds in pursuit of native Canadian coyotes. Their formal hunt clubs spread westward from Winnipeg to Cannington Manor to Calgary hard on the heels of settlement. They had their Calgary Turf Club in operation before the Exhibition was going and a polo club followed quickly. The first horse to be advertised at stud in the Northwest Territories was an imported English hackney.

The immediate result of all this was that while Calgarians were struggling to get their annual exhibition show on the road, the cattle population of Alberta was zooming upwards. Alexander Begg, for example, estimated that by 1884 there were seventy-five thousand head on the ranges abutting the Bow River, and there were many thousands more entering all the time to populate the country between the Cypress Hills, Fort Macleod, and Calgary.

By 1886 and the completion of the Canadian Pacific, Calgary's population had passed the two-thousand mark and that spring the drive to establish the Exhibition was renewed with greater vigor. Major Walker was elected president of the Agricultural Society and vice-presidents were elected to represent Red Deer, Sheep Creek, and High River farmers. While the vice-presidents were rounding up support for the project among their farmers, the Calgary members embarked on a campaign to raise money for the prize list. While one group was soliciting donations from local businessmen, J. D. Geddes was to approach the Territorial Government for a substantial donation. Because of straitened finances, the council could only afford two hundred dollars. Nevertheless by the time the fair dates were set—October 19 and 20—the committees had raised nine hundred dollars for the prize list. Arrangements were made to house all the commercial, handicraft, and vegetable exhibits in the Star skating rink and judging rings for the animals were set up in the adjoining vacant lots.

The decision to get on with the organization of an exhibition was particularly gratifying to the Calgary *Herald* which had been editorially supporting the project since it had first suggested it in 1884. Its editorial expression of this satisfaction on June 19, 1886 might well have been adopted as the prospectus, the credo, which would motivate future boards of directors at the Calgary Exhibition and Stampede. It read:

> ...Apart from the particular advantages of an agricultural fair, any large gathering of settlers in our town for these innocent and festive purposes is to be encouraged. Such assemblies draw our citizens together, farmers, ranchers, trades people and professional men get better acquainted and a harmless vent is given to our Western push and energy, which otherwise might take a less useful direction. The feeling of sodality is one which requires to be fostered in a new community drawn together from all parts of the civilized world. One of the great tasks before us is to make a united Alberta out of all the Canadians, English, Scots, Irish, and Americans who have picked out this fair land for their home. And nothing will tend to further this work so much as an occasional gathering of our citizens together for such purposes as we have indicated.

That the original directors, and those who came after, were profoundly convinced of the worth of the project can be seen from the fact that they stuck with it for the rest of their lives over spans of thirty and forty years. The form to which boards of directors would conform through the years was also set at the very beginning. In both 1884 and 1886 the personnel of the boards was an amiable amalgam of town businessmen, farmers, and ranchers.

In later years the phrase cow town was frequently used to describe Calgary. The use had some legitimacy, but from the very beginning Calgary was first and foremost a horse town. George Murdock, the town's first mayor, noted in his diary that match races were an almost daily event with the streets used as race tracks. As years passed and the population grew, the *Herald* gave voice to complaints about the speed at which horses were being driven and ridden through the streets.

Calgary was both the destination and the jumping off place for the horse traders. William Roper Hull drove a herd of fifteen hundred horses from the British Columbia interior to Calgary through the State of

Washington and the Crowsnest Pass. George Lane built the Bar U into the biggest Percheron horse breeding establishment in the world.

Calgary's love affair with the horse was recognized with the prize list of the first Exhibition. It was dominated by the horse classes. The top prize money of the Exhibition went to the horses: twenty dollars for the first prize thoroughbred stallion and fifteen dollars for the first prize thoroughbred mare. Eleven classes were offered for roadsters—trotters and pacers—and there were five classes for heavy horses. All classes offered first and second prizes. There was a total of ten cattle classes, of which four were for the Durham breed. There were four classes of sheep, three pigs, seven poultry, and seven grain. Prizes were also offered for all kinds of vegetables, flowers, and dairy products. The biggest entry list of all was for "ladies work" which included everything from painting on silk and china to embroidery, plain and fancy knitting, and rag mats.

The less said about the first Calgary Exhibition the better. A blizzard blew up the day before it opened and blocked many of the outlying trails. The implement dealers were sold out of equipment and had nothing to exhibit. The prize list attracted no sheep or pigs; the cattle classes were poorly supported and only the horse classes and ladies' work attracted respectable entries. Nevertheless, the fair attracted an attendance of five hundred over the two days and it concluded with a fall supper and dance that encouraged its sponsors to plan for a bigger and better Exhibition the following year.

It was a following year that would take all their collective optimism to get through. Three weeks after the 1886 Exhibition a disastrous fire destroyed half the Calgary business section. November signalled the onset of a winter that introduced the entire agricultural community to the realities of Alberta climate. For five years the region had enjoyed a stretch of mild winters, showery springs, and moderate summer temperatures. The winter of 1886-87 set in with a vengeance in mid-November. The temperature dropped to thirty below zero before Christmas and stayed there for days on end. Not only that, but the wind blew,

the snow fell so deeply that train traffic was disrupted, and fuel shortages developed everywhere. When spring came at last, the countryside, literally, was littered with the corpses of the animals that had died during the winter. When the losses were eventually totted up, some ranches lost twenty percent of their herd to the storms.

Yet even out of such a disastrous winter some dividends were collected. It demonstrated for all time, to the ranching industry, that summer was no time for traipsing around to cricket matches and horse racing. It had to be a time for putting up hay with which to bring the herds through winter blizzards. It also demonstrated that where ranchers ran their horses with their cattle that the horses helped the cattle battle the storms. Horses pawed the ground to get at the grass beneath the snow, and in the process broke tracks for the cattle through drifts so they could nibble at the grass the pawing uncovered. The experience of 1886-87 gave a pronounced boost to the horse industry of Alberta for it demonstrated that horses could fend for themselves even in the toughest of winters, and that applied to Shetland ponies, shires, and thoroughbreds as well as the Indians' mustangs.

The severe winter was followed by a summer of searing heat and it was the farmers' turn to suffer. Nevertheless, neither cold nor heat diminished the enthusiasm of the Calgarians for their Exhibition and plans were made for an "even bigger and better" Exhibition in 1887. It was neither bigger nor better, but it was held, again combining facilities of the skating rink and the adjacent vacant lots.

In addition, pressure was stepped up to get the Ottawa government to donate the ninety-four acres of land Major Walker had shown A. M. Burgess three years before. These negotiations dragged interminably, and were not completed successfully until after the 1888 Exhibition, when the land was sold to the Agricultural Association for $2.50 an acre. With an eye on the seemingly irresistible urge on the part of Calgarians to convert all land in sight into building lots, Ottawa wisely placed this caveat on the deed to the land: It was never to be subdivided or sold and if any attempt was ever made to do that the federal authority could instantly repossess the entire acreage.

The board of the society did not even wait for the deed to be registered, in 1889, to mortgage the property for three thousand dollars with which they began the improvements. In short order it erected a race track, put in cattle sheds, and erected an exhibition building. From 1889 onwards its exhibitions were held on its own premises which it had christened Victoria Park.

The years that followed the acquisition of the grounds were grim ones for western Canada. A series of hot dry summers marked a steady decline in farm prices. Red Fyfe wheat, introduced at the onset of the decade, proved to be such a prolific producer that a glut developed and the price fell from over a dollar a bushel to under fifty cents. Meantime land was still open for settlement in the Dakotas and Montana, and as a result the appeal of western Canada went largely unheeded by British and European immigrants. Calgary's growth, which had seen its population doubling each year, reaching close to four thousand, slowed after 1890 to near standstill.

In the countryside animosity was intensifying between the homesteaders and the ranchers. The granting of the huge grazing leases to the ranchers was now seen as a positive retardant to settlement. Many of the grazing leases took in lands on which squatters and homesteaders had settled. Two-way shouting matches developed between the squatters and the ranchers over who had illegally branded whose calves. Complicating the situation was the fact that there was endless delay by the federal government in granting titles to the land the homesteaders had proved up. Sam Livingstone and John Glenn, two of Calgary's earliest settlers and prominent farmers, were both active in agitations on the land titles questions. The Cochrane ranch, which straddled the Bow River, was a particularly contentious area where the rights of the farmers and the ranchers collided. Eventually the ranch agreed to surrender two townships of its lease in return for confirmation of the balance as grazing land.

The feud between cattlemen and sheepmen also had its place in early Alberta history. The southern ranchers wanted sheep banned from the range land. The Calgary area settlers wanted free entry of sheep. A compromise was eventually reached that permitted sheep raising north of the Highwood River and cattle only south of the stream.

All these issues divided the community from which the Exhibition expected to draw its support. The Calgary boosters probably overestimated the enthusiasm which the farmers would develop for twenty-mile round trips just to look at wheat, oats, and barley sheaves some other farmers had grown. In any event, for the first decade of its existence the Exhibition never attracted entries that were numerically satisfactory to its supporters. Nevertheless, the entry lists did indicate the progress that agriculture was making in the Calgary area.

In 1890 the Exhibition was scheduled for October 8 and 9. The day before it was to open, the town was hit with so massive a rainstorm that the show was postponed until the tenth and eleventh. Many of the roads were still impassable and many of the farmers failed to bring in the exhibits they had entered. However, there was a good cattle show and that year there were classes for four breeds for the first time—Angus, Hereford, Shorthorn, and Holsteins. The horse classes were also judged to be excellent.

The following year the weather was good and there was little for anybody to complain about the Exhibition. The thirty classes for horses were well filled, along with fifteen cattle classes and five each for sheep and swine. The grain samples were both numerous and of the highest quality yet seen in the Territories. Entries came from as far away as Red Deer, Namaka, and Balgonie. In 1891 there were Indian races, cowboy races, gentlemen's driving classes, and pony races. Thereafter, horse racing was an integral part of the Exhibition. The next year bicycle racing was added to the program.

Not only the increase in classes of cattle, horses, and poultry charted the evolution of Alberta agriculture. Increased entries in butter and cheese exhibits marked the growth in importance of the dairy industry. Increased swine and sheep entries signalled the development of pork and wool as important revenue producers for the farmers.

Following the completion of the C and E Railway to Edmonton and Fort Macleod, Calgary also became the distribution center for western Alberta. Contractors were at work erecting imposing sandstone offices for the chartered banks; James Lougheed was planning a whole string of downtown business blocks. The citizens were making plans to transform their town into a city, but somehow while the town boomed with construction its population growth came to a full stop, and stayed there.

It was the prolonged agricultural depression that did the Calgary and District Agricultural Society in. That and the cli-

By the middle of the 1890s the ranches of southern Alberta were abundantly stocked with livestock — cattle on the Burns Bow Valley Ranch, the brood mare herd on the Quorn Ranch, as well as sheep on the Cochrane Ranch. *Courtesy of Glenbow Archives, Calgary, Alberta.*

mate. The crop of 1895 in the Calgary area was, in August, something to make a farmer's eyes dance with joy. Just about everybody for miles around had a bumper crop ripening in the fields. In the first week of September the country was hit with a two-day combination sleet and snow storm with killing frost. It drove all thought of the fall Exhibition from the minds of the district farmers as they devoted the rest of the fall to herculean struggles to salvage something from their crops. Some were able to thresh some tough wheat and barley. Others cut what they could for green feed for their cattle. Though it survived in legal form, that was the end of

the Calgary and District Society as an Exhibition sponsor.

Victoria Park became mainly a pasture for the dairy cows kept by Calgarians and a sometimes polo field and sometimes cricket pitch. But the Exhibition idea did not die. It was kept alive by the residents of Fish Creek, High River, Davisburg, and Innisfail areas. Each year, came the first week of October, and the farm communities picked a convenient spot and staged their own outdoor exhibitions individually. Usually a good time was had by all, the class of entries judged much improved, but the numbers of entries was always disappointing.

CHAPTER 2

Up from the Ashes

T he worldly hopes the pioneer rushers-in to Calgary set their hearts upon in the 1890s did not exactly turn to ashes, but neither did they burst in the heart-warming flame of a boom-time economy. Indeed, the years that followed upon the completion of the CPR must have seemed more to resemble an anticlimax than any continent-shaking transformation. True, the southern Alberta ranches were filling up with cattle and the Calgary stockyards had become the shipping point for thousands of the critters a month to the far-off markets of the United Kingdom. The railway branch lines were complete from Calgary north to Strathcona-Edmonton and south to Fort Macleod. As a result, almost inadvertently, Calgary became the distribution center for both goods and services for all Alberta.

But, still, somehow or other, the people refused to come—either to Calgary or to the envisioned grain lands that stretched endlessly out from its eastern border. Perhaps it was because doubt was beginning to surface that these lands could grow wheat that could compare in either quality or quantity with that grown farther north. Or, perhaps it was because there was little incentive to go farming when wheat was bringing less than fifty cents a bushel and market steers twenty dollars or less. Or perhaps it was the worldwide depression and recurring financial crises that kept Calgary's growth to a minimum. But, if the population of the town had ceilinged out at

around four thousand, it was also firmly bottomed out at that level. At no time did the city exhibit any signs of serious population decline. The city simply had too many entrepreneurs around who were prepared to look adversity in the eye and toss another poke into the pot.

Pat Burns, his new meat-packing plant on a round-the-clock schedule, was frantically expanding both the plant and the ranch that fed it. Roper Hull was energetically pouring his butcher business and ranching profits into the development of ever newer and fancier limestone buildings on Stephen Avenue, in friendly rivalry with James Lougheed to see who would ultimately become Calgary's biggest real estate tycoon and taxpayer. A. E. Cross was freshly back from Montreal to add the Territories' first brewery to his ranching enterprises. William Sherman had built the biggest roller rink in the Territories and was becoming self-transformed into the city's theatrical impresario. R. B. Bennett, sharing a shingle with Senator James Lougheed in the practice of law, was quickly becoming a one-man investment trust. James Reilly and H. A. Perley operated two of the most imposing sandstone hotels to be found anywhere between Dallas, Texas and Dawson City, Yukon.

Sir John A. Macdonald had gone to what rewards awaited him and in his wake in Ottawa the Conservative politicians were playing musical chairs as administration followed administration. Then, in 1896, the Liberals, under Sir Wilfrid Laurier, swept into office with a newly energized ministry that would forever change the face of southern Alberta and the prairie West. Sir Clifford Sifton, the Minister of the Interior, embarked on a crusade to sell the West to the people of western Europe and eastern Europe, but most of all to the United States. As years passed, people of eastern Europe tended to follow the bordering parkland of the near north to Edmonton and beyond. The people who poured in from the United States tended to fill up the open plains between Estevan and Calgary-Red Deer.

By 1898 the first fruits began to appear of the monster immigration advertising campaign launched jointly by the government and the railways of the United States. The advance guards of the armies of the American land agents who would soon swamp Calgary had done their preliminary skirmishing. American editors were being junketed in special cars to see for themselves what a wonderful country awaited their compatriots north of the border. They went home to write glowing accounts of what they had seen. When the farmers themselves came north from Minnesota, the Dakotas, Nebraska, Kansas, and Missouri, sometimes in small groups, sometimes in train-sized excursions, they found the country at its absolute best and the atmosphere once more became redolent with the spirit of western optimism.

Then, for Calgary, in April 1898, came the cherry on the sundae. The CPR announced that it had decided to make Calgary a divisional point and to locate its main western repair shops and roundhouse in Calgary. This was the announcement civic Calgary had been thirsting after for more than a decade. That the offer was conditional upon the infant city forking over twenty-five thousand dollars to finance the project mattered not at all. A mere bagatelle! The height of the euphoria that the announcement triggered can be illustrated by a single fact: when the proposal went to a vote of the ratepayers it was approved by 176 to 2.

As the roundhouse and shops were going up, and skilled British artisans were being recruited to man them, a long dormant idea was prodded back to life in Calgary. Was it not about time to revive the Calgary and District Exhibition? But not just as a fair to advertise the agricultural productions of the neighborhood; it must also become the showcase for the commercial and industrial potential of the city and of the whole of western Canada! Industrial and commercial development must go hand in hand with agricultural development!

In Calgary in 1899 to dream was to act. A. E. Cross took it upon himself to convince the directors of the Fish Creek and Davisburg exhibitions to join Calgary in staging an authentic regional exhibition. At the same time, Arthur G. Wolley-Dod headed a group that undertook to promote a joint stock non-dividend paying company which would stage the reborn exhibition. It was the grandiosely christened Inter-Western Pacific Exhibition Company. Its purpose in life was to "make Calgary's mid-summer exhibition the most prominent, attractive and educational exhibition between Winnipeg and the Coast."

It should be noticed in passing that the support that the good burghers of Calgary gave the Inter-Western Pacific Exhibition Company was more symbolic than financial. The company was incorporated with five thousand shares of $1 stock and the minimum subscription was for twenty-five shares. However, none of the ordinary shareholders was required to put up more than ten percent of the face value of the stock, or $2.50 for twenty-five shares. Only the directors were required to have their shares completely paid up to qualify for nomination. There was, however, nothing unusual in this kind of corporate financing. The directors could call upon shareholders to put up additional funds if the company needed more capital. The I.W.P.E. made an additional call of five percent on its shareholders ten years later.

Incorporating a company with such high-blown objectives was easy enough. Finding a place to stage their exhibition was something else. Failure of the early Calgary Exhibitions to succeed financially resulted in the Calgary and District Agricultural Society falling behind in payments on its three-thousand-dollar mortgage. It was replaced in 1892 with a mortgage for four thousand dollars. That, too, fell into default and when the Exhibition folded the mortgage was foreclosed and title to the property fell to Mr. R. B. Bennett.

The first order of business for the new Exhibition promoters was to negotiate a deal with Mr. Bennett for the use of the grounds. This they did, and with a one-year lease in hand the directors of the Inter-Western Pacific Exhibition Company were off and running, though "churning about" might have been more aptly descriptive. Most of them, of course, had been part of the previous organization and hence were familiar with all the problems inherent in trying to stage an exhibition in the late fall. The weather was seldom reliable and if the temperatures were friendly, most of the farmers were still busy with their harvesting well into the month of October.

Lack of attendance and lack of entries had been twin handicaps of all the earlier fairs. So, sentiment swung more and more to a midsummer fair, as evidenced by the prospectus of the new company. There were disadvantages there too, of course. The midsummer date would be too early for the showing of flowers and vegetables, although grain exhibits could be held over. There was but a short interval between seeding and the fair for the farmers to get their exhibits ready.

As things turned out, it was physically impossible for the new directors to organize a summer show in 1899 and after several changes of dates, the first Inter-Western Pacific Exhibition opened as advertised for a two-day show on September 27. In substance and form it was very much like every other exhibition. There were competitive classes for every extant variety of farm animal and product of the soil. The clothing merchants exhibited their latest styles of clothing, the furniture merchants exhibited their latest furniture styles, the brewery exhibited rows of beer kegs and the women exhibited their cooking and handicrafts.

Each afternoon there were horse races under flat saddle, horse races under cowboy gear, trotting and pacing races, all in front of the grandstand. In the evening there was a dance in the Hull's Opera House, to the music of the local firemen's band, that went on until two o'clock in the morning.

Though the 1899 Exhibition was accounted a success—it ended up with a small profit despite the failure of expected government grants to be forthcoming—it was clear to all that massive improvements to the grounds were needed. The grandstand, which was more "bleacher" than "grandstand" in the first place, needed substantial renovation and reconstruction. So did the horse barns and cattle sheds. The fencing needed replacement and the race track needed rebuilding.

Mr. Bennett, who had acquired the property as a speculation from the original mortgagor, was unwilling to deal it back to the Exhibition board, or to make the improvements. So the board decided to try to talk the city council into buying the grounds from Mr. Bennett and then leasing them back to the Exhibition company. The city council was persuaded; the ratepayers endorsed the project, but the negotiations with Mr. Bennett seemed to take forever. Talks began early in 1900 but it was not until March, 1901, that the purchase of the ninety-four-acre site was finally completed for seven thousand dollars. As the southern city limits extended only to Seventeenth Avenue at the time, the purchase extended the city ninety-four acres to the south.

Despite the enthusiasm of the company directors, however, a reconstituted annual exhibition did not loom all that large on

Copyright. Oliver.
Calgary.

Copyright. Oliver.
Calgary.

There were always enough horses and riders available close at hand to provide a variety of racing events featured at the early Exhibitions at Victoria Park. Photographs by W. J. Oliver. *Courtesy of Glenbow Archives, Calgary, Alberta.*

Toward the end of the first decade jockey silks and hurdle races were introduced. *Courtesy of Glenbow Archives, Calgary, Alberta.*

any list of Calgary priorities at the dawn of the twentieth century. The burning issue, and the one that excited just about everybody, was "provincial autonomy"—the conversion of the Alberta territory into the Province of Alberta—with Calgary as the capital, naturally. There was also the deeply controversial nationwide Prohibition referendum at which Albertans would give the Drys a substantial majority.

Just when a great influx of American settlers seemed imminent, the United States became embroiled in the Spanish-American War to the distraction of everybody's attention. Then the South African War broke out. It not only interrupted the flow of British immigrants to Alberta, but it also saw a couple of carloads of young Calgarians rush off to the service of the Queen and Empire. As if this was not enough, the Boxer Uprising in China saw both the United States and Britain become involved. So there were distractions, all of which had impacts on trade and finance and population movements. Nevertheless, when the exhibitions were held, as one century melded into another, enough people kept turning up to encourage the sponsors to try again and again.

The Inter-Western Exhibition, like those that preceded it, was very much a commu-

nity undertaking. Everyone who was anybody in the Calgary area as the new century dawned was a member of its board of directors. Included were William Toole, A. L. Cameron, I. S. G. VanWart, A. G. Wolley-Dod, P. Turner Bone, James Smart, A. E. Cross, R. G. Robinson, T. A. Hatfield, H. Neilson, J. A. Turner, George Sharpe, Thomas Wanless, C. P. Marker, L. H. Doll.

They were not only members of the board of directors, but the people who ran the fair. They buttonholed everybody they met for cash donations for the prize list; they arranged for judges, set the judging schedules, and saw to it that classes were judged. They went out into the byways to round up entries and even took tickets at the gates. To top everything off, most of them found classes in which to exhibit, if not purebred animals, then vegetables and flowers.

Naturally, with such an unalloyed amateur and amateurish production there was grumbling along the sidelines. Nevertheless, the newspapers of the day were prepared to award the sponsors of the Exhibitions "A" for effort and urge them on to bigger and better things "next year." From the contemporary accounts of the Inter-Western Exhibitions that followed it is clear that improvements were in everybody's mind during the ensuing years.

Over the two-day Exhibition in 1900 just over twenty-five hundred patrons were persuaded to pay the fifty cents entrance fee to get into the grounds and most of them spent an extra twenty-five cents for a seat in the grandstand. There is no doubt that the bulk of the attendance was attracted by the horse races rather than the grain, vegetable, livestock, and commercial exhibits. Racing was highly popular and race meets were held independently by the turf associations, as well as by the Exhibition. These meetings would commonly attract from 500 to 750 patrons to day-long programs which included every variety of horse race yet devised. All were accompanied by several forms of wagering, of which the most popular was betting with bookmakers at fixed odds. There was also a modified form of parimutuel betting known as "pool-selling" and there were occasional match races in which the owners of two horses were required to pay entrance fees to race, as indeed were all the livestock exhibitors and handicraft and homemakers entrants. The entrance fees provided most of the money for the prize lists. Thus, in 1900 the Exhibition had gross receipts of $8,841 from grants, donations, and entrance fees and distributed $2,324 in prizes, most of it to the horse races.

To attract a crowd of twenty-five hundred out of a city population of just under four thousand was regarded as a commendable beginning by the Exhibition sponsors. But it was also agreed that something more than the horse races was needed to bring out larger crowds. So the freelancing merry-go-round and ferris wheel operators, snake-oil pitchmen, and other itinerant showmen were gradually brought into the operation. But not always with favorable results. Public grumbling developed over the crookedness of some of the gambling games and it was universally resolved that greater emphasis had to be placed on elevating the moral standard of all the attractions at the fair. It was also agreed that something more than a gaggle of enthusiastic amateurs was needed if the Inter-Western Pacific Exhibition Company was to achieve its great potential. The

company directors got their heads together with the leaders of the Calgary Board of Trade in 1903 and decided that if they combined their resources they could hire a full-time joint manager for both organizations. Indeed, they could hire a full-time manager and an assistant.

Of all the decisions taken by the Calgary Exhibition and Stampede over its one-hundred-year history, this was its most important. For one thing, it came just at the time when Calgary, after a somnolent quarter century, was poised to blast off as the fastest growing city on the North American continent, if not the whole world.

The CPR had its new roundhouse and shops in full operation, its Calgary division point the busiest on its system west of Winnipeg. Most important, it had moved its sales offices for its western lands to Calgary. It was to Calgary that the American land agents came to get the land to merchandise across the Great Plains States. It was to Calgary that the land agents came in droves to set up offices for the sale of town lots in every prairie hamlet between Brooks, Bassano, Fort Macleod, and Innisfail.

In the higher reaches of CPR policy-making, plans were being completed to divert water from the Bow River at Calgary into a series of canals and artificial lakes which would irrigate 250,000 acres of eastern Alberta. The CPR also had plans for the mass production of "ready-made farms" which it would merchandise to the immigrating American irrigation farmers. In five years, the CPR alone was responsible for adding more than 1,500 to Calgary's population.

But all this was just the first verse. All along the spur tracks on the south side of the CPR yards, from Second Street East to Sixth Street West, massive wholesale warehouses were being poked five and six stories into the sky, providing employment for building tradesmen by the hundreds, immediately, and laying the foundation for enterprise that would sustain Calgary's commercial life for decades into the future. The building tradesmen flooding into the city had long since overtaxed the city's lodging house accommodation and were beginning to hole up in tents along the Bow

This is where it all began, the manager's brand new office in Victoria Park in 1903. The manager, C. W. Peterson, is shown with assistant, Aimie Hall. *Courtesy of Glenbow Archives, Calgary, Alberta.*

River. The entrepreneurs, promoters, real estate developers meanwhile were bursting out of Calgary's official boundaries to go on a mansion building binge along the northern edge of the south hill. Soon it would be known as "American Hill," in recognition of the numbers of Americans who took up residence on what would one day become Mount Royal.

There was truly, to paraphrase Shakespeare, a tide flowing in the affairs of Calgary, which, if the Inter-Western Pacific Exhibition Company took it at the flood, would lead it on to fortune. The men who enabled it to do so were C. W. Peterson, who became the joint manager of the Exhibition and the Board of Trade and E. L. Richardson, his assistant in both jobs.

C. W. Peterson was a Danish-educated livestock expert who had migrated to Canada in the 1890s and joined the staff of the Dominion Department of Agriculture as livestock commissioner, a position comparable to that of deputy minister for the Northwest Territories. His responsibilities included everything from assisting the individual farmers to improve their skills to organizing them into their particular grain and livestock associations. While at

Regina he had organized the various beef and dairy breeds into their territory-wide associations.

When he moved to Calgary he assisted in the organization of Alberta associations and when he took over the management of the Exhibition he brought all the livestock, grain, and even youth organizations into the Exhibition office. As a result, the Exhibition office became home for all these associations, for their executive meetings and their books which were kept there by the Exhibition staff.

Richardson was a recent graduate of the Ontario Agricultural College who came west in 1901 with a load of cattle and was hired by Peterson as an assistant. When Peterson left the government in the spring of 1903 to take over in Calgary he brought Richardson with him. Then, when Peterson left the Exhibition at the end of 1906 to devote his full time to editing the *Farm and Ranch Review*, he recommended that Richardson be appointed to succeed him.

Prior to Peterson's arrival, the directors of the Exhibition had pushed a rather curious resolution through the annual shareholders meeting of November 26, 1901. In any joint stock company, like

Inter-Western Pacific, members of the public are free to subscribe for company stock without what the lawyers call "let or hindrance." John Doe can become a shareholder simply by paying his money to the company treasurer and getting his shares. Or, if there are no further shares available from the company, he can buy those owned by other shareholders. If he so desires, and has the resources, he can buy the entire issued capital stock of a company and thus become its sole owner.

Something must have happened, in 1901, to arouse the concern of the shareholders that somebody might do just that with Inter-Western Pacific stock and turn the company into his personal monopoly. Why anyone would want to monopolize the shares of a non-profit, non-dividend paying company is difficult to imagine. Nevertheless, an amendment to the company bylaws was passed which stipulated that no one could become a shareholder until his application was approved by the board of directors. That provision has followed through all the organizational permutations that have followed, from Inter-Western Pacific Exhibition Company into the Calgary Industrial Exhibition (1910) to the Calgary Exhibition and Stampede Company (1932).

Another Exhibition rule that goes back to the turn of the century arose from C. W. Peterson's first year of experience as the manager of the organization. At the 1903 shareholders' meeting he read his employers a lecture on how to operate their affairs. They should stop nominating people to the board of directors simply because they were prominent citizens of the community. What the board of directors needed was not only dedicated workers, but dedicated workers with special talents which would enhance their worth to the organization. They should make sure the board contained outstanding dairymen, outstanding horsemen, outstanding grain farmers, and outstanding ranchers. They should be on the alert to get people with special talents in the field of business and finance.

Within a year the board had positive proof of the soundness of Peterson's advice. Peterson had persuaded the city that a comprehensive improvement program of the grounds was needed. A new grand-stand, race track, new exhibition buildings, and new barns were all included. The city agreed to foot the bill of fifteen thousand dollars and work began as soon as the frost was out of the ground in 1904. But when the city went into the debenture market to raise the money to pay the contractors it discovered its credit was exhausted, largely because of the public works expenditures it was forced to make as a result of the building boom. The board of directors was collectively forced to go to the bank and borrow the fifteen thousand dollars for the city on a note backed by their signatures. Those who signed that note were: President I. S. G. VanWart, O. E. Brown, A. G. Wolley-Dod, C. W. Peterson, W. H. Cushing, James Emerson, John Turner, James Smart, R. B. Bennett, Pat Burns, A. E. Cross and W. M. Parslow.

The Exhibition of 1903 was held in July instead of the fall, with nearly disastrous results. All-weather roads, which the Romans had introduced to Britain two thousand years earlier, had still not been developed in western Canada. Heavy rains regularly cut access to Calgary from Fish Creek and in 1903 a particularly heavy rain the day before the Exhibition cut both attendance and livestock entries. Nevertheless, when the question of when to hold the fair in 1904 came up at the annual meeting that fall, the shareholders rejected Peterson's advice to choose October and opted once again for the early July dates. Thereafter no consideration was ever given to a return to the late autumn dates.

Under Peterson's leadership, the premises at Victoria Park began to look like exhibition grounds. It was securely fenced, a substantial office building was constructed, the Turf Club was persuaded to undertake the conversion of the race track from a one-mile oval to a half a mile. The center-field was smoothed out so that it could again double as a cricket pitch, baseball field, or polo grounds, though for the most part these sports were all played elsewhere. Most importantly, the Exhibition could now accommodate all its exhibits on its own grounds instead of having to rent the available downtown halls for certain of its classes.

For the Exhibition itself, strong efforts were made to attract the attendance of more non-exhibitors. Wild horse races, which were more saddle bronc contests than trials of speed, were added, along with equitation contests. Trick riding performers were introduced, along with trained animal acts. A hot air balloonist was brought in to ride a smoke-filled balloon to the height of several hundred feet before dropping to the ground on a parachute. Perhaps most crowd appealing of any of the innovations of 1904 was the decision to cut the entrance fee from fifty cents to twenty-five cents. As a result, the paid attendance for the three-day fair in 1904 reached 6,322 and would have gone higher if the board of directors had not turned greedy the third day. Impressed with the increased attendance on the first two days, they raised the admittance price to fifty cents for the third day and the public stayed away in droves. Admission went back to twenty-five cents for many years to come.

Peterson's first love was livestock and he concentrated from the beginning on making Victoria Park the livestock heart of Alberta. Concerned to upgrade the quality of the beef herds of the Northwest Territories, the livestock men, led by Peterson,

had formed in 1900 the Territorial Livestock Association. The Victoria Park premises were made available cost free to the breed associations for their annual shows. In 1901 the association had staged the first spring purebred bull show and sale at the Exhibition grounds and this became a favorite annual promotion of the Exhibition. A late spring horse show for both halter and performance was started and quickly became a highlight of the social season as well as a livestock event.

But from his first day on the job, Peterson realized that the Calgary Exhibition needed a spectacular performance of some kind to get its show on the road. True, attendance each year was increasing modestly. But it was by no means keeping pace with the growth of population in the city and surrounding countryside. Between 1900 and 1904, Calgary's population doubled and it went on doubling, while the Exhibition attendance only "edged" upwards. What would put Calgary permanently on the Exhibition map would be to have it stage the Dominion Exhibition and

By the turn of the century the cattle industry had boomed to such an extent that it would take forty or fifty cowboys to stage a roundup like this. *Courtesy of Glenbow Archives, Calgary, Alberta.*

that goal became the object of Peterson's attention.

The Dominion Exhibition was a generously subsidized promotion of the federal government which was inaugurated in Toronto in 1903 and shifted from city to city thereafter. Its purpose was to publicize regional production of all kinds and to encourage farmers to improve the quality of their livestock, grain, and dairy products. It was a kind of World's Fair concept miniaturized. Peterson had the campaign to bring the Dominion Exhibition to Calgary well in hand when, at the end of 1906, he resigned from his twin management job. Richardson was appointed to replace him and was barely settled in office when he received word that Calgary had been awarded the 1908 Dominion Exhibition, and that he had barely a year to organize it from the ground up.

Fortunately, Richardson had what amounted to the round-the-clock assistance of President I. S. G. VanWart and the

directors and collectively they turned the event into the greatest thing that ever happened to Calgary, or to western Canada for that matter. In a way it was like a consolation prize that was awarded to Calgary for losing both the provincial capital and the University of Alberta to Edmonton, and Calgary made the most of it. That took a herculean effort for, to bring it off successfully, it had to overcome the impact of the worst Alberta winter in twenty years in 1906–7. It turned cold in early December and kept getting colder until, in mid-February, American newspapers were running sensational stories of cattle, in fifty-thousand lots, freezing to death along the western Canada fence lines. It was not that bad, but it was bad enough. It reached a point where coal famine developed in the cities and towns. Once Calgary was down to a single day's

The descriptive term—The Establishment—had not yet been invented, but if there was such a group this was it in turn-of-the-century Calgary. The picture was taken, ca. 1900, on the steps of Pat Burns' Bow Valley Ranch and many of those included were directors of the Exhibition. Top row: *L-R:* Capt. James G. Gordon; A. E. Bannister; Major James Walker; William Roper Hull (holding straw hat); George K. Leeson; W. Robert Newbolt. Second row: *L-R:* Supt. James O. Wilson, NWMP; Amos Rowe; Dr. Harry Goodsir Mackid; Ed H. Hodder. Third row: *L-R:* William Pearce; H. A. (Dusty) Rhodes; Patrick J. Nolan; Judge David Lynch Scott; John Brazier. Seated: W. B. Graveley. *Courtesy of Glenbow Archives, Calgary, Alberta.*

supply on hand and if coal trains had not made it into town from the mines, disaster would have struck. It took the farmers and ranchers months and months to recover from that winter. But recover they did and, when the Exhibition's spring livestock show and sale was held in May 1908, the entrants broke all previous records in numbers.

As a first step in preparation for the Dominion Exhibition, Richardson and VanWart went on brain-picking expeditions to the exhibition offices in Winnipeg, Toronto, and Chicago. They soaked up advice like sponges and returned to set up the organization needed to bring the show to fruition. For the first time they had no money worries. The Dominion Government donated $50,000. The province of Alberta contributed $35,000, the city of Calgary $25,000 and with entrance fees from exhibitors and gate receipts, the Dominion Exhibition had a budget of

$145,000 with which to operate. In 1908 dollars, it was truly a king's ransom, enough to erect half a dozen new buildings on the grounds, subsidize the freight charges for all the exhibitors from near and far, and bring in the kind of super attractions that only American state fairs could usually afford.

The directors of the Inter-Western Pacific Exhibition Company learned more about organizing a king-sized fair that year than they ever knew existed. They set up committees to canvass all the communities between Winnipeg and Vancouver to send community entries. They had an attractions committee screening attractions. They had committees working with the purebred cattle associations, horse breeders, chicken fanciers, and swine breeders. They catalogued every handicraft known to man and went out to have contests for each of them at the fair.

The Dominion Exhibition ran from July

Poster for Dominion
Exhibition, 1908. The
Exhibition opened with
a historical pageant on
July 1. *Courtesy of
Glenbow Archives,
Calgary, Alberta.*

The Indians from Calgary's nearby reserves were prominent in the Exhibition parades from the beginning. This picture of the Indian section of the 1908 Dominion Exhibition extravaganza demonstrates that the traditional travois was still a fact of Indian life. So, indeed, were Hudson's Bay blankets.

1 to July 8, with a day off for the intervening Sunday which fell on the fifth. It began, on the morning of Wednesday, July 1, with a historical pageant, the likes of which no one in western Canada had even imagined, let alone seen before. The streets of downtown Calgary were cleared of all construction material shortly after dawn and the parade units were assembled on Sixth, Seventh, and Eighth Avenues. Shortly after 10 A.M. the process of melding the units into a cohesive whole began and the serpentine parade began moving back and forth through the downtown streets and avenues preparatory to the march to Victoria Park, with the Grand Marshal, Fire Chief James Smart, in charge.

The first carriages held the usual digni-

taries, Lieutenant-Governor Bulyea, Chief Justice Sifton, Senator Lougheed, President I. S. G. VanWart, then Premier Rutherford and his Cabinet and Mayor Cameron, Superintendent Deane, A. E. Cross, and Colonel Steele. Just about every ethnic and racial group in the province had a float entered, including the British, Canadian, Scandinavian, German, American—both white and black—and French Canadian.

There were industrial floats, commercial floats, and a temperance float rubbing axles with a brewery float. There were bands without number, Indians from all southern Alberta reserves, and more than one hundred American cowboys and Indians from the Miller Brothers 101 Ranch Wild West Show which was in town for a

one-day stand at the Exhibition. One of the most famous of the traveling American shows, it moved across the country in a special forty-five-car railway train and had performed recently at Madison Square Garden in New York.

By Dominion Day, 1908, Calgary's population had zoomed past the twenty-five thousand mark most of whom lined the streets for the parade and then followed it through the gates that day for the Dominion Exhibition. Within the fair buildings, there were substantial displays from the four western provinces and no less than forty communities had display booths advertising the features of their communities. There were 601 horses entered in competition, dominated by the Clydesdales, 675

beef cattle headed by the Shorthorns, and a grand total of 2,500 animals that took days to judge. The dog show was an enormous success and more than 625 entries were received for the poultry show.

The outstanding attraction on the grounds was Strobel's airship, a propeller-driven dirigible that made three flights daily in front of the grandstand. Competing with it for attention, of course, was a full program of vaudeville acts on a large central stage and several special events in the infield of the race track. The most crowd-pleasing was a demonstration by Calgary Fire Department horses of how they responded to a fire alarm. Feeding on pasture when the alarm rang, they dashed to their places at the fire engines, and in

The early parades were strong on pageantry, as this float of John Bull and the British "bull" dog demonstrates.
Courtesy of Glenbow Archives, Calgary, Alberta.

Thanks to federal, provincial, and civic largesse, this was Victoria Park at the opening of the Dominion Exhibition. The new construction included the Exhibits Building in the center, the roofed grandstand, and the Livestock Exhibits building in the center foreground, along with half a dozen new stables. *Courtesy of Glenbow Archives, Calgary, Alberta.*

Milady without a parasol, or a hat that shaded her face, was considered only half-dressed as she strolled into the Dominion Exhibition in 1908. *Courtesy of Glenbow Archives, Calgary, Alberta.*

This hydrogen-filled balloon made five successful flights over Victoria Park at the Dominion Exhibition. On the sixth attempt it caught fire and burned in front of the grandstand. *Courtesy of Glenbow Archives, Calgary, Alberta.*

seconds were tearing around the track with their engines and ladders.

For the Exhibition, the biggest day of the fair, financially, was not Dominion Day but the Fourth of July. Special trains brought excursionists from Spokane and there was a large influx of Americans from all the border towns. The Calgary Americans took over promotion for the day, brought in a band from Iowa State University, staged an American Day parade that rivalled the Dominion Day parade, and filled the grandstand for both afternoon and evening performances.

Midway through the American Day festivities, there was an unscheduled spectacular. As Captain Jack Dallas was preparing the Strobel airship for takeoff, a sudden gust of wind blew it against the grandstand where it exploded and burned.

When the results were all in, E. L. Richardson was able to report that 100,051 persons had passed through the turnstiles during the seven-day Fair and that the Exhibition board emerged with a surplus of $24,000 to finance future expansion.

More important than money, however, was the learning process which the Dominion Exhibition provided. And, of that process, the most valuable lesson was how to take care of the great mass of visitors which such an event could attract from outside a community like Calgary. Special excursion trains provided passengers with overnight accommodations on the sidings. The hotels naturally filled to overflowing. Anticipating even heavier demand, the board made an arrangement with the Public School Board to turn the city's schools into billets for visitors. It bought one thousand beds and set them up in the schools. As a result, nobody had to sleep in the streets and up to seven hundred found sleeping accommodation in the schools.

CHAPTER 3

The Stage is Set for Guy Weadick

I n the years before the First World War, for Calgary even the most outstanding achievement was but the prelude to something greater. In seven years the city's population soared from 4,000 to 25,000 but in 1908 it already had a group of super-boosters beating the drum for 100,000 and when it reached 50,000 in 1912 the group was considering extending its goal to 200,000. The CPR shops and yards located with such euphoria in 1898 were outgrown so quickly that a whole new complex had to be built at far-out Ogden in 1912. Building permits broke through the $2,000,000 level in 1900, passed $5,400,000 in 1905, doubled again in 1907, and zoomed to $62,747,000 in 1911. Release of the 1911 figures was accompanied by a prediction that 1912 permits would exceed $100,000,000.

The epitome of Calgary reacting to achievement was the Exhibition board of November 1908. It had staged the greatest exhibition the West had ever seen, and had done it with a flair and efficiency that would have done P. T. Barnum proud. So what did it propose for 1909? More of the same, only bigger and better. And this despite the fact that it would not have the $100,000 in government money to subsidize its efforts as it had in 1908. Nevertheless, it voted Ernie Richardson a five-hundred-dollar increase in pay, to twenty-five hundred dollars a year, and sent him to Edmonton with President VanWart to get Alberta's permission to convert the Dominion Exhibition of 1908

into the Alberta Provincial Exhibition of 1909. Not only did they get permission, they got an eight-thousand-dollar grant from the province to assist with the agricultural exhibits.

After becoming accustomed to "thinking big" the Exhibition directors could not even contemplate going back to the prosaic kind of exhibitions they had had before. An example of the new approach was their pioneering in the use of motion pictures to publicize their activities.

The motion picture business in 1908 was barely into its infancy. Calgary's only such theater, the Empire, like all the others was starved for material for its screen. It was frequently reduced to trying to get by with reruns of old prize fight newsreels, like those of the Jeffries-Fitzimmons, Gans-Herman, and Corbett-McCoy fights it was showing during the Dominion Exhibition week. To take advantage of this need for material the CPR was preparing a newsreel to publicize its Canadian resort hotels in the motion picture theaters of the continent. "Hey," said the directors, in effect, "let's do some of that too." They persuaded the city council to appropriate one thousand dollars with which to have a newsreel produced of the 1909 Exhibition parade—pageants they were called then —to be part of the CPR film. With that the parade became a permanent part of the Exhibition promotion.

wild animal circus. Four free acrobatic and animal acts performed several times a day on the midway. But to the thousands of visitors from the countryside, the main attractions were still the exhibits. By 1909 the grounds were dotted with fine new buildings in which the exhibits could be displayed. That year there were no less than 616 horses on display, along with 256 cattle and hundreds of grain, horticultural, and craft exhibits. There was a grand total of 1,954 animal entries including over one hundred dogs.

The rains which fall on the plains of western Canada in July mean the difference between bumper crops when they do and crop failures when they don't.

From 1886 onward, display of women's needlecraft artistry was a vital part of the Calgary Exhibition. This is one of the few photographs capturing the event for posterity. *Courtesy of the Calgary Stampede.*

Once again the show in 1909 focused upon Alberta agriculture in all its aspects. But, as a special added attraction, it staged the biggest art exhibition ever seen west of Toronto. It consisted of 113 oils and watercolors by Canadian artists and 110 by French, British, Dutch, Italian, and German artists. For the grandstand it brought back the Navassar Ladies Band, which had been the hit of the Dominion Exhibition. It reached into the famous Hippodrome in New York for a three-girl motorcycle act in which the girls raced each other around the inside of the gigantic wire cage. They were followed by the Eight Mirza Golems— "Acrobats from the court of the Shah of Persia"—and Howard's Dogs and Ponies.

On the grounds there were the C. W. Parker Carnival shows and Al G. Barnes's

Thus, to have a viable agriculture which will exhibit at and attend the Calgary Exhibition a lot of rain must fall. But when it does fall in July it puts the kibosh on managers' dreams of new attendance records. And no matter how the dates were switched in those early years, the rains always came down in torrents sometime or other during Exhibition week.

At the Dominion Exhibition, which ran for seven days, it rained on two days. In 1909 it rained one and one-half inches on the second day and forced cancellation of a number of events. In 1910 heavy rains on the fourth day cut attendance in half. In 1911 there was a cloudburst the first day and the rain continued for the next two days. Nevertheless, with Calgary's population soaring the way it was, attendance at

Poster advertising
Calgary Industrial
Exhibition, 1911.
*Courtesy of Glenbow
Archives, Calgary,
Alberta.*

the fairs was bound to rise each year. Thus, in 1909 the board was more than satisfied with the 55,375 paying customers who passed through the gates though that was far short of the 100,000 Dominion Exhibition record. The paid attendance rose to 77,804 in 1910 and 91,097 in 1911. In these years the Exhibition always operated at a small deficit, as might be expected from a twenty-five-cents admission price and another twenty-five cents for the grandstand. It added to its income with government grants, commercial grants, and exhibitors' fees. Rental of concession stands, profit sharing from the midway concessions, and fees from the bookmakers who operated betting booths at the horse races also contributed revenue.

There were a number of innovations in those years. In 1910 more than six hundred came in on special trains for American Day on the Fourth of July. As a special added attraction for them it was arranged to have an announcer with a large megaphone rebroadcast a blow-by-blow description of the heavyweight championship fight being held in Reno, Nevada, between Jack Johnson and the unretired Jim Jeffries. The announcer read the reports coming in to the grounds on a special newswire.

The growing interest in aviation was reflected in the number of aviators who turned up at the Exhibition. In 1911 Henry De Van, the boy aviator, had all kinds of trouble getting airborne. On the first afternoon he hit the top of a fence on takeoff and crashed. The plane repaired, he tried it again the next afternoon but it was too windy to take off. That evening he did get airborne and flew around for five minutes at a height of three hundred feet in front of the grandstand and landed without mishap in the centerfield. The following year Jimmie Ward came in a bigger plane and made two flights in front of the stands.

The ownership of automobiles had become common enough in Calgary that the 1909 parade could, for the first time, feature an automobile section of more than a score of cars gaily festooned in colored ribbons and carrying bevies of brightly dressed school girls. Fireworks were introduced as a super feature in 1905 by L. H. Doll, one of the directors who undertook to underwrite the cost of the first perfor-

mances. In 1910 the fireworks were combined with an Indian pageant replicating the signing of the 1877 treaties. Thereafter pageants and fireworks were combined as an attraction. The 1910 Exhibition was also staged as the Alberta Provincial Exhibition, but when the directors asked the province to designate Calgary as the site of the permanent Alberta Provincial Exhibition, the government refused. Indeed it put an end to all "provincial" exhibitions. It was better for all concerned, the government ruled, for each community to operate its exhibition as a vehicle for publicizing its own community.

Calgary had better luck that year with another promotion. It originated a drive that led to the establishment of the western summer fair circuit composed of Calgary, Edmonton, Prince Albert, Saskatoon, and Regina. The big dividend that accrued from getting the circuit going was it enabled all the exhibitions to obtain better attractions at less cost by offering them five weeks' work.

Naturally, Calgary wanted to be the starting point of the circuit, which would give it both Dominion Day and the Fourth of July. It was a moot point whether the first or the fourth of July produced the biggest crowds in Calgary. Usually it came down to the weather, and on which day it rained. Edmonton balked at this suggestion, not so much because of concern with the Fourth of July, but it wanted its share of Dominion Days. The compromise was to alternate the first weeks of July between Calgary and Edmonton.

The big innovation of 1911 was the introduction in Canada of parimutuel betting on the horse races, and the gradual increasing of the purses for the races to attract better horses. Until then betting had been with local bookmakers who rented space at the race track and posted fixed odds for each horse. Gambling with bookmakers had fallen into public disrepute in the United States, and when it was outlawed in the State of New York in 1905 there was fear that it would kill horseracing. Parimutuel machines for recording bets were introduced as an alternative in other states.

In Calgary the introduction of parimutuels, additional to bookmaking rather than a substitute for it, was by no means an instant success. Indeed, the horse players of the day were so suspicious of the new-fangled machines that they avoided them. They much preferred the fixed odds offered by the bookmakers. The small volume of betting through the machines prevented realistic payouts and that discouraged further patronage. For all that the board persisted and used the machines again in 1912. With the steadily increasing crowds the machine play increased slowly to a point where the board could foresee the time when they would be able to run the bookmakers off and rely solely on the parimutuels to take care of horse racing betting. What eventually turned the scales in favor of the machines were increasing numbers of occasions when the machines paid off at greater odds than the bookies.

The year 1911 was notable for the beginning of the construction of the magnificent new $55,000 livestock and horse show arena which had a 200 by 84 feet ring and seating accommodation for three thousand. That brought to $138,500 the money expended by the city on capital improvements on the Exhibition grounds since it had acquired title in 1901. Impressive as this sum was, it by no means indicated that Victoria Park was turning out to be a financial drag on the city. The city had pre-empted at least ten acres on

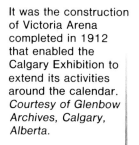

It was the construction of Victoria Arena completed in 1912 that enabled the Calgary Exhibition to extend its activities around the calendar. *Courtesy of Glenbow Archives, Calgary, Alberta.*

the east side of the property for its street car barns, an electrical power station, and a warehouse for its stores department. The way land values were skyrocketing in the city, it would have been impossible to have bought the car barn sites alone for $55,000.

It was this real estate boom that caught the Exhibition up in a noisy controversy during the 1910–13 period. As the last vacant building lot within half a mile of Victoria Park had long since disappeared, the real estate promoters hungrily eyed its wide open spaces. Did it make sense, they asked, to utilize such valuable property for a race track and the Exhibition? Would it not make eminently better sense to move the Exhibition onto the vacant pasture land beyond the city limits and turn Victoria Park into building lots?

The city administration in 1912 actually gave some serious consideration to relocating the Exhibition in the vicinity of the Shaganappi area, five miles to the west. It was then that it discovered the caveat Ottawa had placed on the title to the original grant—the land had to be used for an exhibition or it would be reclaimed by Ottawa. This put the responsibility up to the directors of the Exhibition Company and they opted to stay in Victoria Park.

The Exhibition, by this time, had undergone another reorganization and name change, partly as a result of the refusal of Edmonton permanently to allot it the title

of Alberta Provincial Exhibition and partly because of a change in the focus of the Exhibition. If, as the Alberta Government insisted, each exhibition should promote and publicize its own community, the name Inter-Western Pacific Exhibition Company did nothing to publicize Calgary. So, in 1910 it was decided to change the name and the one chosen was indicative of the changing times.

Calgary was moving rapidly away from the role of market town for the surrounding farming community and becoming, in its own eyes at least, the primary commercial and industrial center for the western prairies. No one who contemplated the round-the-clock shunting of the railway box cars in and out of its wholesale district could dispute that fact. The commercial and industrial exhibits at the Exhibition were increasing every year. With the expansion of manufacturing that was bound to keep pace with the city's population growth, Calgary's industrial future was assured. Ergo, what better name than the Calgary Industrial Exhibition Company, Limited? It still remained a non-dividend-paying company of shareholders given prior approval by the board of directors, of whom four members were to be city aldermen. But the Calgary Industrial Exhibition Company was barely settled into business before it, and Calgary itself, was vigorously recalled to its roots by a chance encounter with a meandering American cowboy turned rodeo performer, vaudeville entertainer, and sometime spectacle-stager. His name was Guy Weadick, and the time was late winter of 1911-12.

Born in Rochester, New York, on February 23, 1885, Guy Weadick was cowboying it on the cattle ranches of the northwest after the turn of the century when he was bitten by the rodeo bug. The essential skill which ranch hands acquired in the course of their daily work—breaking wild horses to the saddle, roping horses, cows and calves, wrestling three-year-old steers to the ground—had, after 1904, become marketable commodities in the entertainment world. Trick riders, trick ropers, steer wrestlers, had already moved from the local fairs to the county fairs, to the state fairs. In the wake of the universal audience appeal of Buffalo Bill Cody's wild west

extravaganza they were moving into the vaudeville circuits and onto the New York and London stages. Weadick had become part of that movement. He was a trick roping performer with the Miller Brothers 101 Ranch Wild West Show when it made its one-day stand at the Dominion Exhibition in Calgary in 1908.

Weadick was quite familiar with Alberta before that, however. He had worked on the McIntyre Ranch in 1904 and toured the West in 1905 as the agent for Will Pickett, the Negro cowboy who had invented "bulldogging." Pickett had performed the stunt as a grandstand attraction at the 1905 Calgary Exhibition. It took the form of leaping from the saddle of his galloping horse to the back of a full-grown steer, grabbing its horns, and twisting until he could reach its upper lip with his teeth. Then, biting the lip, he would release the horns, raise his arms, and twist the animal to the earth with his mouth. That was the spectacular forerunner of steer wrestling and steer decorating.

Weadick and Pickett worked a number of neighborhood rodeos across the Prairies and had a full dress rodeo going in Winnipeg when a gang of American rustlers stole their horses and fled back to the States with them. By then, Weadick had polished his skill as a trick rope artist sufficiently to catch a place with the Miller Brothers Show.

A brash, outgoing extrovert, who in the showbusiness phrase was "always on," Weadick was the focus of any gathering. A natural showman! Yet seemingly from the very beginning he had set his goal in life high above being a mere entertainer. Being the impresario who exploited the talents of other performers was his idea of a more suitable role in life. Thus, while barely out of his teens when he visited Calgary with the Miller Brothers in 1908, he found the time, and the effrontery, to approach H. C. McMullen, the general livestock agent of the CPR with the proposition that they should join forces and stage a week long rodeo in Calgary.

McMullen, who himself had found his way to Alberta with the first cattle drives from Montana in the late 1870s, did not think the time was ripe for such a promotion. But he was impressed with Weadick, liked the idea, and promised to contact him if the times became more propitious.

Weadick went on with his performing career that took him in and out of every state of the Union and to London, Paris, and Berlin. As the Calgary boom rushed toward its climax in the winter of 1911–12, McMullen happened into conversation with A. P. Day, a Medicine Hat farmer. One-day rodeos had been springing up in the cattle ranching country and the two discussed whether a full blown rodeo might be a promotable proposition for the city of Calgary. McMullen persuaded Weadick to come back to Calgary for another look. Weadick, by this time, was on a first name basis with practically every

performer in the rodeo business, from Canada to Mexico, and with most of the stock contractors as well. He was also the rodeo correspondent for *Billboard* magazine, the bible of show business. He put a rough outline of a week-long show together for McMullen. A. P. Day was contacted and he agreed to put up ten thousand dollars to get the show on the road. Their next stop was the Calgary Industrial Exhibition management. Neither Ernie Richardson nor President VanWart found Weadick's sales pitch convincing and they refused to have anything to do with it. They even boggled at letting Weadick use the Exhibition's facilities.

McMullen then contacted George Lane, who contacted Pat Burns and A. E. Cross and the three contacted A. J. McLean. Together the "Big Four" agreed to back

Before he became a show-biz impresario, Guy Weadick was a working cowboy on several southern Alberta and Montana ranches. He posed for this picture at the inaugural Stampede in 1912 in front of the Calgary City Hall. *Courtesy of the Calgary Stampede.*

Weadick and McMullen to the extent of one hundred thousand dollars to finance his "Frontier Days and Cowboy Championship Contest" which he eventually christened "The Stampede." They also twisted all the arms necessary to have the Exhibition grounds made available to him at a nominal five-hundred-dollar rental and for Richardson to take charge of the financial management of the enterprise.

By the end of March, the deal was wrapped up and Weadick took off for the United States to line up his troupe of performers. McMullen undertook with the assistance of A. P. Day to round up the livestock obtainable locally. The Big Four turned down Day's offer to help finance the project but he became the main supplier of bucking stock. The Indians, hundreds of them from all over southern Alberta, were supplied by the Rev. John McDougall of Morley who pocketed a $390 fee for his services. For a cultural touch, Weadick persuaded two of the West's outstanding artists, Charles Russell and Ed Borein, to come north to exhibit their work in Calgary during Stampede week. McMullen organized the parade and became the official director general of the enterprise. A. P. Day was arena director.

The news that the Stampede was coming to town was broken to the citizenry of Calgary in a large advertisement in the *Albertan* on June 15, in which it was announced in black-faced type that it would bring fifty thousand visitors to the city. Thereafter, until the show opened on Labor Day, September 2, 1912, Guy Weadick bombarded Calgarians with regularly placed half-page and full-page advertisements extolling various aspects of his show. In one, using an Ed Borein drawing as an illustration, he heralded the coming of the champion cowboys and cowgirls from the Cheyenne Frontier Days, the Pendleton Round-Up, and from "all the leading Wild West Shows and from every cattle district in Mexico, the United States and Canada" to compete for twenty thousand dollars in prizes. In another ad Weadick claimed, "We wish to state that the management of The Stampede are putting on the greatest Frontier Days Celebration in any man's country heretofore. It is one which will do credit to the Dominion

of Canada and the city of Calgary." In keeping with such an event, he urged all Calgarians to lay in supplies of ribbon and bunting with which to decorate their houses and businesses.

When Weadick discovered that the governor-general, the Duke of Connaught, and his family were to be in Calgary during the week of the Stampede, he fired off an invitation for them to attend, increased the run of the show from four to six days to accommodate them, and ordered the construction of two special royal boxes for them across from the grandstand.

It was Guy Weadick who introduced the war-whoop "Whoooop-ee-eee" that became a Calgary trademark. He did it as a heading on a half-page ad announcing he was arranging "to secure certain plots of ground on which those who desire may pitch tents and we will provide ample police protection for people coming to these plots."

Tickets for the great event at one dollar general admission plus fifty cents for the grandstand, plus tickets for special shows inside the horse show arena at one dollar each, went on sale on August 5 and by the seventeenth, Weadick was able to announce that the advanced sales had reached twenty thousand dollars. And this despite a lot of grumbling about the high gate price compared to the twenty-five cents charged by the Exhibition. Weadick answered the complaints by pointing out that he was encircling the entire race track with free bleachers.

There is little doubt that Weadick became infected by his own propaganda for he imported a hundred Indians from the United States who gloried in parading around in their war paint; he persuaded several hundred cowboys and a troupe of Mexican rodeo performers to come to Calgary. His group of fancy riding and roping cowgirls was the cream of the American rodeo circuits.

The prize for the champion bucking horse rider, steer wrestler, and calf roper was for each one thousand dollars in cash, a new saddle, and a silver belt buckle. Smaller prizes were awarded in other events and for the top finishers in the preliminary contests. For all Canadians the highlight of the show was the winning of the bronc riding championship by the Blood Indian, Tom Three Persons, who rode the notorious outlaw horse Cyclone to a standstill in front of a packed closing day grandstand. The champion Canadian all round cowboy was Clem Gardner while the champion all round Canadian cowgirl was the felicitously named Alberta McMullen, daughter of H. C. McMullen. While Americans won most of the prize money, several Canadians managed to take subsidiary prizes and collectively pocketed $3,200 of the $15,992 prize money actually paid out.

The show itself was kicked off on Labor Day morning with what the Calgary *Herald* described as the "grandest pageant in all history." That description was to be found in an eight-page special supplement with which the *Herald* celebrated the Stampede with column after column of superlative-peppered prose. It estimated that no less than 80,000 watched the pageant-parade and that 25,000 then trooped to Victoria Park for the show, which consisted of seventeen events staged each day.

It was purely, simply, and completely a western frontier days extravaganza, the ultimate refinement of the kind of things that were once part of the daily grind on the cattle ranches of the West. A measure of Weadick's dedication to the western theme can be judged by a single fact: in one of his early ads, he appealed to all Albertans to ride in his Stampede parade but warned that full western equipment and dress was required as no one riding with a flat saddle would be allowed to participate. The full program each day was:

1. Trick and fancy riding by cowgirls on race track
2. Stage Coach Race
3. Roping Steers by Cowboys
4. Cowgirls Relay Race
5. Cowboys Bareback Bucking Horse Contest
6. Cowboys Steer Bulldogging
7. Cowboys Steer Roping, Continued
8. Fancy Roping by Cowgirls
9. Fancy Roping by Cowboys
10. Cowboys Relay Race
11. Cowgirls Bucking Horse
12. Cowboys Bucking Horse
13. Cowboys Steer Roping, Continued

The winner of the bronc riding championship at the Calgary Stampede of 1912 was Tom Three Persons of Cardston, shown here with his wife Ambush Woman. Long after age and injury took Tom Three Persons out of competition, he was still an infield fixture at the Calgary Stampede of the 1920s. *Courtesy of Glenbow Archives, Calgary, Alberta.*

14. Cowboys Fancy and Trick Riding
15. Cowboys Steer Riding
16. Indian Relay Race
17. Wild Horse Race

It was a program that would have taken all the skills of a well-trained rodeo crew to run off efficiently. Weadick's managerial skills, still in their infancy, did not begin to match his promotional skill. There were interminable delays between events. There was too much parading around and posturing and too little action. Only in the final hours of the Stampede did it begin to operate with any semblance of order and professionalism, though in all fairness, the weather that week was almost impossible to contend with.

Much of the cause for the delays in the program could be traced to the environment of the Exhibition grounds. There were no chutes in which the bucking stock could be closely penned for saddling. The wild horses were roped and snubbed to the saddle-horn of the roper on horseback. The buckers had to be blindfolded with a blanket or sack, sometimes even hobbled, before they could be haltered and saddled. The cowboy, or cowgirl, had to climb on

The Stampede midway in 1912 was a ramshackle affair in which the carnival games and "grease joints" were located in the middle of the Indian Village by the main entrance. Improvements to the midway evolved rather slowly over the next decade. *Courtesy of Glenbow Archives, Calgary, Alberta.*

the still tightly snubbed horse and begin the ride when the horse was turned loose. That ride might take the bucker from one end of the infield to the other for the horse had to be ridden, sometimes for several minutes, until it ceased to buck.

Similarly, the calves to be roped were turned loose in this vast centerfield of the race track to be chased often for a quarter of a mile by the roper on horseback. The steer wrestlers too often chased their animal far afield. As a result, many of the performances were out of sight of the audience in the grandstand.

The Stampede was certainly a promotional and crowd-producing success. It drew more people into Calgary than any other event had ever done. The CPR was reputed to have carried forty thousand passengers on its half-fare excursion from as far away as Winnipeg. All the hotel keepers and merchants were ecstatic. The show played to over one hundred thousand admissions and grossed over $120,000. After all expenses were paid it disbursed $3,100 to Guy Weadick, in addition to the $425 he was paid in salary, $4,000 to H. C. McMullen and $5,000 to A. P. Day. The

Big Four promised in the beginning that if there was any profit they would donate their share to local charities. Alas, for them there was no profit to donate. But, Burns, Lane, and Cross made donations anyway. Pat Burns put up $2,000; George Lane and A. E. Cross each kicked in $250. The General and Holy Cross hospitals each received $1,000 and the Victorian Order of Nurses got $500.

However, a public relations, artistic, and managerial success it was not. In fact, it was from these perspectives a disaster. On the first day the program moved so slowly that the show was eventually called because of darkness. On the second day bad weather hit and everything came unstuck. Despite the unfavorable word-of-mouth publicity it was getting it continued to attract crowds ranging from twelve to twenty thousand a day until the Friday of the governor-general's appearance when disaster struck in the form of a sudden thunderstorm. The grounds were already soaked from rains during the week. The thunderstorm hit just as the afternoon performance was getting under way. The management announced that in deference

Getting a cowboy, or as in this case a cowgirl, Hazel Walker, on a bucking horse took forever at the first Calgary Stampede. Only when the horse was ridden into submission was the ride over, and that might take up to five minutes. Photograph by Marcell, Calgary. *Courtesy of Glenbow Archives, Calgary, Alberta.*

The area in which the bronc riding and roping took place took in the entire centerfield of the Victoria Park race track. As a result, when this competitor finally got her steer roped, she was clear over to the backstretch and out of sight of the spectators in the grandstand. *Courtesy of Glenbow Archives, Calgary, Alberta.*

to the governor-general, the show was being transferred into the horse show arena. The Duke of Connaught's carriages were whistled up and, while the vice-regal party was being loaded aboard, the six thousand people in the grandstand stampeded for the arena and its three thousand seats. Ultimately, the vice-regal party had to push and shove its way through the crowd to get into the building.

Eventually the royal couple escaped from Calgary to an irrigation dam opening ceremony at Gleichen and Calgarians had time for a post-mortem on the first Stampede. There was a consensus that it was

such a success that it would have to be made an annual event. But with changes. The way in which the bulldozed long horn bulls spewed blood in all directions when the cowboys, wrestling them to earth, tore their horns out by the roots, offended squeamish Calgarians. Certainly there would have to be no more of that, and there was not for the next fifty years after the Stampede was revived. The depths of animosity which Weadick and his assistants aroused can best be illustrated by quoting a front-page editorial the *Herald* ran on September 7 as the show came to a close.

"The Stampede"

Today marks the last of Calgary's great Stampede. After a week of strenuous entertainment and hearty enjoyment the residents of this city and their thousands of guests will rest. It has been a record week among the cities of western Canada and perhaps, indeed, of the Dominion, and to most of those connected with it must be extended the heartiest congratulations on the successful result of their efforts.

To the public spirited group of gentlemen who made the Stampede possible by their financial support and cooperation Calgary owes a debt of gratitude. The names of Messrs. P. Burns, George Lane, A. E. Cross and A. J. McLean will long be remembered in connection with this affair. The good that has been done to Calgary will remain in their credit as their only reward for their remarkable and generous action.

The management of the Stampede must be congratulated on the ability with which the affair was organized. It cannot be congratulated, however, either on its demeanor towards the public or its treatment of the public on several occasions. In fact, if there is anything of which Calgary feels a little bit ashamed today it is the management of the Stampede itself. As the days passed the impression became prevalent, and events appeared to justify it, that those who had the affair actively in charge were out after the money and did not care much for anything else as long as they got it. They broke faith with the public on several occasions. They turned thousands of people away from the grounds one day without giving them more than a few minutes of a show and without endeavoring to return them their money. They charged an admission fee to see the Calgary Cadets honored by the Governor General of Canada, thus making a circus spectacle of a public event for their own pecuniary benefit. Then, when they had taken the people's money, they excluded them from the inspection.

Last night they got the horse show building jammed with people at so much per head, rushed through a hasty programme, and turned their audience out at a quarter to ten in the evening. Towards the press which has so loyally supported them, the attitude of the management has been arbitrary and discourteous on many occasions. It is the hope of Calgary people that if this performance is repeated another year, it will be placed in the hands of those who will see that faith is observed with the public after the public's money is taken just as well as before. The Herald refers to this matter today instead of keeping it for a later reference in order that visitors to Calgary may know that residents of this city condemn just as much as they do some of the incidents which have marked the conduct of this great event.

But the show was not revived, not just then. Weadick went back to the United States and for the next six years, honed his promotional and managerial abilities and stored up experience promoting shows that took him all the way to New York's Madison Square Garden and to London, England. But for Calgarians the skill of the cowboys and cowgirls, the quality of their horses, and the enjoyment of the frontier days entertainment became a carved-in-granite memory. The directors could call it the Calgary Industrial Exhibition if they liked, but Calgary was still ever so much closer to the frontier than it was to industrialization; a fact that would be emphasized again and again as the years passed into decades within the confines of Victoria Park.

CHAPTER 4

A Master Plan that the World War Blighted

The doubling and redoubling of Calgary's population, increasing to 63,305 in 1912, could alone have made it possible for the Calgary Industrial Exhibition to go on building an unbroken string of attendance records. But the burgeoning of the Exhibition into the outstanding organization of its kind on the Prairies had less to do with Calgary's population than with the population implosion that was filling up the plains of southern Alberta with farm families and farm animals. Between 1901 and 1911 Alberta's population skyrocketed from 73,000 to 374,000 and at the next census in 1921 had reached 588,000.

Exhibition entries first reached the one-thousand mark in 1906. By 1913 they touched 5,909—a number that included 1,105 horses, 393 cattle, 196 pigs, 119 sheep, 1,179 poultry, 529 dogs, 853 ladies' work, and 316 art exhibits. Not only did numbers multiply, but varieties increased as well, emphasizing the rapidly broadening base of agriculture development in southern Alberta. For example, sheep breeds increased from two to ten; swine from a single variety to six. There were ultimately a dozen poultry varieties on display. Within the breeds, the steadily increasing numbers of classes were indicative of the healthy expansion of herds. Thus a breed which started with a couple of classes for each sex would expand to a point where it could fill ten classes, as with the sheep and swine, and up to sixteen classes for the Holstein dairy cattle.

With the 1913 show, E. L. Richardson could look back on his first ten years of employment by the association with pardonable pride. Working in tandem with President I. S. G. VanWart over the last six of those years, he had expanded the activities of the Exhibition in directions never envisioned when the first Exhibition was organized. Richardson operated on the principle that there ought to be an appropriate class at the fair for everybody with a hankering to exhibit anything in competition. It did not matter whether that urge was related to draft horses, beef cattle, dairy cattle, warbling canaries, Dresden lacemaking, or oil painting on satin pillows. Once any class was opened to competition, it usually underwent a weed-like growth in entries. By 1913 so many entries flooded into the Exhibition office as soon as the entry forms were out that the board was stymied in its efforts to mount a campaign to attract the kind of high quality entries it wanted. It had no place to put them.

The close relationship which existed between the Exhibition and Alberta agriculture derived from the original C. W. Peterson policy of making the Exhibition the secretariat for the purebred animal associations. More than that, it was the permanent staff of the Exhibition that stage-managed such occasions as the fat stock shows and sales spring and fall, the spring horse show, fall poultry show and sale, for all these associations. Nominal fees were charged to the exhibitors, but the fees were scaled barely to recover the costs, not to create profit.

The Exhibition office collected memberships for the various associations, charged on the sales of animals a small commission which was turned into the associations to finance their operations. The money handled on behalf of the livestock associations reached $200,000 in 1912 and $870,000 in 1919 before the post-war slump brought the ever onward and upward progress of the Exhibition to a grinding halt.

When Richardson succeeded C. W. Peterson as general manager in 1907, Victoria Park consisted of some ninety-four acres of land and very little else. After the city took title to the property, it advanced money from time to time for the construction of stables, cattle sheds, rudimentary buildings to house exhibits, and the reconstruction of the race track and erection of a grandstand. By 1905 the city's expenditures totalled $19,587. The newly operating spring and fall fat stock shows and sales were then attracting such a flood of entries that substantial expansion was called for. In 1907 the city provided another $13,332 with which to build two additional race horse stables and a grandstand at the outdoor livestock show ring. These improvements were hardly in place before they were proving to be totally inadequate. Fortunately, the federal, provincial, and city governments all made substantial contributions to remedying the deficiency. More than $55,000 was spent in 1907–8 on a large industrial exhibition building, improvements to the race track and grandstand and in the construction of poultry and dog show buildings.

Within two years, however, the organization was again suffering from growing pains, and the Exhibition board decided to "go for broke." It asked the city to submit a bylaw to the ratepayers for permission to borrow an unheard-of $55,000 with which to build a proper horse show arena and livestock pavilion. Richardson pointed out that entries for horse show events had risen from 80 in 1908 to 600 in 1909 and 915 in 1910. Show horses from Vancouver, Spokane, and Saskatchewan were being stabled in Sherman's roller rink and in downtown stables because of lack of accommodation in Victoria Park. Moreover, the horse shows, along with all the other outdoor livestock shows and sales, were still at the mercy of the weather. The $55,000 bylaw was submitted in 1911 and passed with but eleven dissenting votes, and the Victoria Arena was rushed to completion in time for the 1912 Exhibition and the first Stampede.

As it evolved, Victoria Park was becoming a year-round activities center for the city of Calgary and the surrounding countryside. Certainly, it was the prime Calgary community sports center. Track and field sports interest was reaching its peak and half a dozen separate organizations used its race track centerfield for their annual sports days. In addition, the Calgary schools and minor sports organizations held their track meets there. The race track was used by the Calgary Turf Club for its horse races. It was also rented for motorcycle races. Barney Oldfield, the famous American auto racer, brought his troupe to Calgary for an auto racing spectacular in 1912. Local baseball, cricket, and football teams used the park for practices and games. A touring Australian Cricket Club made it the site of a four-day stand. Touring lacrosse teams also played there. All these were interspersed with horticultural shows, dog shows, pigeon shows, and poultry shows.

Despite all this however, the life blood of the Exhibition still flowed from the countryside. By 1913 it had settled into a formula for success patterned very much after the American State and Country Fairs, which were very much agriculture orientated. So voluminous were the entries that judging of livestock took most of the week. The winners were always paraded before the assembled grandstand on Friday afternoons. For the exhibitors the fair was a dawn to dark, week-long event.

The Exhibition gave the farm families an opportunity to see what other farmers were producing, to compare their breed of cattle, horses, sheep, or goats with others. And they made these comparisons while tirelessly touring the barns and pens inspecting the new breeds and varieties appearing every year. They made more such comparisons while seated for hours on end around the judging rings watching the winners being separated from the losers.

Around the showrings, murmurs would run through the crowd when one animal was put up, applause would break out when another winner was announced, gasps of surprise would be audible at still another award. That happened, in 1918, the Calgary *Herald* reported, when the Percheron judge from Illinois placed Keota Jalap, owned by E. A. Davenport of Acme, over George Lane's sensational three-year-old stallion, Newport.

In 1913 the Exhibition reported receipts of just over $100,000 which included $36,528 from gate receipts, $25,000 in grants and something new, and a harbinger of more to come—$10,061 from the pari-mutuel machines which completely replaced bookies for the first time. The

No Calgary organization was more enthusiastic about the construction of the Victoria Arena than the Horticultural Society. Every August, from 1913 onward, it broke out in a riot of colorful blooms from hundreds of Calgary gardens. *Courtesy of Glenbow Archives, Calgary, Alberta.*

overall attendance of 104,529 and the number of exhibitors—1,251—broke all previous records.

The 1913 Exhibition marked the end of I. S. G. VanWart's presidency of the Calgary Industrial Exhibition Company Limited. He had taken over in 1907 to direct the organization of the Dominion Exhibition of 1908 and then stayed on for the next five years of unbroken success. He was succeeded by E. J. Dewey, who served through good times and bad until 1923.

It was during the last year of VanWart's presidency that the directors decided to have done with piecemeal wrestling with plant expansion, adding some barns here, an exhibition building there and a sports facility elsewhere. What was needed was to come up with a master plan which would provide all the facilities they would need for the next fifty years, one which would enable them to concentrate on the quality of the operation not on wrestling with a makeshift physical plant.

In the designing of the master plan for the new Victoria Park, everybody got into the act. Richardson, VanWart, Dewey, the directors, the city engineers, the commissioners, the aldermen, the editors of the newspapers and magazines. They made on-the-ground inspections of the park and went back and debated priorities. The leaders of the various agricultural associations were brought into the discussion when they got down to details. Most important perhaps was the way in which all the aldermen and city commissioners were informed of developments and consulted about all aspects of the master plan. As a result, when the plan eventually went before council for approval it whizzed through without a dissenting vote.

The proposal for the long-range development of Victoria Park called for the following expenditures of $352,625 to finance the rebuilding program:

Grandstand, fireproof, seating 11,000	$127,700.00
Manufacturers' Building	58,300.00
Implement Building	10,000.00
Moving Race Track	24,000.00
Horse Barns — 6 @ $3,500.00	21,000.00
Cattle Barns, to accommodate 420 head	37,200.00
Sheep & Swine Building providing 108 large pens	19,600.00
Superintendent's Cottage	2,400.00
Remodelling Sheep & Swine Building to add to poultry accommodation	3,000.00
Painting — 2 coats & roof, changing color to gray with green roof, 34 buildings	7,600.00
Water Connections ($2,958), 2 new stables ($7,467) already completed pending refund	10,425.00
Water & Sewer Connections	10,000.00
Roads & Sidewalks	12,000.00
Permanent Lighting	4,000.00
Remodeling Present Stables & moving Stables	2,400.00
Roadway for City Stores east of R.R. to 17 Ave.	3,000.00
	$352,625.00

The key to the entire project was moving the race track from the west to the southeast side of the grounds. That area was too close to the river to attract commercial or industrial exhibitions. Spotting the race track on this waste space would release other better land for building sites if, as and when needed.

The changes would add 168 stalls to the horse barns and raise the horse accommodation to 631 head. A fireproof cattle barn and judging building 90 feet square would provide accommodation for 420 head. Space was reserved for ultimate expansion of capacities to 1,500 head of cattle and 850 horses.

The city council rounded the numbers off to $360,000 and made it part of a five bylaw package which it submitted to the ratepayers for approval on June 26, 1914. In addition to the Exhibition's $360,000, there were bylaws of $360,000 for the electric department, $90,000 for street railway extensions, $50,000 for parks, and $17,000 for contingencies.

The Exhibition directors mounted as comprehensive and imaginative a campaign to get ratepayer approval as the city had yet seen. A personal canvass was launched to get pledges of affirmative votes from individual leaders with requests they send copies to customers and suppliers. All the directors embarked on buttonholing blitzes. It is well that they did. Money bylaws had to be approved by sixty-six percent of the electors. Both the electrical and transit bylaws passed easily but the Exhibition barely squeaked through with 33 votes to spare. The vote was 820 to 373. The other two bylaws were defeated.

It was a very small turnout of electors that day. But that should not be taken as evidence of a declining interest in the Exhibition. The simple truth was that public attention in Calgary that June was concentrated elsewhere. The Dingman Well in Turner Valley had just discovered crude oil. Scores of real estate agents, going broke with the collapse of the real estate boom, were hurriedly converting to oil-stock brokerages. The opening of the 1914 Calgary Exhibition on June 29th was driven completely off the front page of the *Herald* by the report from Turner Valley and by a somewhat lesser important news story about the Grand Duke Francis Ferdinand being assassinated at Sarajevo.

Thereafter in 1914, in comparison with the attention it had previously received, the Exhibition fulfilled its dates almost anonymously. In 1913 the *Herald* devoted column after column to listing the winners of all exhibition contests. In 1914 most of the results were crowded out by page after page of oil stock advertisements. As for the assassination of the Grand Duke, the *Herald* noted editorially that people who studied the Balkan affairs closely were convinced there "would be hell to pay" as a result. Payment began on August 4, 1914, with the outbreak of the First World War.

The fact that the ratepayers voted the money to the Exhibition did not mean it would be able to begin bringing its plans to early fruition. The way the system worked, the city treasurer had to go into the bond market and sell city debentures for the amount approved by the ratepayers. By 1914 the collapsed real estate market had ruined the market for municipal debentures. And even if there had been money available, the war would have siphoned

away material essential for its construction. Despite the directors' enthusiasm, expansion plans were filed away until peace returned. For the next four years, the Exhibition had to make do with what facilities it had. Even its use of its own facilities was drastically curtailed because many of its buildings were taken over by the military.

When time came for the 1915 Exhibition to open its gates, it naturally did so to the sound of martial music and the tramp of army feet. The parade that opened the celebration stretched for more than two miles along Seventh Avenue. It was composed of more than four thousand soldiers in two cavalry regiments, three infantry regiments, and medical and service corps. They marched from the Sarcee camp to Victoria Park and assembled there for a demonstration of close order drill and other military exercises. Thereafter throughout the week the military was very much in evidence.

The army was back again in full force in 1916 and while one battalion set up a model bivouac, another put on a demonstration of trench warfare with real trenches and dugouts.

Calgarians got their first glimpse of a woman flying a heavier-than-air airplane in 1917 when Kay Stinson, the barnstorming American aviatrix, turned up as a super-attraction at the Exhibition. She was billed to take off and land in the centerfield but unusually high winds that week kept Miss Stinson on the ground most of the time. She returned the following year to race a car around the race track, but even higher winds prevented her from making the sharp turns needed to keep pace with the car.

That was the year, 1917, when automobile races were a major attraction and a group of touring auto racers from the United States was hired to do the racing. Unhappily, an amateur Calgary speeder also wanted to get into the act and refused to take "no" for an answer. While the manager of the racing troupe was otherwise involved, Fred Siegel wheeled his car onto the track, floored his accelerator to demonstrate his prowess as a race driver. He demonstrated only his inability to negotiate the sharp race track turns at high

31st Battalion CEF on parade at the Exhibition grounds, 1914. *Courtesy of Glenbow Archives, Calgary, Alberta.*

The Calgary Exhibition's interest in aviation moved from balloons to airplanes in 1917 when Kay Stinson, the famous American woman aviation pioneer, paid the first of her many visits to Calgary. She is shown here with her plane with Ernie Richardson posing as pilot. *Courtesy of Glenbow Archives, Calgary, Alberta.*

Automobile racing became a regular feature of the afternoon show at the Calgary Exhibition in 1917 but when the Stampede was revived in 1923 it was phased out. *Courtesy of Glenbow Archives, Calgary, Alberta.*

speed and was killed when he crashed into the fence.

Kay Stinson made a surprise return in 1919 to demonstrate some trick flying for her twice disappointed admirers. She was unintentionally upstaged by a local flyer lately back from the war. He was Captain Fred McCall, who took E. L. Richardson's two sons on a flight over the race track during the auto races. Suddenly his engine died and he was faced with the choice of landing on the race track among speeding cars or alighting on top of the merry-go-round on the midway. He opted for the merry-go-round, made it with a great

crash, and walked away unhurt from the experience, along with his schoolboy passengers.

The super crops at super prices which the farmers enjoyed during the war years were, of course, reflected in the increased attendance, exhibits, and exhibitors. The Exhibition had recorded small deficits in its operating accounts prior to the war but it got into the black, wiped out the accumulated deficits, and came to the official end of the war in 1919 with an accumulated surplus of $51,896.

As soon as the fighting ended in Europe, the Exhibition board returned to its concerns for expansion and the $360,000 the ratepayers had voted for it in 1914. While 1919 brought peace in Europe, it also brought industrial strife to western Canada. As a result there were delays in getting the renovation of Victoria Park underway. However, the city council was able to find $115,000 to advance to the board and

tually outlived their usefulness and were replaced, but the livestock pavilion never was. Named the Victoria Park Pavilion it consisted of a judging ring surrounded by seats for fifteen hundred people, stalls for 150 animals, wash racks, shower rooms and an exhibitors' lounge. With an additional $102,410 the city was able to ad-

One of the most spectacular events in all Exhibition history was the July 5, 1919 crash landing of an airplane on top of the midway merry-go-round. Captain Fred McCall had taken E. L. Richardson's two sons for an aerial tour of Victoria Park when his motor stalled. Neither pilot nor passengers were hurt. *Courtesy of Glenbow Archives, Calgary, Alberta.*

despite the strikes and material shortages, the Exhibition had a new concrete fireproof grandstand seating five thousand spectators in place for the 1919 Exhibition, along with a steel and concrete livestock show and sales pavilion. The plan to relocate the race track was abandoned as an economy measure and the combination grandstand-exhibition hall was located on the opposite side of the track to the original structure. For that fair in 1919, the Exhibition had two grandstands in operation with the old one functioning as a free entry set of bleachers.

The race track and old grandstand even-

vance later in the year, a steel and concrete addition to the pavilion provided fireproof stabling for a total of 600 animals. For over sixty years, it has provided Calgary with an unmatched facility for livestock shows and sales, auction sales, concerts, and, in later years, wrestling matches.

At its 1919 Exhibition, the board went all out for crowd-attracting "spectaculars." It brought in the most famous of American bands—John Philip Sousa's—to provide afternoon and evening concerts. Its performance of a blend of classical, popular, and martial music drew round after round of applause. The Exhibition also had better

Poster advertising Calgary Exhibition, 1919. *Courtesy of Glenbow Archives, Calgary, Alberta.*

luck with a couple of homegrown aviators than it had had with Miss Stinson.

Fred McCall and Wilfred "Wop" May took turns, one in the afternoons, the other at night, thrilling the crowds with the "loop-the-loops," "Immelman rolls," and "falling leaf" manoeuvres that had enabled them to survive the dog fights over the western front in the recent war. The military motif of the war years was carried into the 1919 Exhibition when McCall landed Brigadier General H. F. McDonald in the centerfield of the race track officially to open proceedings.

Super-successful as the 1919 show undoubtedly was, it seemed destined to serve only as a preliminary for the 1919 Stampede. Smack in the middle of Exhibition week, the Calgary newspapers broke out full-page advertisements over Guy Weadick's signature announcing the great Calgary Victory Stampede which would be held from August 25 to 30 at the Exhibition grounds. It would also be sponsored by the Big Four who backed the 1912 show —George Lane, Hon. A. J. McLean, A. E. Cross, and Pat Burns.

The idea of holding a Stampede to celebrate the victory of the allies in the First World War was E. L. Richardson's, grafted onto a British inspiration. Early in 1919, while the peace treaty was still being

One of the star performers at the Victory Stampede of 1919 was Clem Gardner. He is shown here aboard great bucker "High Tower" and with his outfit after a spill in the chuckwagon final. Gardner made his first rodeo appearance at the 1912 Stampede, drove in the first chuckwagon race in 1923, and was an active participant well into the 1930s. Then he confined his activities to riding in the jumping classes at the Calgary Horse Show until well into the 1950s. *Courtesy of the Calgary Stampede.*

An enlargement of this picture has been a mural at Stampede headquarters for fifty years. In addition to the Big Four, it includes two of America's most famous western artists, Charles Russell and Ed Borein, who accompanied Guy Weadick to the 1912 Stampede and exhibited their work. From left to right in the picture: White Headed Chief, unknown, Mr. Galbraith, George Lane, unknown, Mrs. Charles Russell, Mr. Blackstock, Archie McLean, Alex Newton, Pat Burns, unknown, Charles Russell, A. E. Cross, unknown, Ed Borein, unknown, unknown. *Courtesy of J. B. Cross.*

negotiated in Versailles, the British decided the war should not be allowed to end without some sort of a Guy Fawkes Day Spectacle of Commemoration. The government decreed that there should be a Peace Festival on July 19. Canada naturally seconded the proposal and declared that day a national holiday on which all the communities across the country could celebrate with mass outpouring of the citizenry for fun, games, and patriotic speeches. For the Exhibition board, however, this date came much too closely upon the heels of the annual Exhibition.

Richardson's idea from the beginning had been to stage Calgary's Victory Stampede some time in late summer or fall. In early May he contacted George Lane to inquire if Lane, Cross, Burns, and McLean would be prepared to bankroll such a celebration as they had done in 1912. The success of that event had completely reversed Richardson's original conviction that a rodeo in Calgary would never pay its way. It had, almost, and he was now convinced it would again. Lane persuaded his colleagues and then located Guy Weadick who was performing in Spokane and

negotiated a deal with him. Weadick agreed, for a fee, to restage a Stampede in Calgary if the Big Four would again guarantee its solvency.

When he returned in early May, Lane announced the completion of the deal for the Victory Stampede. But he did so with an uncharacteristic note of caution. Such promotions could lose money as well as make money, he warned. Recent experiences in the United States had proved that point. It would be promoted in Calgary for the benefit of local charities and it would only succeed if the citizens of Calgary backed it to the limit of their enthusiasm.

In the process of negotiating a deal with Weadick, Lane learned that there was a rodeo scheduled for Bozeman, Montana for the middle of August and that the Calgary Stampede could be quite conveniently slotted into the fourth week of August. That was smack in the middle of harvest; but it would enable Weadick to bring all the Bozeman rodeo stock and seventy-five competitors and performers to Calgary, along with some skilled behind-the-scenes rodeo workers. They settled for August 25 to 30 for the celebration.

The Calgary Victory Stampede guaranteed $25,000 in purses for participants like bucking horse riders, steer ropers, and bulldoggers. There were also stand-up chariot type races, girls saddlebronc riding and relay races, and the usual trick roping and riding acts. As the show dates approached, Weadick put on a super advertising and publicity drive climaxed by a special twelve-page Calgary *Herald* Victory Stampede edition in which the advertisers joined to publicize the Stampede.

Naturally, with A. E. Cross's longstanding membership of the board of directors, it was no problem for the Big Four to get free use of the Victoria Park facilities along with E. L. Richardson's service as treasurer and general factotum for the Stampede. The format was the one that had worked in 1912, but with some refinements.

This time rigidly constructed saddling chutes were provided in sufficient number to get the broncos saddled quickly and the events run off the same way. The bronc riders still rode their animals to a point where the will-to-buck was broken. A horn then sounded to end the ride. The events were all divided into daily heats with the top contestants competing for the championships on the final day.

The show was widely advertised for its charitable objectives. All profits would be split three ways between the Great War Veterans Association, the Salvation Army, and the YMCA. Unhappily for all concerned, there were no profits to split.

The attendance at the Victory Stampede was:

Monday	5,678
Tuesday	7,354
Wednesday	15,490
Thursday	9,241
Friday	8,412
Saturday	11,281
TOTAL	**57,456**

Despite Weadick's publicity, including published claims before the show opened that the grandstand was sold out for the first three days, attendance was shatteringly disappointing. Only on Wednesday, a specially declared civic holiday that featured the morning Stampede parade, did the grandstand fill to capacity. That was the day that the *Herald* ran a front-page editorial commenting on the poor crowds and urging more general public support. On Friday E. L. Richardson issued a special public appeal for a big turnout on Saturday to push receipts to the break-even point.

When the show closed and the money was counted, it had taken in $82,728, which barely paid expenses and left nothing for the charities. Richardson was inclined to blame the failure to attract Exhibition-sized crowds to the decline in crop prospects that summer. But was a show that delighted 57,000 spectators during the week, and almost made money, all that big a disaster? Not for the spectators certainly, who soon came to appreciate the fine points of the performances they were seeing and returned again and again for more of the same. Not in the eyes of Calgary merchants who avowed that it had been a superbly profitable week. Not for the hotel keepers whose premises were filled to capacity all week. Not for the management of the trolley system, who said the street cars carried more passengers that week than ever before in history.

Calgarians and visitors alike had become accustomed to a twenty-five-cent admission to the Exhibition grounds. The Victory Stampede, like its 1912 predecessor, charged a dollar admission and an additional fifty cents for a grandstand seat. The Exhibition's twenty-five-cent admission of only six weeks previous undoubtedly set off invidious comparisons and created resentment on the part of many prospective customers. Moreover, the Victory celebration came just when post-war inflation was reaching its peak and the high cost of living was on everybody's mind and grabbing for everybody's purse. The resumption of the 1912 building boom, which everybody expected with the coming of peace with victory, did not happen; so jobs were by no means plentiful, and money was tight.

In essence, the "failure" of the Calgary Victory Stampede was only a failure to achieve expectations that were excessively unrealistic in the beginning. On all other counts it had to be declared a success.

CHAPTER 5

Branching Out

As it moved into the 1920s, this could be said about the Calgary Exhibition: the years had been subtly changing its form and direction, but the more it changed the more the men who guided it remained the same. The founders of the Calgary Exhibition were the most durable of men. Col. James Walker served as a director for forty-eight years and A. E. Cross served for forty-five. James "Cappy" Smart, the fire chief, was a director and the chief parade marshal for over thirty years and Col. A. G. Wolley-Dod, Dr. C. P. Marker, P. Turner Bone all served more than thirty years on the board of directors, going back to well before the turn of the century, some to the very beginning.

By 1920 the Exhibition had a permanent staff of six and a spanking new administration building. But to make all the wheels go round in the multitude of activities the institution was becoming involved in, it depended on volunteer committees. It had always had such committees, but in 1919 it underwent a reorganization which tied the members of these committees more closely to the policy level than ever before.

Prior to 1919 its fifteen-member directorate, plus four city representatives, had had the usual slate of patrons, honorary presidents, and honorary or associate directors. Most of the latter were ex-officio appointments—presidents of livestock associations, the superintendent of the CPR, deputy minister of agriculture, civic bureaucrats, and the like. Then they dispensed with the ex officios and began to draw the bulk of their associate directors from their 130-odd shareholders. The second step was to reach into the associate directors for replacements when active directors retired or died. Ultimately a system was evolved in which people were elected to the Exhibition board only after having served as associate directors. Naturally, as the activities of the Exhibition expanded during the 1920s, more and more volunteers were needed and the associates' roster expanded and expanded.

By the latter half of the 1920s being a member of the Board of Directors of the Calgary Exhibition and Stampede had become *the* prestige thing for Calgary citizens. And for the Johnny-come-latelies who were absent when the first directors were appointed, membership on the roster of associate directors was not anything to spurn either.

What was happening was that the business and community leaders of Calgary were joining with the farm and ranching leaders of southern Alberta to turn something that had been a summer agricultural fair into a year-long celebration of life in the great southern Alberta outdoors. It was, in part, the coopting by the Exhibition of the minds and muscles of Calgary's outstanding business and community leaders for service on its committees; and it was in part the growing awareness of the business and community leaders of the city of the possibilities of the Exhibition as a vehicle to advance the business and community interests, of the city. This twin process may be said to have begun with one of Calgary's most spectacular fires. That was the fire that destroyed the Sherman Rink in February 1915.

The Sherman Rink was located a couple of blocks up Seventeenth Avenue from the Horse Show Arena, and was a summertime roller rink, a wintertime ice rink, and an inbetween setting for theatrical performances and dances. The fire left Calgary without an adequate indoor hockey facility and hence was a sports disaster of the first order. Elsewhere in the West, where winter came in early December and stayed until March, outdoor hockey was possible. In Calgary the players needed protection as much from the chinooks which turned skating rinks and curling rinks into mud puddles as from the freezing winds. What with postponements because of severe temperatures, plus postponements because of chinooks, it was frequently impossible to complete any kind of a hockey season. Not even a covered rink was completely chinook-proof, though it was protection against cold spells. So, when Sherman's rink went up in smoke, just when he was contemplating installing an artificial ice plant, agitation arose to turn the Arena into a hockey rink.

Such agitation arose naturally with Calgarians who had become accustomed to turning to the Exhibition when a problem required solving. Thus, prior to the war, when the baseballers had been nudged out of their playing field by the house builders,

a site for the baseball diamond was located on the race track infield in Victoria Park. Similarly, when the footballers needed a playing field, the Exhibition board leveled out a spot for them south of the race track. All this, of course, was consistent with the city's conception of Victoria Park as a sports and community center. But when the agitation for the closed hockey rink surfaced it set going a mumble or two from the curlers of the town.

Indeed, when the Arena was being sold to the ratepayers in 1910, part of the sales pitch was that its 200 by 100 feet show ring "would be flooded in winter to provide curling ice." That notion was quietly filed and forgotten when the Arena was built. The curlers already had a couple of rinks—the Thistle and the Granite—and another group had flooded the CPR's abandoned downtown roundhouse to provide a third. Fundamentally, Richardson had grave doubts about the wisdom of flooding and freezing the dirt floor of the Arena. When spring came, would it be possible to melt the ice and dry out the ground in time for the horse show? Or would the soil remain saturated well into the summer? As long as such questions remained in the air the Arena went unflooded.

Eventually Lloyd Turner was able to talk Richardson into taking a chance. Turner had been manager of the Sherman Rink and after it burned operated an open air rink in downtown Calgary for a couple of years. He knew all about freezing and thawing skating surfaces, and he was able to convince Richardson the job could be done without risk to the horse show. The trick was to cover the surface of the show ring with straw prior to freezing. The straw would absorb most of the water as the ice thawed and could be bulldozed out of the Arena in a semi-frozen state in the spring before it could penetrate too deeply into the dirt below.

The Arena was turned into a hockey rink for the 1918–19 season and Turner was hired to operate it on a joint-venture, profit-sharing basis. At the same time the interest of the curlers was taken care of with the construction of the stabling area of the Victoria Pavilion. When removable partitions and stalls were cleared away there was room for a fourteen sheet curling rink. So enthusiastically did the curlers take to the rink that more ice was soon needed. Richardson provided it by flooding the sheep-swine building. This conversion added five more sheets to Victoria Park's capacity.

The curlers took to the pavilion with as much enthusiasm as Calgary skaters took to the Arena. After the loss of the Sherman Rink they had been served by three or four corner-lot outdoor rinks in downtown Calgary and the Crystal Rink at Fourth Avenue and Ninth Street. When Turner invited Calgarians to skate the old year out and the New Year in at the Arena, the response was like a charge of the light brigade. The newspapers reported that no fewer than 1,250 donned their skates and so jammed the ice surface that it had to be cleared and swept after every half dozen band numbers.

One of Turner's first moves on taking over the Arena was to persuade Calgary businessmen to sponsor two Calgary teams to play in a Big Four Hockey League with Edmonton. Out of those teams evolved the Calgary Tigers which became a fixture in the Western Canada Hockey League composed of Calgary, Edmonton, Saskatoon, and Regina. The four prairie teams arranged an interlocking schedule with the Pacific Coast League but that only lasted one year.

Although keeping professional hockey leagues in operation in the West was an excessively marginal undertaking, hockey from the first was a financial winner for the Arena. Until Turner came upon the scene in 1918, the building had been a financial drain. The horse shows, spring and summer, paid their way. But for the rest of the year the Arena did not take in enough to pay for building maintenance and fire insurance. Under Turner's administration the Rovers-Canadians-Tigers were only the beginning. He soon had junior teams, commercial teams, ladies' teams, and schoolboy teams playing in the Arena along with public pleasure skating and evenings set aside for figure skating club practices, "art" skating as it was called then. By 1921 the facility was completely out of the red and contributing over $9,500 to the net income of the Exhibition.

The Arena, moreover, was not only a hockey center. As time passed, the Arena became Calgary's "everything center." It was to the Arena that Aaron Sapiro came to launch campaigns that got the Alberta, Saskatchewan, and Manitoba Wheat Pools into operation, where Aimee Semple McPherson came to preach her "four square" revival gospel.

Expanding hockey and curling facilities in Victoria Park was just the beginning. In March 1920 Richardson launched the largest project ever undertaken by the Exhibition without financing by the city—a baseball diamond and stand for the Calgary team in the newly formed Western Canada Baseball League. It would have teams in Calgary, Edmonton, Saskatoon, Regina, Moose Jaw and Winnipeg. The league was an artistic success, attracting one hundred thousand spectators to Victoria Park in 1920, but in the end it was a financial disaster, wrecked on the shoals of exorbitant travel costs on an across-the-board attendance collapse. The Calgary Bronks won the league championship in 1920 and repeated in 1921. The league, however, barely made it to the playoffs which drew less than one thousand fans a game. The next year Calgary and Edmonton got Vancouver and Tacoma into a league but that lasted but a single summer. Over the next decade the board quietly wrote off the $12,150 it sunk in its foray into professional baseball.

Baseball was not its only artistic success and financial disaster of that super-expansionist era. Another was the decision to sponsor the Calgary Winter Carnival of 1921. In the back of everybody's mind seemed to be the idea of staging something like a midwinter Stampede to counteract the post-Christmas business blahs in Calgary. There could be a week-long winter carnival with hockey games, a prize fight, a curling bonspiel, speed-skating, snowshoeing races, and ski-jumping.

A world class ski-jumping contest? In plate-flat Victoria Park? How?

Easy! Build a seventy-five-foot-high steel tower on one end of the grandstand roof and slope a slide from the top of the tower to the other end of the roof with a take-off curve for the skiers! This would shoot them into the air and they could land

The wackiest promotion in the history of the Calgary Exhibition and Stampede was indubitably the ski-jumping championships of 1921 from the grandstand roof. The top picture shows the superstructure from which the jumper has just taken off. The second shot is looking down from the take-off platform. More than ten thousand attended the first year, but the next year the event was blown away by a snow-melting chinook and a howling blizzard *Courtesy of Glenbow Archives, Calgary, Alberta.*

on another slide sloped from the end of the roof to the ground.

Not only did Richardson and the board of directors conjure up such a project, they embarked upon it!

And they completed it! Tons and tons of snow were hauled to the roof of the grandstand and manhandled onto the sloping surface of the slide from the top of the tower. More snow had to be packed on the much wider slide from the grandstand roof to the ground. Then more than a score of ski-jumpers from Minnesota and British Columbia, including the world champion professional, Augen Haugen, were persuaded to come to Calgary, lug their skis to the top of the tower, and make the jump, not once but several times.

The Calgary *Herald* hailed the ski-jumping caper as the "greatest sporting event in western Canadian history." It may well have been. It attracted more than eleven thousand spectators, no doubt of the sort who go to auto races in anticipation of smash-ups. None of the contestants broke a neck, or even a leg, though most of them crashed heavily on landing on their first practice runs. Then more snow was hauled in, some adjustments were made in take-off and landing areas, and over the two-day tournament a number of jumps were completed. The longest distance however was in the 110–15 feet range, barely half the distance the Revelstoke jumpers were recording at home.

Construction of the ski hill cost the Exhibition $8,535.61, which was $5,846 more than the net after expenses for operating the carnival. The next year real disaster struck, in the form of a chinook, a week before the carnival, the chinook's warm winds and fifty degree temperatures melting the Calgary area snow cover. Then the weather turned cold, but brought no snow. To make the ski jump operative the Exhibition board had to import railway gondola cars full of the stuff from Lake Louise. Then, just when the ski-jumping was about to begin the weather turned bitterly cold, an arctic gale blew across Victoria Park, and the crowd dwindled to well under one thousand spectators. The winter carnival lost money. The steel tower was dismantled and the cost of the episode written off over the next ten years.

The winter carnivals, the Arena hockey promotions, curling, baseball, and football, were good examples of the "try-anything-once" attitude that Richardson brought to the job of general manager of the Calgary Exhibition. True, he had scorned the Stampede idea when it was first presented to him in 1912. But when he saw its impact on the crowd it attracted he was instantly convinced that this was a promotion with a future. Thus, when Calgary was looking around for a suitable form of victory celebration in 1919 it was Richardson who suggested that the city should stage another Stampede.

In the process of Guy Weadick's selling rodeo sports to southern Albertans in 1912 and 1919, southern Alberta had sold itself to Guy Weadick. In the summer of 1920 Weadick bought a ranch in the Pekisko country, on which he proposed to operate an American style dude ranch. It was located southwest of High River, eleven miles north of the E P Ranch which the Prince of Wales had acquired on his visit to Calgary in 1919.

Weadick's presence in the Calgary area led Richardson to add a rodeo touch to the Calgary Spring Horse Show. In 1921 he hired Weadick and his wife to put on their trick riding and roping act as an intermission feature at the evening horse shows. An instant hit, it became an added attraction to the show, with the following year a miniature rodeo added to the Weadick act.

In 1923, when Richardson was casting about for something to arrest the declining attendance of the Exhibition, it was to Weadick that he turned and the Calgary Exhibition *and Stampede* was born. It would not, however, legally become the Calgary Exhibition and Stampede Company Limited for another full decade. For 1923 it would be the Calgary Exhibition, Stampede and Buffalo Barbecue.

To all intents and purposes until 1920, the Calgary Industrial Exhibition Company Limited had been a company-on-paper without visible means of supporting itself, or with bankable assets. The city held title to Victoria Park and everything in it. The Exhibition held a dollar-a-year lease on the premises but functioned very much as an ordinary city department. Thus it ordered

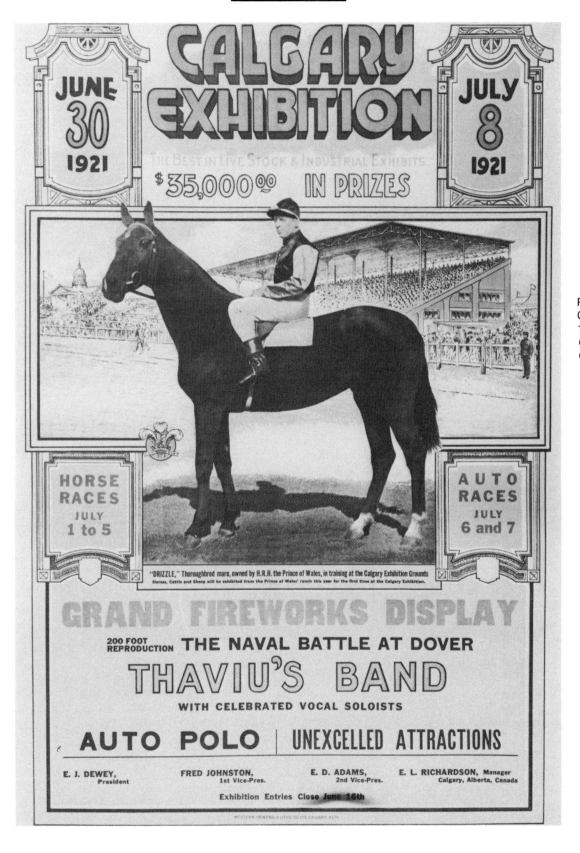

Poster advertising the Calgary Exhibition, 1921. *Courtesy of Glenbow Archives, Calgary, Alberta.*

its supplies through the city purchasing agent, and negotiated important expenditures with the city commissioners. However, except for a five thousand dollar annual city grant toward maintenance costs, and another five thousand-odd to cover insurance premiums on the Victoria Park buildings, the Exhibition maintained itself out of income. Except, that is, for the debenture debt which had been floated for various construction projects. Servicing that debt was charged to the Calgary taxpayers. In 1920 the Exhibition board took the first small step toward a declaration of its financial independence from the city and toward having a life of its own. It decided that henceforth it would no longer accept the operating grant and would take over the payment of the insurance premiums on its buildings.

It was able to make these gestures because of the profit of $23,893 it made in 1919 which boosted its accumulated war-time surplus to $51,896. This surplus probably contributed to the surfeit of optimism that led to the involvement in hockey, baseball, and winter carnival promotions. It was a mood of optimism that died hard on the shoals of post-war depression that pounded Calgary's dreams of the future to pieces.

From a peak of $2.80 a bushel in 1919, the price of wheat sank to $1.00 in 1921. Prime steers that had brought $12 per hundred pounds went begging at $4.50.

Instead of round-the-clock hammer-banging on construction jobs, the city was counting up the hundred thousand building lots it had taken for taxes, and the nine hundred destitute unemployed seeking relief of some kind.

The farmers were angry and getting angrier, the workers were morose and getting more so at talk of wage cuts instead of wage increases. The politicians were frustrated and the electors were out of sorts. In 1920 for the first time in a decade attendance at the Exhibition dropped sharply from 127,000 in 1919 to 103,000 and instead of 1919's $23,000 surplus it wound up with a $5,700 deficit.

Instead of bouncing back in 1921, as everyone expected, things got worse, though the operating loss was down to $4,624. Attendance was down again too, to 96,000. The decline in attendance was arrested in 1922, but the deficit jumped to $14,888 and reduced the accumulated surplus to $22,811. The financial statements would not have been so depressing if the Exhibition had not foregone the city's grant and paid the insurance premiums. But they were depressing enough to convince the directors that the mini-stampede they had been staging at the horse show should be expanded into a full dress rodeo and slotted into the Exhibition programme in the hope of arresting declining attendance and getting it back into the black.

Weadick was hired as Stampede Man-

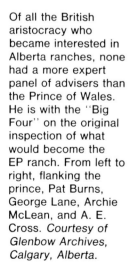

Of all the British aristocracy who became interested in Alberta ranches, none had a more expert panel of advisers than the Prince of Wales. He is with the "Big Four" on the original inspection of what would become the EP ranch. From left to right, flanking the prince, Pat Burns, George Lane, Archie McLean, and A. E. Cross. *Courtesy of Glenbow Archives, Calgary, Alberta.*

ager for $5,000 for a six months' stint. He was to come on staff in January and work putting the show together and staging. When the Exhibition closed he was free to take off in pursuit of his own performing career until the following January. In the context of the times it was a remarkable arrangement. Full-time managers of Calgary banks, in 1923, earned from $2,500 to $3,000. The city commissioners were also paid $2,500 a year while Mayor George Webster earned $5,000, and in 1923 there was a lot of talk around city hall of reducing both stipends rather substantially. The Exhibition was prepared to pay Guy Weadick as much for half a year's work as it was paying its own general manager for full-time employment!

The 1923 Stampede differed somewhat from previous editions. More attention was paid to recruiting Canadian contestants and less to bringing in Americans. More emphasis was placed on trophies and less on cash for prizes. Stampede cash awards were held to $10,000 compared with the $25,000 offered in 1919. But the trophy prizes almost made up the value difference, and several of them became permanent fixtures of the Stampede prize list.

As a challenge trophy to be competed for each year for champion Canadian bronc rider, the Prince of Wales donated a solid silver statue of a horse, plus a sterling silver cigarette case. Mary Pickford, Douglas Fairbanks, and Henry Birks each provided a case of Community Plate. Riley and McCormick, Great West Saddlery, and Calgary Saddlery each donated western saddles. There were buffalo heads and buffalo robes, Stetson hats, silver plated bits and spurs, Navajo blankets, cases of mounted birds, and a dozen other items to add to the cash prizes. There were also $1,750 in special cash awards by members of the board of directors through their companies. The Prince of Wales personally presented his trophy to the first winner, Pete Vandermeer, later that summer at a party at his ranch.

Guy Weadick was a history buff with a nostalgia streak a foot wide running down his back. His entire promotional life, he

440 - CHIEFS OF THE STONEYS, SARCEES AND BLACKFEET WITH GUY WEADICK, STAMPEDE CHIEF. - © W. J. OLIVER.

There is surely a spectacular contrast between these Indians with Guy Weadick and those who appeared in the Stampede Parade in 1912. Gone are the travois and the Hudson's Bay blankets. In their place the superbly crafted ceremonial costumes of the chief of the Stoney, Cree, and Blackfoot. *Courtesy of Glenbow Archives, Calgary, Alberta.*

was then thirty-eight years old, was spent trying to recapture a romanticized version of American western life before the turn of the century. In Calgary, and in particular on the Exhibition board, he encountered more kindred soul mates than he ever suspected existed. When he and Richardson asked Mayor George Webster to ban all vehicular traffic from the busiest section of Calgary's main street for two hours each morning, so that cowboys and Indians could ride around on their horses, the mayor acquiesced. When they suggested that downtown merchants fancy up their store fronts with rough lumber decorations in imitation of the old frontier town, the merchants fell in with the suggestion. When they proposed that the highlight of the week be a free buffalo barbecue for all attenders on Saturday night, the Dominion Government supplied the buffaloes, a local bakery supplied the buns, and a local creamery all the butter.

What set Weadick apart was not so much his ability to stage a rodeo, although he certainly fine-tuned that talent in the decade that had elapsed since his first Calgary appearance, but in his ability to *promote* a rodeo. To bring off the kind of show he wanted he recognized that it took weeks stretching into months of advance promotion. Thus the cow town he envisioned Calgary becoming for Stampede Week had to look like a cow town. In early spring he was out persuading the downtown merchants to bedeck their store-fronts with crude-lumber facades, mangers, and hitching posts in imitation of Calgary of the 1880s. Such a slab-coated street would be incongruous unless the populace was suitably clothed. So he was off on a campaign to promote the wearing of western dress during Stampede.

In a real sense, the 1923 Exhibition and Stampede set the pattern for everything that came after. Calgarians wearing "west-

ern" clothing became the fashion when the downtown merchants offered daily prizes for the best dressed cowboys and cowgirls—urban variety—on display. Not, of course, that the authentic variety was not prominently on display as well. They too got daily prizes for their horses and tack. The Indians turned up en famille in all their beadwork finery, and their presence helped turn the downtown mornings into fashion promenades.

On Tuesday morning, July 10, shortly before noon, a cowboy Stampede contestant named Eddie King gave rein to an impulse, rode his cowpony through the open door of the Club Cafe, ambled it quietly in past the cashier, down the aisle behind the customers at the lunch counter, circled around the kitchen and into the dining room where he threaded his way between the tables and back out to the street. Out of that episode grew the legend of cowboys riding horses in and out of

hotels as a regular thing during Stampede week in Calgary.

Another first to be established during that week was the chuckwagon breakfast on the downtown streets. It began when a couple of the chuckwagons that were competing at Victoria Park drove into the city on Thursday morning, unloaded their stoves, lit the fires, and began cooking beans and bacon and flapjacks and serving them to the assembled multitudes.

The chuckwagon races that first year were a far cry from those that came after. In concept they were devised to give the Stampede patrons a glimpse of an event that sometimes occurred at the end of a roundup when the various outfits that participated packed up and headed for home. The chuckwagon, so called because it was the dining center for the cowboys, was a heavy farm wagon with a canvas top from the rear of which an eight-foot canvas canopy extended to two upright poles. The

Another tradition, or more accurately, another legend was born when Eddie King was persuaded by a Calgary *Herald* photographer to ride his horse into, through, and out of the Club Cafe on Eighth Avenue. *Courtesy of Glenbow Archives, Calgary, Alberta.*

Here is the authentic model of a chuckwagon—a heavy farm wagon converted into a mobile kitchen for a cattle roundup. They raced wagons like these during the formative years of "The Greatest Outdoor Show on Earth." *Courtesy of Glenbow Archives, Calgary, Alberta.*

camp cook prepared the food on a heavy cast iron stove and served it under the canopy. Breaking camp consisted of dismantling the flap, gathering up the branding irons and other paraphernalia, and loading everything, including the stove, into the chuckwagon. Usually drawn by a single team, the wagon in rough country was sometimes pulled by two pairs of grade Percherons, Clydesdales, or other heavy breeds.

When the wagon was loaded and the teams hitched to it, the homeward bound horses quickly broke into a fast trot. If a couple of outfits were going the same way a race at full gallop might develop. If there was a town en route there was likely to be an all-out race for the nearest saloon. And that was what Weadick and the Stampede committee had in mind when they scheduled the first chuckwagon race, a race from campsite to saloon at a full gallop!

Their first hurdle was to convince the neighborhood ranchers they should risk their horses and wagons in such a contest. The resistance they encountered was most discouraging. Then they urged groups of ranchers to club together to enter a rig and spread the risk. In this they were more successful and had eight groups entered. At the last minute two dropped out so the first chuckwagon race was in two heats of three wagons each.

The course to be raced was around half the race track, starting and finishing in the centerfield in front of the grandstand. The inner race track rails were removed and the wagons were assembled, facing across the centerfield, adjacent to a couple of spaced-out barrels for each rig. At the starter's signal the four outriders of each rig were to dismantle the tent-fly, gather the branding irons, and load the stove into the wagon. The wagon would then start and make a figure eight around the barrels while the outriders mounted and followed it across

One of the most popular features of Stampede Week in Calgary is the downtown serving of flapjacks and bacon from the chuckwagons. It began as a spur of the moment impulse in 1923. Weadick had persuaded a number of the chuckwagon drivers to stage an informal parade through the downtown streets. Horace Inkster, who was the C-X ranch camp cook, went along with the Jack Morton wagon. He lit a fire in the stove, put on some pancakes, and began dishing them out to the gathering crowd. A tradition was born. *Courtesy of Glenbow Archives, Calgary, Alberta.*

the centerfield to the backstretch. There the wagons made a sharp left turn onto the track and around the far turn for home. Back at the barrels the riders would dismount, unhitch the horses, reerect the canopy, set up the stove, and light a fire in it. The first outfit to get smoke emerging from the chimney won the race.

That was the concept. The result of the first races was confusion worse confounded. First to get the stove smoking was the Clem Gardner rig from Pirmez Creek. But he had his team facing the wrong way and was disqualified. The third rig turned everything into shambles when its outriders, seeking to get more speed from the team, rode alongside and began applying their whips. They caused, instead, only a bucking, pitching pile-up as they hit the centerfield.

The rules were instantly amended to ban the use of whips by outriders. And, as the week progressed other changes were made,

all of which enhanced the excitement of the race itself and diminished the importance of the authentic touches of the roundup.

At the conclusion of the five days of racing the judges decided that Bill Somers of Mosquito Creek, a seventy-year-old former stagecoach driver, was the winning driver and that Dan Riley of High River should get the Stetson hat awarded the winning owner, even though he shared ownership of the outfit with A. E. Cross, Jack Drumheller, and Rod MacLeary.

In chuckwagon racing the Calgary Exhibition and Stampede had a spectacular hit on its hands. There was no doubt about that, either from the reaction of the audiences or of the ranching community. In 1924 the ranchers' reluctance turned to enthusiasm and more than a dozen rigs were entered. The trend to lighter rigs and lighter, faster horses began. The race was extended to a full half mile and the following year the after-the-race riga-marole in the centerfield was abandoned. The age of chuckwagon racing as real horse racing had begun.

It was the chuckwagon races that en-abled the management to reschedule its entertainment more effectively. The chuckwagons, the Indian races, chariot races, and vaudeville program were all shifted from afternoon to evening. With the band concert and fireworks there was thus created a full fledged evening's enter-tainment. In effect, for those who spent a full day on the grounds, it was two shows for the price of one, though separate grandstand tickets were required for each show.

Here is how Weadick described the chuckwagons in the 1927 promotional lit-erature:

Primitive, rattling, lumbering, range-scarred, mess wagons fully equipped. Their daring drivers on the swaying seats handling the ribbons on the fastest four-horse team their ranch can pro-duce. Old-timers who know no fear, and daredevil young "uns" desperately pit-ting their skill in racing rivalries. They break camp, load their wagons, cut a figure eight around two barrels, and run half a mile on the track to finish under the wire in just under two minutes. The sensation of any race course. The mad glories of the chariot races of the Roman Coliseum eclipsed by the rangemen of the west.

When it came to publicity, Guy Wea-dick tended always to get the bit in his teeth and run. His approach was pure Phineas T. Barnum—to exaggerate the glories of whatever he was publicizing, but to give the customers more than they paid for. Left to his own devices, he would not have stopped until every newspaper on the continent was carrying stories promoting the Calgary Stampede. And if there was a newspaper anywhere which did not feel the brunt of Weadick's publicity it must have been a mean and shrunken specimen of the fourth estate. Weadick's familiarity with the newspapers of the continent was all embracing.

In their annual report to the sharehold-ers for 1923, President E. J. Dewey and E. L. Richardson were only slightly exaggerating when they opined: "It is not too much to say that this year's Exhibition received as much publicity as had been secured for the exhibitions held annually in Cal-gary for, say, the past fifteen years."

The pre-Stampede blitzkrieg in Calgary was indeed too successful in one way. So many people turned up at Victoria Park on Sunday before the show to ogle the pre-liminary preparations that the gates had to be locked. There were so many people wandering around the grounds that there was no room on which to erect the rides, games, and displays.

The result of the enthusiasm was appar-ent again in the parade that kicked off the celebration on July 9. More than two thousand Calgarians, mainly on horses, participated, if the hundreds of Indians from the nearby reserves were counted as Calgarians. Headed by Mayor Webster and Guy Weadick, with a forestry airplane overhead, and half a dozen bands in-terspersed, the parade took an hour to pass the thirty thousand spectators that lined the streets and was adjudged the best such spectacle Calgary had ever seen.

The show itself was certainly the most spectacular and the most successful in Calgary history. Eighteen carloads of thor-oughbreds were rushed in from the Bran-don summer fair to participate in the first all-running-horse race meet. Over the years entries of harness horses had dwin-dled steadily until a point was reached in 1922 when there were not enough entries to fill the races. It was not until 1961 that a trotter or pacer again set foot on a Calgary race track in a major race meet.

The part played by the Indians in the summer party reached the highest point yet. The women erected their teepees in a village of their own in Victoria Park and participated enthusiastically in the down-town jamboree. And the Indians continued to take part in the daily Indian pony races as they had done for many years.

The chuckwagon races, wild horse races, chariot races, calf roping, and steer riding had the public coming back again and again. A record of 137,825 were attracted through the gates and filled the grandstand to capacity most days. It was, for the first time in years, blessed with perfect weather throughout the show.

One of the wildest events at the rebirth of the Stampede in 1923 was the wild cow milking contest. *Courtesy of the Calgary Stampede.*

This is the disaster that might have been in 1923—a flash flooding of the Elbow River in June that turned Victoria Park into a lake only days before the Stampede. *Courtesy of Glenbow Archives, Calgary, Alberta.*

The 1923 weather was regarded as a minor miracle. A month before the show, torrential rains in the mountains caused flooding over wide areas of southern Alberta. The Elbow River went seven feet over its banks, flooded the basement of the power house in Victoria Park and the low lying area of the park itself. However, the flood subsided before doing any damage to the race track and left no permanent impression on the park.

Over the first Stampede week itself, two events were outstanding. The first was the monster Cowboys and Old Timers western dance on Friday night. In the beginning it was conceived as an affair that would be comfortably accommodated in the main ballroom of the Palliser Hotel. But tickets sold so quickly that the main dining room was booked as well. Still the demand came until the sponsors sold tickets to everybody who wanted them, hired four additional bands, and roped off the street in front of the hotel for the crowd of four thousand who participated in a party that began at 10:00 P.M. and continued until 2:00 A.M.

The event was equalled and even topped by the buffalo barbecue that was the final event on the week-long program. The buffalo was cooked in Pat Burns's packing plant and made into sandwiches for free distribution to the patrons on the grounds. The logistics of cutting the meat and the bread, making eleven thousand sandwiches, and then distributing them to the patrons without evoking a riot, were horrendous. They involved an army of volunteers that included Calgarians of every walk of life from the mayor, the aldermen, and everyone on down.

What made the events particularly noteworthy was that both were carried through without untoward incidents of any kind. The barbecue was embarked upon with misgivings that people could be trampled in the rush of a crowd of 10,000 to get at the food. There was a rush, and a crush, but an incipient mob melted into orderly lineups before the scores of distribution points and the multitude feeding went off without a hitch.

The closing night barbecue was repeated intermittently over the next few years but the increasing attendance precluded it becoming a permanent feature and it was eventually dropped entirely. The dance, on the other hand, went on expanding and expanding until by 1928 the entire block of Ninth Avenue between First and Centre Streets was needed to accommodate the fifteen thousand who attended.

For the board of directors, the 1923 Exhibition and Stampede was the end of the red ink era. When the books were closed for the year they revealed a surplus of $22,142.56. It was the first of many to come. But outranking the artistic and financial triumphs of 1923 was the spiritual lift that the Calgary fun week gave to southern Alberta. After three years of depression it again became possible to look on the bright side, to refurbish one's lagging faith in the country. It was a fun week, in just about every way "fun" could be defined. Troubles were shucked, and once shucked, diminished in importance. It was more than a fun week, it was an augury of better things to come for, as the visitors returned home, their eyes fell on the greatest wheat crop in Alberta history beginning to ripen in the fields.

CHAPTER 6

Horse Races and Hollywood

I t was one thing for Mayor Webster to tell the assembled patrons at the conclusion of the 1923 Exhibition that the chuckwagon races would be back in 1924. That would mean bringing back the Stampede as well, and in the cold light of the after-the-show assessment of 1923 there were some directors who were not so sure.

True, the Exhibition, Stampede, and buffalo barbecue had ended with a whopping net profit. But bringing it off had been a monumental undertaking which had taxed the human resources of the whole community, Exhibition directors and an army of volunteer citizens. The parade committee needed the services of several hundred volunteers to move its various units into place. Scores of downtown merchants and their employees were coopted for the downtown street performances. The work done by the directors on the various committees was vital, of course, but without the contributions of brain and brawn of the hundreds of volunteers the entire project could have collapsed in a snarled disaster.

Could the Exhibition count on the reenlistment of the citizenry if the project became an annual event? The short answer was "yes." Volunteerism had become so much a part of the Exhibition operations that it could almost be said that the Exhibition had invented it. The volunteers were people with passionate interests in the aspects of the Exhibition for which they

volunteered. Thus, the Exhibition directors knew that they could count on the horse lovers to run the horse show, the flower lovers to run the flower show, the dog lovers to run the dog show, the cattle breeders to run the livestock shows.

It was E. L. Richardson's genius for keeping people involved that kept all the balls in the air. But was volunteerism enough? Staging the Stampede as part of the Exhibition was an immense undertaking altogether aside from the increased number of volunteers required. A small army of cowboys and great herds of horses and cattle had to be hired for the operation. Prize money running into the thousands of dollars had to be guaranteed. The net cost of staging the 1923 Stampede alone exceeded $12,000.

The 1923 show had been blessed with perfect weather from start to finish. But what if it rained? What if public interest in the Stampede turned out to be a one-time thing?

The state of the weather was always a worry. It seldom if ever rained on the Exhibition parade, but an all-day rain

By 1900 George Lane had a thriving thoroughbred breeding enterprise going on his Namaka ranch as this herd of mares and foals indicates. *Courtesy of Glenbow Archives, Calgary, Alberta.*

anytime during the week could put a deep dint in the net income of the operation. What worried the directors and their 147 shareholders was the organization's lack of financial reserves. An even mild disaster, like a wet week, might cause such a financial shock as to make the shareholders personally liable for a whopping deficit. So there was good reason for looking long and hard before they leaped. The wonder was that they had plunged so often into unplumbed promotional depths.

Guy Weadick assumed that the success of the 1923 show meant it would become a permanent feature of the Exhibition. But he had assumed the same in 1912. When he left to resume his vaudeville acting career the day after the 1923 show closed, he had no assurance that running the Stampede was to become a permanent appointment. His contract was for one year and if the show was to be continued, he would be notified of the extension of his contract by December 1. Eventually the directors decided to take a chance on having a Stampede for a second year and instructed Richardson to notify Weadick that his contract would be extended—again for one year. There was nothing foolhardy or

precipitous about the decision of the Calgary Industrial Exhibition Company to make Weadick's rodeo an integral part of its operation.

All unknowingly, the Calgary Exhibition in 1923 was caught up in a series of events that would profoundly affect its future, and the future of the greater Calgary community. One such was the deal it made with a Winnipeg promoter, R. James Speers, to take over the operation of its horse racing department. It was a deal that would prove to be a tremendous boon to the thoroughbred horse business of western Canada, as well as to the Exhibition itself. Indeed it marked the birth of the thoroughbred horse business in western Canada.

Thoroughbred horses had been a part of the ranching industry from the beginning for the thoroughbred had qualities of body and spirit that made it invaluable to the cattle ranching business. It was faster afoot than any other horse, it was unmatched for stamina, and it could be trained to skills essential in riding herd on cattle or horses. Thus when the cattle industry was moving into Alberta the first requirement of the ranch owner was to acquire thoroughbred stock for his horse herd. In the 1880s the

Quorn Ranch imported the bay stallion Eagle's Plume which became one of the great names in western thoroughbred history. He was the sire of May W which was foaled in 1894 and went on to make racing history across the United States before being shipped to England. Other Quorn importations were Yorkist, Acostic, and Grand Coup.

It was not, of course, that thoroughbreds monopolized the attention, or the affection, of the early ranchers. There was a French Coach Horse Association and Hackney Horse Association in Alberta well before the turn of the century and Pat Burns had established a fine herd of Morgans. It was Calgary horse, Robin Adair, owned by the Rawlinson Brothers, that won the Hackney stallion championship at the Madison Square Garden, New York, horse show in 1901. In the main, however, the others were specialty breeds. The thoroughbred was the all-purpose horse. He was a workhorse and a fun horse that could be ridden to hounds, over jumps, and even

hitched to a plow or a jogging cart. But most of all it was a speed horse.

Wherever there were thoroughbreds, there were arguments about speed and stamina. In the pioneer years there was not a town in southern Alberta whose life was not periodically excited by match races down the length of its main street, often with side bets running into the hundreds of dollars. Farther east, and to the north where farming predominated, the races tended to be more between the owners of pacers and trotters. In southern Alberta when the government began looking to the

production of remounts for its cavalry regiments, it was to the thoroughbred that it turned. After establishing a remount center at Millarville, it imported thoroughbred stallions to stock it and regularly kept four or five stallions on hand to service the ranchers' mares.

Next to Eagle's Plume, the most notable stallion imported into western Canada was Yorkshire Lad, by Dinna Forget, out of Rose Marjorie by Roseberry. Born in 1902, he stood at stud at C. E. Wilkinson's farm at Millarville for twenty-five years. Of him it was said: If there had been available to him mares that matched his quality he might have sired offspring of international racing caliber. As it was he sent winner after winner to the races of western Canada, including Yorkshire Maid, York Road, and Yorkist.

The first *Canadian Thoroughbred Horse Association Stud Book* was published in 1915. Until then registration of thoroughbreds had been via the American or British books. There was but a single Alberta entry the first year. The following year thirty-two births were recorded, which was also the average for the next six years. After R. J. Speers became the manager of thoroughbred racing across the Prairies, registrations doubled and redoubled, in Manitoba and Saskatchewan as well as in Alberta.

In 1925 registration in Alberta jumped to 67, increased again to 103 the following year, and never looked back. Part of the explanation for the Alberta increase was the instant popularity at stud of Will Somers, the royally bred black stallion King George V gave the Prince of Wales when he bought the E P Ranch at Pekisko and stocked it with Shorthorn cattle and thoroughbred horses.

Speers had built a new race track in Winnipeg, Whittier Park, and to get horses for his 1924 meet he combed the "bushes" of Minnesota, Iowa, Nebraska, and Montana. By organizing the prairie racing circuit he was able to offer the owners a continuous summer of racing at the fairs in Brandon, Calgary, Edmonton, Saskatoon, and Regina. At the same time he could assure the fair managers of an adequate supply of horses to enable them to run a full racing program. By moving the horses

Calgary's, and southern Alberta's, love affair with the thoroughbred horse began with the arrival of the first settlers and bloomed triumphantly during the 1920s. Konrad was probably the first thoroughbred imported into Alberta from Kentucky. He stood at the Bow River Horse Ranch in the early 1880s. *Courtesy of Glenbow Archives, Calgary, Alberta.*

One of the most revolutionary changes in thoroughbred racing occurred when a Calgarian, Charles Cowell, invented a portable starting gate that enabled thoroughbred races to get off to perfect starts. This Cowell gate, however, was replaced the following year by a more refined and sophisticated model that had been developed in California. *Courtesy of the Calgary Stampede.*

on a special train, Speers got a cheap freight rate, which he permitted the owners to pay out of whatever purses they earned on the circuit.

Speers established too a large thoroughbred stock farm in Manitoba in 1925 by importing stallions and mares from Kentucky. For almost ten years he sold off all his production stock to neophyte owners, often at give-away prices. He also persuaded A. E. Cross, E. D. Adams, George Addison, and a number of other Calgarians to incorporate the Chinook Jockey Club and construct a mile race track at Calgary's southern city limits.

In the early years the American horses completely dominated racing, though there was always at least one race a day restrict-

ed to Canadian breeds. As the Canadian horses increased in numbers more races were made for them. By 1928 there were enough two year olds at Victoria Park to schedule the first race for Canadian-bred two year olds, four of which were sired by Will Somers and three by Jas T. Clark, the Meeks brothers Kentucky bred stallion. A Will Somers colt, Willmarnock, finished first with a young apprentice jockey named Johnny Longden aboard. A Jas T. Clark filly, Silent Sister, finished second. Both were owned by the Jacques brothers of Calgary who enjoyed considerable success over the years racing other Jas T. Clark progeny, two of which were Silent Pardner and Silent Messenger.

The equine quality competing on the

prairie circuit was, of course, basic bush-league, as was only to be expected from the two- and three-hundred dollar purses offered for horses entered to be claimed for two, three or four hundred dollars. But it was bush-league with standards. Thus, Calgary built a proper jockey's dressing room and an adjacent saddling paddock. Speers imported professional presiding stewards, racing secretaries, and starters from the United States and saw to it that their authority extended across the entire circuit. Any malefactor ruled off one track was ruled off them all; a jockey grounded in Winnipeg was grounded on all other tracks.

Speers introduced innovations that not even the major tracks in Toronto, Louis-

ized the horse players were contributing a net profit of eight thousand dollars a year to the Exhibition coffers. If credit had been taken for the contributions the bettors made to the gate and grandstand revenues, the racing income would have exceeded twenty thousand.

During the first half of the 1920s, however, it was hockey which was the most pleasantly profitable enterprise in Victoria Park—pleasant because the Exhibition board had nothing to do but sit back and wait for the profits to be divided under the terms of the Lloyd Turner leases of 1918–19 and after. But it all came to an abrupt end with the death of the professional hockey league in 1926–27.

E. L. Richardson had been moving spirit

The Calgary Tigers who challenged for the Stanley Cup in 1924. *Courtesy of the Calgary Stampede.*

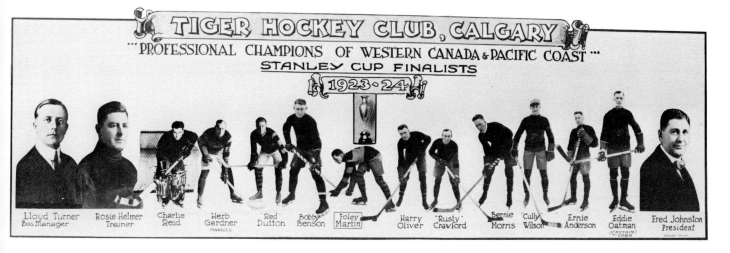

ville, and New York had yet adopted. The daily double and the quinella were introduced to North America on the western Canadian fair circuit. Speers provided prairie patrons with programs on which the past performances of all the participants were printed. It was this program that got the Calgary service clubs into Victoria Park. The Gyro Club members sold the racing programs along with the Stampede programs for fifteen cents each and kept a nickle commission to fuel their community projects.

So popular did parimutuel betting on the horse races become that in 1926 the auto races, which had been the main feature of the closing Saturday afternoon, were called off and an additional seven–horse race substituted. Five years after the prairie racing circuit was organ-

in the organization of the Western Canada Hockey League in 1921–22 and became its first commissioner. That league was a sort of spinoff from the triumph at the 1920 Winter Olympics of the Winnipeg Falcons hockey team. It sparked an outburst of interest in hockey all across the West and in the northern states where rink construction and new league organizing went hand in hand. When the Falcons came home from Europe they were set upon by the promoters from the western cities and lured into professional hockey careers with offers of twenty-five hundred to three thousand dollars a year.

And not only from the Falcons, which was composed mainly of young Icelandic Canadians from the Winnipeg west end. Winnipeg with its three enclosed and a score of outdoor corner lot rinks, was a

The greatest jumping horse Canada ever produced was Barra Lad, a rugged gelding of uncertain lineage. During the early 1920s he was shown at horse shows all across western Canada. He is shown here with fifteen-year-old Louis Welsh up easily clearing a seven-foot jump. *Courtesy of Glenbow Archives, Calgary, Alberta.*

tremendous incubator of hockey talent. The Calgary Tigers managed to recruit Bobby Benson from the Falcons but also lured Mervyn "Red" Dutton, Herb Gardiner, Harry Oliver, Eddie Oatman, Rusty Crawford and Ernie Anderson from other Winnipeg teams. Among other early players who went on to the National Hockey League when it expanded into the United States were: Bill Binney, Foley Martin, and Jimmie Gibson. The Tigers in 1923-24 went on to win the western championship and ultimately went to the finals for the Stanley Cup, losing to the Montreal Canadiens in two straight games.

That was the Mt. Everest for professional hockey in the West. The next year the National Hockey League expanded to Boston, Detroit, Chicago, and New York. The Patrick brothers folded their Pacific Coast League and sold their players to the expansion teams. Calgary lost all its best players,

as did the other prairie teams, and the league was doomed.

The annual horse show, which the Exhibition staff managed for the Alberta Horse Breeders' Associations, expanded in size and greatly improved in quality during the 1920s. In addition to the conformation and performance classes of the various breeds of light horses, audience pulling spectaculars were being slotted into the programs. Trick and fancy riding acts became staple fare and the high jump and broad jump were outstanding features.

High jumping had been a feature of horse shows across the country for many years. Sir Clifford Sifton had raised highjumpers that cleared seven feet by crossing thoroughbreds and French coach horses. Peter Welsh, a Calgary breeder and dealer, raised several horses that cleared seven foot, six inches and owned the greatest jumping horse of them all. He was Barra Lad, a great favorite with Calgary crowds.

Jumping at a show in New Westminster, Barra Lad broke his own world record by clearing eight feet, one and one-half inches on September 12, 1925, ruptured internally, and died five hours later.

By the middle of the 1920s the writing was already on the wall for the heavy draft horses as lightweight gasoline powered tractors were beginning to appear on the market. Thus Clydesdale entries, which had topped 120 in 1921 and 1922, dropped to 64 in 1923 and 41 in 1925, while Percherons declined from 65 to 23 and Belgians from 35 to 7.

Out on what was left of the cattle ranges, and in the bull rings of the growing numbers of purebred farms, the battle of the beef breeds was beginning. From the first days of settlement in the West, this had been Shorthorn country. From the first purebred bull sale in 1901 until the Lacombe sale was united with the Calgary sale in 1921, the Shorthorn entries outnumbered the combined entries of Hereford, Aberdeen-Angus, Galloways, and Red Polls, often by a substantial margin.

Following the collapse of cattle prices in 1920-21, entries of all breeds declined sharply. But as recovery occurred both the Hereford and Angus began to challenge the Shorthorn for primacy among the breeds.

The breed rivalry enhanced the importance of the Calgary Bull Sale as years passed until it was attracting exhibitors from all across the West and buyers from the northern States. The importance of the Calgary Bull Sale to the livestock industry may be illustrated by a single statistic—it took 130 railway cars to move the bulls into and out of the sale in 1922.

All these, however, were main-ring activities. Around the edges, the Exhibition was becoming a full-time undertaking. It had, for example, evolved into the main shipping center for the wool growers of southern Alberta. Between two hundred and three hundred sheepmen regularly brought their annual wool clip to Victoria Park where it was graded and packaged and sent off to the Canadian Co-operative Wool Growers' marketing office in Montreal. These shipments varied in size from 93,451 pounds—five carloads—in 1924 to 205,000 pounds—ten carloads in 1926.

During the course of any year, the Exhibition could expect to receive upwards of 4,400 entries for its various events, each accompanied by an entrance fee that had to be accounted for, and an entry that had to be stabled, penned, benched, or otherwise taken care of. In no year did the annual Exhibition ever account for more than half the revenue that passed through its office.

For the Calgary Industrial Exhibition, the expansion of horse racing simultaneously with the incorporation of the Stampede created an overabundance of activities with which it was not set up to cope. For one thing, it found itself once again desperately short of horse barns, a shortage that seemingly could never be completely overcome. Mostly, however, there was a shortage of time for its skeleton staff to carry out their multifarious duties.

In 1924 Richardson's permanent staff consisted of W. N. Gibson, the assistant manager, Thomas Bellew, the livestock superintendent, Robert Spencer, the grounds superintendent, Fred Stanford, the accountant and cashier; and Annie Hall, who was officially the manager's secretary but who doubled in brass in all other jobs from file clerk to publicity agent.

Whenever assistance was needed beyond what the volunteers could provide, it was obtained on a day-labor basis. The organization's approach to administrative overload can be illustrated by the reaction to staff needs for the early Stampedes. Richardson and Weadick pondered whether to take Jack Dillon and Dick Cosgrave on staff for a week or for a month before the Stampede to organize the rodeo livestock and facilities. They settled for hiring them for just a week. It was only later, when the work load had intensified that their employment was extended to a month. Even when, still later, they were appointed in turn to the high-sounding positions of "arena director" neither was made a full-time salaried employee.

What made the melding of the Calgary Industrial Exhibition *and* the Calgary Stampede possible was the empathy that developed between Guy Weadick and Ernie Richardson toward the Stampede. Both were utterly convinced of the Stampede's viability in Calgary. For his part, Weadick had such a deep paternalistic, proprietary interest in the Stampede that he seemed convinced that he had invented the word itself. Actually, it had been in common usage in the Mexican border country for almost a hundred years, and there had been rodeos billed as "stampedes" long before Weadick hit Calgary. But the Calgary Stampede was Weadick's creation and promoting it and protecting it became the passion of his life.

Richardson's dedication to the interests of the Stampede was akin to the convert's commitment to a new religion. But, as the poet Byron said of love, the Stampede to Richardson was a thing apart while it was Weadick's whole existence. Richardson had all the Exhibition's other activities to be concerned about, and the financial health of the whole operation to safeguard at all costs. It was he who had to justify Weadick's promotional activities to the board of directors and shoulder the responsibility for bringing the show to a financially successful conclusion. For Richardson, a single financial disaster could have meant the end of the Calgary Industrial Exhibition for, to make the point again, it had no financial reserves to fall back on.

Empathy made it possible, but no two more disparate personalities ever worked in double harness. Richardson was a rolypoly little man, Weadick was the gaunt, classic cowboy six-footer. Richardson was quiet, serious, and deeply religious. The depth of his commitment to his faith may be measured by the fact that it took the persuasive powers of the entire Stampede committee to get him to undergo lifesaving surgery for a ruptured appendix. He neither drank nor smoked.

Weadick was a thoroughgoing extrovert who smoked, drank, and took his fun where he found it. Richardson was the administrator who made sure that everything would happen as it was supposed to happen. Weadick was the front man who was in his element entertaining visiting celebrities and old cowhands in the Stampede's Palliser Hotel "snake room." Richardson was the cost accountant and Weadick was the quintessential vaudevillian and the most imaginative promotional genius Canada had ever seen.

With the coming of autumn Weadick and his wife, Flora La Due, took off on a three months' vaudeville tour of the United States, playing split weeks on the Keith-Albee, Orpheum and Pantages circuits, as they had been doing for a decade or more. But as far as the Calgary Stampede was concerned, Guy Weadick never left home. The truly voluminous correspondence between Weadick and Richardson is replete with discussion of every aspect of the rodeo operations. They discussed the advisability of acquiring herds of bucking horses, importing a large herd of Brahma bulls for the bull riding events, changing the regulations governing the rodeo events. Above all there was a bombardment from Weadick of suggested names of big wheels to invite to the fair, of new acts to bring in, for improvements even to the company letterheads.

Richardson, for his part, though he was definitely Weadick's boss, treated Weadick with deference in all the interchanges, sent him drafts of publicity being prepared, deferred to his judgment about who to deal with, and who to avoid, when it came to obtaining livestock for the show.

The fertility of Weadick's mind can be illustrated with a couple of examples. When he learned that the Texas Rangers had organized a polo team he urged Richardson to find out if the RCMP had a polo team and if an international match might be arranged between the two. When he heard that Colonel Theodore Roosevelt, the big-game-hunting son of a former American president, might visit the Stampede, he managed a lunch date with Roosevelt in the hope of persuading him to bring a mounted posse with him.

On his theatrical billboards, Weadick billed himself as the "Producer of the World Famous Calgary Stampede" and wherever his performing jobs took him he functioned as the publicity agent for the Stampede. His typewriter was as much an essential of life as his ropes and cowboy boots and hat. From it flowed a steady stream of Stampede publicity for local newspapers, theatrical magazines, New York travel agents, and anybody else who came to mind. Weadick, like all publicists, knew that big names were attention-grabbers around the copy desks of newspapers. So he was forever on the alert for big

names to invite to the show. And a mere rumor that the Prince of Wales, the governor-general, or a theatrical celebrity might attend was enough to set his typewriter aclicketing.

The Weadicks never did make it to the Palace Theatre, that Mecca of all vaudevillians. His circuit was mainly the small cities of West Virginia, Pennsylvania, New York, and Ohio. But in his time he had crossed paths with most of the stars who had made it to the Palace, and he never lost a name or misplaced an address. So he whiled away his leisure hours on the road firing off invitations to them to come to the Calgary Stampede. Amazingly, he drew acceptances from all over the world. Peter B. Kyne, the famous western author, came. So did Frazier Hunt, the editor of *Cosmopolitan* magazine, who bought a ranch west of High River after his first visit to Calgary. For those who did not come, he put the arm on for donations of trophies for Stampede events. Among them was E. F. Albee, the vaudeville impresario.

The cherry on the topping of Weadick's promotional career was undoubtedly the movie *The Calgary Stampede*. The 1920s were the golden age of the horse operas on the silver screen. Every Hollywood studio had its western star and such names as William S. Hart, Tom Mix, William Farnum, Dustin Farnum, and Hoot Gibson were legion. Many of the stars and featured players in the horse operas were old Weadick pals from his early barn-storming days. On his first jaunt to Calgary to try to promote a stampede he had been accompanied by Tom Mix, who then gave up rodeoing for movie acting. So did Hoot Gibson, who by the mid twenties was earning fifteen thousand dollars a week making pictures for Universal Studios.

Weadick persuaded Gibson to come to Calgary and to use the Calgary Stampede as the backdrop for one of his westerns.

Thanks to Guy Weadick's arm twisting among his show-biz friends, the Calgary Stampede got more than its share of movieland attention. Hoot Gibson's **Calgary Stampede** was a box office hit and Weadick's own movie, **His Destiny**, ''wasn't the worst movie ever made.'' Both Gibson and Weadick used Calgarians to the limit and here is a movie being made on Seventh Avenue in the wake of the Stampede Parade in 1926. Interestingly, the crowd is intently watching the action, not ogling the camera. *Courtesy of Glenbow Archives, Calgary, Alberta.*

The movie, fittingly entitled *The Calgary Stampede,* became a box-office smash all over America and probably did more to spread the fame of the show than any other promotion. Certainly it spurred Weadick on a campaign to persuade all the other Hollywood studios to follow Universal's example. None did, but the Canadian government put together several short movies which were used as tourist promotion around the world.

The relationship between Richardson and Weadick in the beginning got the show on the road. It was the outstanding success of the 1924 show that permanently banished all doubts and insured that the union of the Calgary Exhibition and Stampede would become permanently established. It broke all previous attendance records by 30,000 when it attracted 167,000 for the six-day show. Gate receipts were more than double what they had been for the last pre-Stampede Exhibition. The cowboys, Indians, and chuckwagons took over the downtown streets each morning to the delight of the citizenry. Highlighting the downtown festivities was a thirty-two-horse team hauling eight loaded grain wagons through the streets. The driver, Slim Moorehouse, successfully manoeuvred the team around the corners of Calgary's narrow streets in a demonstration of the teamster's art in what could be truthfully called the swan song of horses as beasts of burden. Moorehouse returned the following year with a thirty-six-horse team of matched Percherons hauling ten wagons full of grain.

The local ranchers twigged quickly to the excitement of the chuckwagon races introduced in 1923 and in 1924 entered no less than ten rigs without the need to be sold on the idea, so there were two heats of five rigs each daily. The five wagon races guaranteed spills and collisions that made them the most exciting spectator sport since the chariot races of ancient Rome. Indeed, one of the other exciting features of the Stampede derived directly from ancient Rome. It was the Roman race, in which the competitors rode two horses standing astride their backs. Still another event with ancient roots was the California cart race.

Ironically, the success of the 1924 Exhibition and Stampede might have been its undoing given a difference in circumstances. Contemplating the rodeo events from the grandstand, Peter Welsh, a prominent Calgary horseman, was fascinated by the excitement of the crowd. If bucking horses, wild cow milking, and bull riding could create such a frenzy of excitement in small-town Calgary, why could it not be repeated in such metropoli as Winnipeg, Toronto, and Ottawa, and Minneapolis, Chicago, and Detroit? To the immense profits of the promoter? All you needed was a couple of carloads of bucking horses, some bulls, and a couple of dozen cowboys! It was an idea that Welsh could not resist.

After the 1924 Calgary Stampede he bought up as many of the top bucking horses as he could find. Within a year he had acquired such buckers as Midnight, Bassano, the tops at the 1923 show, Stand Clear, Grave Digger. Then he became incorporated as the Alberta Stampede Company Limited and went off to promote stampedes at Winnipeg, New Westminster, Ottawa, Toronto, and Detroit, accompanied by most of the top cowboys from the Calgary Stampede.

Weadick regarded Welsh's use of the word "Stampede" as a personal affront, and a barefaced attempt to cash in on the publicity Weadick had been generating for the Calgary Stampede. He went after Welsh with all guns blazing. From his vaudeville tour he continually urged Richardson to persuade the publisher of the *Albertan* to shut off the publicity blurbs Welsh was getting in that paper. Richardson then headed a delegation to Edmonton to persuade Premier Brownlee to interdict the use of the word "Stampede" for any more corporate registrations. Weadick also embarked on a poison-pen campaign to all the newspapers, magazines, and promoters on his mailing list. When he wrote to the owners of the new Detroit Olympia attacking the integrity of Welsh and his traveling rodeo he provoked Welsh into instructing A. L. Smith to sue Weadick and the Calgary Industrial Exhibition Company for one-hundred-thousand-dollar damages. In the letter, written on a company letterhead, Weadick had identified himself as "Manager, Calgary Stampede."

At what might best be described as an elaborate nose-thumbing gesture at the oncoming generation of truck driving farmers, Slim Moorhouse dramatized the teamster's art by driving a wagon train through downtown Calgary. The first year the wagons were drawn by an even mixture of thirty-two horses and mules. The next year he took his place in the 1925 Stampede Parade with sixteen teams of matching Percherons and amazed everybody by making turns around Calgary's narrow street corners. The outfit was owned by Glen House of Gleichen, sixty miles east of Calgary. *Courtesy of the Calgary Stampede.*

Weadick aside, Welsh soon discovered there was a lot more to the Calgary Stampede than cowboys and bucking horses; that what moved Calgarians to whooping and hollering was a unique variety of environmental circumstances that were absent in Ottawa, Toronto, Winnipeg, and Vancouver. Among them was forty years of ranching history blended with forty years of grain-growing history, and just about the perfect mixture of British, European, Canadian, and American people needed to appreciate the nuances of artistry in saddle bronc and bull riding.

If Welsh had only asked, Weadick would have warned him of the financial disasters his road show would encounter in such places as Ottawa and Toronto, as a result of unattractable and unappreciative audiences. Winnipeg in 1913 had demonstrated that the Stampede was not exportable, a fact that was confirmed by Sheephead Bay, N.Y., the following year when Weadick's financial hide was hung out to dry. The same fate overtook Welsh in Toronto in 1927 when the sheriff walked in and wrote finis to Welsh's Alberta Stampede Company.

Not, of course, that Welsh was Weadick's only major problem with the Stampede. In truth it was loaded with problems, of which the most vexing was trying to devise rules for its various contests which the contestants could understand and the judges were capable of enforcing. It took the better part of five years before the chuckwagon races evolved rules that could be enforced with sufficient severity to minimize the risk to the lives of contestants. As Weadick was to report to Richardson, he was hearing rumors that one particular wreck in 1925 was orchestrated the night before by cowboys conspiring to "get even" with Clem Gardner, the unfortunate wreckee.

The biggest headache, and by a substantial margin, centered on the bucking horses. The bronc riders, both saddle bronc and bareback, were of course required to ride their horses to exhaustion; that is, until they ceased to buck, if that took one minute or fifteen. Horses which managed to unseat their riders quickly had their bucking instincts reinforced, became

more determined than ever to dislodge the riders. But when ridden to submission they got the idea they were being taught to accommodate themselves to having a man on their backs. Some learned that lesson quickly; some took all summer. But when they did they lost the urge to buck and their usefulness to rodeo operators ended.

It all added up to a continuing search for reliable buckers. Horses that would be star performers one year would be hired back the next and refuse to buck. The result was demands by the cowboys for rerides and the intolerable stretching out of the program. By 1927 a solution was found. The length of a qualified ride was cut to ten seconds and a new system of grading the performances of the horses and the riders was adopted. This not only resulted in getting the rodeo events run off before the evening show was scheduled to begin, it solved the main problem of a supply of bucking horses. An outstanding bucker seldom had its spirit broken and the Stampede was able to buy up the outstanding performers and assemble its own herd of bucking stock. As time passed it also added several crowd pleasing new events to the afternoon program—boys steer riding, wild horse races, Brahma bull riding, and steer decorating.

A change in the bureaucracy of the Department of Indian Affairs was responsible for almost subtracting one of the most colorful and attractive features of the annual Exhibition: the Indians who flocked in from the neighboring reserves by the hundreds. The bureaucrat was W. M. Graham, the Indian commissioner, who had a jaundiced view of the monkeyshines in Calgary. What he required of the Indians was they stay on the reserves and get on with the business of learning how to be farmers. Suddenly, in 1925, he placed Calgary and its Exhibition out of bounds for Indians.

The edict sent panic shock waves through Victoria Park. This was the fiftieth anniversary of the arrival of the NWMP at the future site of Calgary. That was to be the theme of the 1925 Exhibition. The historical pageant which was organized in cooperation with the parade was the most ambitious ever attempted. In addition the mounties brought in their musical ride and

Of all the celebrities who graced the Stampede over the years, few enjoyed themselves more than Earl Haig, the governor-general and former commander in chief of the British army in the First World War. He is shown here, after being made an honorary Indian chief, with his guard of honor, 1925. *Courtesy of Glenbow Archives, Calgary, Alberta.*

the countryside was combed for surviving members of the great trek of 1874–75. To try to stage such a celebration without Indian involvement was unthinkable! Eventually the commissioner was persuaded to compromise. All the able-bodied Indians still had to stay at work on the reserves, but the elderly Indians and their wives were permitted to bring in their regalia and teepees, camp at Victoria Park, and participate in the celebration.

Also participating to the hilt were the field marshal of the British forces in World War I, Lord Douglas Haig, and Lady Haig. Haig was made a chief of the Sarcees, had breakfast at two of the downtown chuckwagons and mingled enthusiastically with the Indians, cowboys, cowgirls, and the jam of tourists who combined to make the downtown celebrations the most spectacular in Calgary history.

It was also the most successful Exhibition and Stampede yet, despite the appalling weather. It rained two days, turned the infield into a swamp, and fouled up the rodeo events. And just when the entries of contestants for all events broke all previous records. There were 104 entries for the calf roping, 73 wild cow milking, 68 saddle bronc riding, 61 steer riding, and 53 bareback bronc riders. Most important of all, there were 21 wagons entered in the chuckwagon races and four heats of five wagons each were run off each night.

Despite the rain, attendance and gate receipts broke all previous records but because of the extra expenses of the pageant, advertising, and the closing night barbecue, the net profits were down sharply from the previous year. Nevertheless, there was a profit of $5,060 after writing off $11,336 in expenditures on building improvements. More important than the money however was the demonstration that the Calgary Exhibition and Stampede was weatherproof. Despite the rains, people came and kept on coming; and the Stampede committee demonstrated that it could rearrange its schedule of the rodeo events so as to complete all the programs.

Where the weather was a factor was in the flow of tourists into Calgary for Exhibition week. It was beginning to count on an influx of thousands, mostly by train. But automobile tourist traffic was also becoming important with the opening of a highway to Lake Windermere and to Medicine Hat and Regina. Though gravelled, Alberta highways had improved but little over the trails of the 1880s. A two-day rain could still turn the Calgary-Macleod "highway" into an impassable quagmire. Even the Banff highway, which was fairly well gravelled, could become impassable. What saved the Exhibition from disaster when the rains came was the irrepressible enthusiasm of the Calgarians for their show.

CHAPTER 7

Surviving Difficult Times

As time passed it became obvious that the melding of the Calgary Stampede with the Calgary Industrial Exhibition was a ten-strike, a grand-slam on every count. The presidential reports to the shareholders fairly dripped with enthusiasm for the artistic triumphs of the enterprise, glowed with pride in the worldwide publicity generated for Calgary. The reports of the financial committees joyously converted increasing patronage figures into increasing totals of money in the bank.

It could no longer be argued in 1928, as it had been possible in 1912, that the attendance growth could be attributed to the tenfold increase in the city's population. For the whole prairie region in the 1920s, burgeoning population growth was no more than a dimming memory. An economic pall hung over the region. Save for the construction of single department stores in Calgary, Saskatoon, Regina, and Winnipeg, and railway hotels in Moose Jaw, Saskatoon, and Regina, the construction industry languished in a decade long depression. Emigration from the Prairies exceeded immigration into the region. Prairie agriculture, debt burdened from wartime expansion, rode an economic roller coaster between good crops and bad, high prices and low prices. Economic stagnation froze wage rates so that general increases were virtually unheard of.

Calgary was a minor exception to all this in one way. Its Turner Valley oil boom made it the only half-exciting place to be, economically, on the Prairies during the last half decade. The burning gas flares on "hell's half acre" which lit up the southwestern sky added an eerie after-glow to the nightly fireworks display at Victoria Park. And the speculative heat generated by the oil stock boom that erupted with the arrival of I. W. C. Solloway from Toronto helped fill Calgary's numerous vacant downtown stores and vacant office space with stock brokerage firms and oil well promoters.

So while things were marginally better in Calgary than anywhere else in the prairie region, the slight difference could not account for the dramatic advances at Victoria Park. Here, in tabular form, is what was happening:

Year	Attendance	Total Receipts	Profit (Loss)
1921	96,120	$125,000	$(4,625)
1922	97,732	95,000	(14,884)
1923	137,838	136,000	22,142
1924	167,279	156,000	15,582
1925	178,668	162,000	16,396
1926	197,471	184,000	32,263
1927	210,879	186,000	6,114
1928	243,985	239,000	37,696
1929	258,469	254,000	41,846

Not all the credit for the spectacular attendance growth and improved finances could, however, go to the Stampede and such superb crowd attracters as the Royal Coldstream Guards Band and visiting royalty. Much of it had to go to the automobile. With the increased use of the motor car and farm truck, the population of Alberta reached new highs in mobility during the 1920s. Motor vehicle registration more than doubled from forty thousand to almost one hundred thousand. Each year, more and more Calgary patrons were making their way to Victoria Park by car.

Perhaps more important, farmers and ranchers were turning to motor trucks for primary transportation for both their families and farm animals. Until the trucks came into general usage, farmers who lived beyond a day's journey to Calgary by horse and buggy relied on trains to get them to the city. This not only retarded access of farm families to the Exhibition, but reduced the flow of agricultural exhibits as well. The motor car extended the intensive patronage area for the Exhibition from a dozen miles to a hundred.

It also created an excruciating headache for the Exhibition Board. Clogged streets around the Victoria Park gates caused agitation for increased parking inside the grounds. Each year more space was provided, but it was never enough though by 1927, there was parking space for five thousand cars. One trouble was that paved parking lots had not yet been invented. Indeed, in Calgary residential areas, paved streets had not yet been invented. It was not until after the Second World War that Calgary's definition of a paved residential street ceased to be the spreading of gravel

doused with a heavy coating of a tar-black-oil mixture.

From the Victoria Park parking lot, there arose daily clouds of dust that blackened the sweating necks of grandstand patrons, then drifted through the Mission to settle on the newly hung washing on the clothes lines of Mount Royal. Or, so it often seemed to the bleary-eyed patrons, the parking lot dust kept eddying in and around the race track and rodeo ring to add to that being raised by the bucking stock and thoroughbred race horses.

The increased patronage imposed other strains on the Victoria Park facilities. There were barely sufficient toilet facilities for the 1922 crowds, let alone those of 1925. The attendance explosion brought the city health department inspectors down on the association. Despite the building department's best efforts, the supply never did catch up with demand until the great depression brought the crowds down to a manageable size. Until that happened, medium-sized small boys were banned access to the facilities unless accompanied by parents.

Each year, sometimes out of income, sometimes out of advances from the city, the facilities at Victoria Park were expanded and improved. Thus in 1928 a one hundred foot extension to the grandstand doubled the amount of space available for exhibits underneath the stand and in-

For over thirty years, Fire Chief "Cappy" Smart was the Stampede Parade marshal, marching at the head of the procession. *Courtesy of Glenbow Archives, Calgary, Alberta.*

creased the seating capacity of the grand-stand and bleachers to fourteen thousand, the largest in Canada with the exception of the Toronto Exhibition. The livestock pavilion was also enlarged to provide for the stabling of 832 cattle and a sales ring with seats for two thousand. Permanent chutes, catching pens and corrals were constructed in the infield for the rodeo events. Because of the substantial sums spent each year on improvements and replacements, the annual profit figures in the foregoing tabulation are understated, perhaps by as much as forty or fifty percent on the average.

The growing pains which the Calgary Industrial Exhibition experienced during the 1920s were physical rather than mental for there is no evidence that any strains developed between the Stampede and Exhibition sides of the operation. Indeed the evidence all pointed to a blending of interests between the two. One explanation for the unity of effort may have derived from the interest of the individual directors. They, without exception, were Calgary businessmen, but with strong ties to farming and ranching. A. E. Cross was a pioneer rancher before he was a pioneer brewer. Frank Collicutt was a pioneer Hereford breeder and J. H. Laycock was a major dairy farmer. T. M. Carlyle and Peter Pallesen were dairy farmers before they became the operators of Calgary creameries. G. H. Hutton who served for many years as both director and livestock judge, was superintendent of the Lacombe Experimental Farm. Fred Johnston was the owner of a large draying and storage company with a large stable of horses and an interest in thoroughbred breeding and racing. Nat Christie operated the city's largest laundry and bred race horses and chaired the racing committee. Christie even insured his posthumous participation in the racing activities of the association by so arranging his substantial estate that there would be seed money to establish a seventy-five-thousand-dollar stake for Calgary competition. E. D. Adams combined stock brokerage, Galloway cattle breeding and horse raising—with over a long period the presidency of the Alberta Horsebreeders' Association. C.M. Baker divided his interest between his wholesale business and farm.

The strain which the amalgamation

placed upon Ernie Richardson and his full-time staff was kept just a shade south of intolerable by the way in which the services of the shareholders were coopted for the working committees. The roster of associate directors was increased from 50 in 1923 to 116 in 1927 and 133 in 1928. There were fifty members on the parade committee, eighteen on the morning street display committee, a like number on the cowboys ball committee, and fifteen on the Stampede committee. What set the organization apart was the near absence of deadwood on any of its committees. Some of the committees served but briefly during the fair and some were active most of the year.

The heart of the organization was its executive board and its executive committee. From the fifteen-member directorate, President N. J. Christie, Vice-President C. M. Baker, Past President Fred Johnston, Peter Pallesen, and E. D. Adams with Richardson formed the executive committee. Each of the other members of the board was a chairman of an important operating committee. The subsidiary committees, usually presided over by an associate director, were chosen exclusively from people of special knowledge and experience germane to the committee. Thus the educational committee, which arranged for the entries, named the judges, and put up the displays for the schools exhibits, were all educators; the publicity committee was composed of the editors of all the local newspapers and magazines.

The euphoria that gripped the directors over the success of 1926 can be gauged by the fact that everybody but Richardson was given a raise in pay, the first in years. W. N. Gibson, the assistant manager, was raised from $3,000 to $3,720 a year; Fred Stanford, the accountant, Robert Spencer, the grounds superintendent and Thomas Bellew, the livestock superintendent went from $2,540 to $2,840, Miss A. E. Hall from $1,200 to $1,600.

Richardson's salary had been raised to $5,000 in 1920 when he had been offered the post of Dominion Immigration Commissioner and by 1926, his take home pay reached $7,200. That, however, included $1,000 he received as commissioner for the Western Canada Hockey League, and sev-

The celebrations fill the streets, street dancing a favorite with the crowds. *Courtesy of the Calgary Stampede.*

eral smaller annual honoraria from livestock associations for which he was secretary. The permanent payroll, it should be
noted, was not all a charge on Exhibition
income. Of the 1926 budget for office and
administration expenses of $23,753, a total
of $3,417 was cannily charged to the
livestock associations for clerical and other
services.

Strains did develop around the edges of
the fair, however. The campaign by Guy
Weadick to recreate a frontier ambience in
downtown Calgary created favorable excitement and enthusiasm, except among
those downtown retailers whose business
was being interfered with by all the foo-
foraw. Complaints from them to the mayor
were shunted to Richardson who passed
them on to Weadick. Weadick's solution
was to get the merchants to organize their
own committee and select a chairman and
help run the downtown show. That was
done, the street shows were limited to
certain days and certain areas, and everybody was happy, for a while at least.

The exception was the unhappiness of
the restaurant owners with the late closing
of the Friday night cowboy and old-timers'
street dance. Allowing it to run till 2:00
A.M., they complained, meant the restaurants had to stay open till 3:00 or 3:30 A.M.
That did not allow the kitchen help to get
home and back to work in time to get
things ready for Saturday operations, and
Saturday was always their biggest day of
the week. That turned out to be a problem
without a solution for as long as the street
dance continued.

One reason that little interior tension
developed may be that the success of the
Stampede made it possible for each committee's Exhibition activities to be expanded. New facilities were provided for the
dog show, the poultry show, flower show
and above all else for the schools, arts, and
handicrafts divisions. The prize lists for all
classes were increased out of Stampede
earnings. And the exhibits of everything
from farm machinery to insect collections
grew beyond anything imagined by the
most enthusiastic drumbeaters for the
turn-of-the-century exhibition.

By 1927, for example, it took better than
two and a half columns of tightly set
newspaper type to tabulate the winners of

the first, second, and third prizes in fancy
work exhibits alone. From the sheer volume of the work displayed, it was obvious
how the women of southern Alberta spent
their free time—in frantically embroider-
ing, crocheting, knitting, and quilting for
the Exhibition. The categories in which
they might specialize were unlimited. The
embroiderers could practice their art on
dinner mats, towels, underwear, pillows,
collars, and cuffs. There were even classes
of knitting for "old ladies' work."

That was the only function "old ladies"
were permitted for the Calgary Industrial
Exhibition—entering examples of their
handiwork. If there were any women in
business in downtown Calgary, you could
not prove it by any Exhibition board. The
only woman asked to belong was Mrs. P. S.
Woodhall, who made it onto the associate
director roster in the reorganization of
1925. And this after years of running the
entire women's section of the annual Exhibition with a skeleton staff of anonymous
assistants. Later on, when women began to
nose into city politics, a couple more made
it to the same roster as civic representatives. Among them were Alderman Edith
Patterson and Alderman Pansy Pue.

Over the years, others became associate
directors but none was ever elected to that
great bastion of male chauvinism, the
board of directors of the Calgary Exhibition and Stampede Limited, until Eleanor
Bailey made it in 1979.

For those women who did not fancy
fancywork, there were classes for emerging
artists. Prizes were offered for oils and
watercolors, crayon sketches, charcoal
drawings of landscapes and still life, and
portraits. The biggest display of all came
from the schools of Calgary and district.
There were competitions between schools
and between pupils, hundreds of entries in
all categories from handwriting to the
manual arts. The bonanza which the Stampede was creating did more than enable the
institution to increase its prize list: it
enabled the Exhibition to become an increasingly important promoter of the cultural life of Calgary.

This aspect, indeed, had been an integral
part of the institution from the time of the
Dominion Exhibition onward, when the
new buildings constructed for that event

provided the facilities in which art and photographic exhibits could be mounted. The first major traveling art exhibit in western Canada was held at the Exhibition of 1909. That came about because the National Gallery in Ottawa functioned under the Minister of Agriculture, who arranged for the showing.

Alex Calhoun, Calgary's chief librarian, became the first chairman of the Exhibition board's art committee and served in that capacity for many years. It was he who arranged in 1922 for the National Gallery to exhibit in Calgary a portion of its Wembley Exhibit, the exhibit which Canada put together to acquaint the British with the work of such artists as Lawren Harris, A. J. Casson, A. Y. Jackson, S. F. Turner, F. Carmichael, C. W. Jeffreys, Arthur Beaumont, and Ann Savage.

Calhoun earned a master's degree in classics at Queen's, had done post-graduate work at Chicago and taught high school at Fort William before coming to Calgary. He was an avid enthusiast for bringing traveling art exhibitions to Calgary. When none was available he devised the plan for borrowing works from local patrons of the arts to exhibit during Stampede. Tried for the first time in 1928, this turned out to be a surprisingly popular attraction. During the week more than 30,000 people visited the art gallery to view the $200,000 worth of painting on display.

The Exhibition's interest in the art of the photographer went back almost to the beginning, both in the mounting of photographic displays and in the encouragement of picture-taking. Thus, when putting the final arrangement together for the 1912 Stampede, it appointed Millward Belmont Davis Marcell its official photographer and set up special facilities for him.

The Calgary Exhibition and Stampede in 1927 demonstrated how well it could survive a week of bad weather, still attract record crowds, and turn a profit. In 1928 it demonstrated how well it could do when the weather was favorable. It even was able to jam an all-time daily record attendance of 51,920 through the gates on the only rainy day of the week.

For Guy Weadick, if all this success were a dream, let him never awaken! Every dream he had ever had for the Stampede had come true. He himself was recognized wherever he went and had achieved the ultimate in celebrity status—he had been hired to contribute a testimonial to a cigarette advertisement! In a half-page ad for Buckingham cigarettes, centered by his picture, he was quoted: "When trying to work 24 hours a day during the great Calgary Stampede, I sure enjoy a Buckingham—the one cigarette I have found easy on my throat. . . ."

During the 1928 show, Weadick got to rub shoulders with Viscount and Lady Willingdon during the entire week they spent in Calgary, mostly around the Stampede. Everything about that show broke records: the attendance by a whopping 33,000, profits touched $37,696, the exhibits, the prize money, the horse races, and above all the quality of the rodeo events. No previous show had ever received such worldwide publicity, nor such a steady inflow of complimentary mail from the four corners of the earth. American cameramen had come from New York and Los Angeles to make extensive newsreel pictures for showing on the movie screens of the world. And when it was all over, the Exhibition board voted Weadick a bonus of one thousand dollars for his services!

But perhaps more satisfying than anything else that year, Guy Weadick got to produce and act a prominent role in a full-length feature movie, mainly filmed at the Calgary Stampede. The movie was *His Destiny* or, for American patrons, *North of 49* and featured Neal Hart, Barbara Kent, a bevy of Toronto actors, and the members of the Calgary Elks Lodge. There was also a part in the script for Mary Cross Dover but it wound up on the cutting room floor. The project was financed by Pat Burns, A. E. Cross, and John I. McFarland and was also filmed on the Cross ranch, and on Weadick's own spread at Pekisko.

As Weadick himself said, in introducing the show to the grand opening crowd at the Palace Theatre, "it was not the worst movie ever made." It was made specifically with an eye on the British market which had provided an exemption in its restrictive tariff against American movies to permit Canadian-made films to enter. At the same time, it was cast to capture the attention of American audiences. Like all westerns of

There is a legend abroad in Calgary that the city's white hat trademark was an invention of Mayor Don Mackay for the 1948 Grey Cup safari to Toronto. Here are Viscount and Lady Willingdon in white hats twenty years earlier. No vice-regal party ever enjoyed themselves more at the Stampede than the Willingdons did in 1928, or participated more actively in all its activities. *Courtesy of Glenbow Archives, Calgary, Alberta.*

the era, its hero was squeaky clean and its villains unspeakably villainous. If it was no great box office smash, and it was not, it nevertheless paid back the sponsors their investment. And like everything else Weadick did, it was all publicity grease for the Stampede wheel.

Ironically it was almost to the hour of Weadick's lifetime high that a nemesis was taking shape in Hollywood which would ultimately destroy his way of life. The nemesis was Al Jolson, who was making a movie called *The Singing Fool* while Weadick was putting the finishing touches on *His Destiny.* Coming as it did on the heels of *The Jazz Singer* which introduced the human voice to the movies, *The Singing Fool* added enough music to revolutionize the entertainment industry and sound the death knell for vaudeville, almost overnight. And vaudeville had been as much a

part of Weadick's life as stampeding had been for more than twenty years.

By 1931 vaudeville was dead. When the deep snows buried the high country for the winter and the Weadicks took off, it was no longer to absorb the warming applause of the vaudeville audiences. Instead it was only to cut up touches with old trooper friends in California, Oklahoma, and Texas, shielded from the worst of the depression by his five-thousand-dollar Stampede salary and one-thousand-dollar bonus.

For a couple who had been living off audience applause for their entire adult lives, it must have been an emotional trauma of the first order for the Weadicks. True, what happened to them—unemployment—was happening to hundreds of thousands of factory workers. But there was a difference. For the latter the factories were still there, giving hope of a reopening some day. For the Weadicks, their "factories" were gone forever. But Weadick still had the Stampede and during the winter sojourns in the south, he kept bombarding Richardson with suggestions for additional improvement to the program and to the plant itself.

Richardson, however, as early as 1930, was beginning to have other things on his mind than bigger and better attractions for the Stampede, despite the fact that the 1929 show scaled new heights in attendance, net income, and profitability. The exhibition side attracted a record 7,275 entries including more than nine hundred cattle, almost double the 1928 entry. New classes were established for Alberta bred cattle and in the open categories entries came in from ten American states, New Brunswick, Ontario, Manitoba, and British Columbia. And when it took almost an hour to parade the prize winners past the grandstand audience, the executive could concede that this was the kind of Exhibition they had been aspiring to for these many years.

But—

A new race track had opened in Butte, Montana, and drained away many of the horses that had been racing in Calgary. As a result, racing profits in 1929 did not rise with the attendance. And there were some other figures that were troubling to the canny, Scottish general manager. For one thing, expenditures were also breaking records. Since 1923, the Stampede prize list had grown from around $9,000 to over $18,000 and other Stampede expenses had ballooned to $30,742 from $8,000. Over the same period expenses of all kinds had just about doubled.

There were indications here and there as well that Calgarians were not quite as gung ho as they had been. The downtown merchants grumbled about having the downtown celebrations on Eighth Avenue, thus impeding entry to their stores, and succeeded in having them nudged over to Ninth Avenue away from the main shopping area. Dressing up the store fronts with old-time motifs fell into disfavor and after the show was over in 1929, Richardson publicly chastized the downtown merchants for their lack of participation. After all, the Exhibition was attracting thousands of tourists to the city and its retail establishments. It was hardly too much to expect those who profited from the effort to get into the swing of things.

Before the 1930 show got underway, Wall Street had crashed, bringing the once out of control Calgary oil stock boom to a dismal conclusion that shut down the industry itself. The price of wheat had dropped below a dollar a bushel and the number of jobless single men trooping into the city was becoming an embarrassment to the civic administration. In such an environment a repetition of the record accomplishments of 1929 could hardly have been expected. Even so, the extent of the decline was a blow to the confidence of the Calgary establishment.

Despite superb weather conditions, attendance in 1930 dropped by 56,000, receipts were down $57,000 and a $41,846 profit of 1929 disappeared in a $14,000 deficit. As it looked around, the Exhibition board discovered that all the other fairs were in the same boat, that the economic downturn hit the amusement industry first everywhere.

Plans for the 1931 show included the biggest birthday party the country had ever seen. It would be the seventy-fifth birthday of the patron saint of the Calgary Exhibition—Pat Burns, who had always been its anchor to windward. When financial help had been needed, he was always there. When staff and facilities were required to process thousands of pounds of meat for monster barbeques, he provided them. As there was nothing like a birthday party to cure the blues, the board began planning for the Burns party the week after the 1930 show closed.

It was well that it did, for on May 3, 1931, fire destroyed the main exhibits building on the grounds. The building had housed most of the commercial and industrial exhibits since its construction for Dominion Exhibition in 1908. The Exhibition board and the city administration went into emergency session to consider alternatives. There were two choices: the 1931 exhibition could be called off, or an attempt could be made to clear the site and replace the building in no more than six weeks. The decision was overwhelmingly for the latter. A small army of unemployed single men were rounded up and put to work for their relief clearing away the fire debris. With $14,000 in fire insurance and a $17,000 grant from the city, the company was able to erect a 64 by 264 foot exhibits building in five weeks, just in time to house the exhibits for the 1931 show.

The Bessborough building marked the beginning of a new continuing role for the Calgary Industrial Exhibition Company—acting as an unemployment relief agency. Most of the artisans employed were drawing unemployment relief from the city. The work was spread around so that each worker got at least a week's work which, at current union wages of a dollar an hour, provided them with forty-eight dollars, the first cash many had seen in months.

When the time came to hire the hundreds of ushers, ticket-takers, gate keepers, grounds keepers, etc., for the Exhibition, this too became a relief works. Preference was given to the unemployed and because the applicants were so numerous, an effort was made to dole the work out in half-day dollops. That was a practical impossibility so the work week for each employee was ceilinged at three days. It added $15,000 to the money in circulation among the unemployed in Calgary during Exhibition week.

Despite the deepening economic depression, however, the 1931 Exhibition and Stampede was adjudged an outstanding success. Perhaps the euphoria that permeated Calgary was generated by the parade of which Pat Burns was the grand marshal. Perhaps it was the distribution of pieces of his birthday cake to fifteen thousand at the opening day show. Perhaps it was the super birthday banquet for seven-hundred at which his appointment to the Canadian Senate was announced. Whatever it was, for one week in 1931 Calgary forgot the depression.

Two days of rain failed to dampen attendance which was within 4,000 of that of 1930. The number of exhibits actually exceeded those of 1929. The threat from Butte to the racing profits evaporated and the take from the parimutuels increased slightly, thanks to the introduction of daily double betting. Nevertheless, the overall

deficit for 1931 was $16,364 and this was an ever-present consideration in the minds of the organization when plans were being laid for the 1932 show, a fact which brought it into head-on collision with Guy Weadick. It was a confrontation that was easy to understand.

Weadick had spent the winter in the south, isolated from the economic storms that were sweeping Calgary and western Canada. The city council had so antagonized its electors with its spending on unemployment relief that an aroused electorate was circulating recall petitions which would have vacated most of the council seats. There were eighteen-hundred families on unemployment relief in Calgary, along with several hundred single men. The city had seized 684 houses for unpaid taxes, along with thirty stores and nine Chinese laundries. Out in the countryside the price of wheat had been driven to the lowest point in recorded Canadian history, to below forty cents a bushel at the farm gates.

All the governments—national, provincial, and municipal—were desperately short of money with which to finance the increased demands for unemployment and agricultural relief. All were searching for budgetary fat that could be trimmed and diverted to urgent needs. One such pocket of fat was identified as the grants budget. In the winter of 1932 it was rumored that the Dominion and the province would together abolish the $14,000 annual subsidy to the Calgary Industrial Exhibition Company. That sparked another rumor that the organization was considering abandoning the Exhibition altogether for 1932. Ultimately the two governments agreed to come through with $5,500 and the rumors of abandonment died away.

When plans were being made for the 1932 show the watchwords were economy, retrenchment, frugality, and thriftiness—or, in two words, cheeseparing stinginess. After almost ten years of more or less openhandedness in spending money to make money, the Calgary Industrial Exhibition went on a budget-slashing campaign that left no single item intact. Staff salaries had already been reduced by ten percent, for Richardson and Weadick as well as for the clerical employees. Substantial cuts had been made in several items in 1931, in race purses, parade expenses, and attractions. These were all cut again, along with every other category, from Stampede prizes to judges' fees and the art exhibit expenses.

The biggest cuts of all were where the largest growth had been—in the Stampede prize list and Stampede expenses. The first was cut by $7,000 from $17,000 to $10,000 and the second from $25,000 to $19,000. This translated into up to a fifty percent reduction in the day money and finals prize money for all the Stampede events. Day money prizes of $175 in 1931 were reduced to $125 for the North American Saddle Bronc Riding Championship. The bareback final money was cut from $650 to $375. The chuckwagon prizes were reduced from $1,810 for the week to $1,190.

To Weadick, the board was violating all the promotional rules he had lived by for twenty-five years. When business slackened you went out and brought in bigger and better attractions! And you pumped up promotional campaigns! Most certainly you did not cut the advertising budget from $16,400 to $11,120!

Richardson had kept Weadick abreast of the way the administration was thinking by correspondence during the winter and Weadick had entered his caveats in rather mild and polite tones. Nobody was therefore prepared for his reaction at the final board meeting in May at which everything for the 1932 show was finalized.

Over the years this meeting had become a forum for a Weadick pep talk in which he forecast bigger and better attendance and profits and public enthusiasm. The 1932 show, he predicted, to the consternation of the directors, was headed for absolute disaster. There was no way in which the cowboys would turn up to compete for the kind of money they proposed to offer! There would be no Stampede!

When the directors recovered from their shock at Weadick's performance, they attempted to allay his concerns. Some concluded that Weadick simply had two or three drinks too many before the meeting. The directors stuck to their guns and despite his outburst, Weadick went ahead

with preparations for opening the show as he had always done.

The show opened on time, the parade was one of the best in years, attendance, while down 23,442 from 1931, exceeded everyone's expectations. Certainly the number of cowboys who turned up far exceeded Weadick's expectations, although entries from the United States were down. Weadick, in simple truth, had misread the nature of the cowboy who would challenge a bucking horse for "pennies, marbles or chalk" if fancier prizes were not available. And in any event the reduced prizes offered by the Stampede were eminently worth competing for in the context of the times. Thanks to the achieved economies, the show wound up with a profit of $181.66. Unhappily, it also wound up without the services of Guy Weadick as Stampede manager.

Weadick never really got over his disenchantment with the economizing splurge of the board of directors. Toward the end of the show there were reports that Weadick was telling people that he was through with the Calgary operation at the end of the show. As if to emphasize his dissatisfaction, on the final evening of the show, he turned up somewhat the worse for wear and fouled up the prize presentation ceremonies at which a British brigadier general, William Allison, was doing the honors before twelve thousand spectators.

If Weadick was fed up with the directors, the Stampede committee was equally disenchanted with Weadick. Before the August meeting of the board, several of the directors, perhaps jokingly at first and then with increasing seriousness, started asking each other: "When we come right down to it, what do we really need with Weadick"? The answer they kept coming up with was "Not much, really."

The Stampede section of the Exhibition did not differ fundamentally from the livestock and other sections. The livestock section also had to bring in and look after large numbers of livestock. Both required the hiring of judges and extra help to take care of the animals. Indeed the hiring of the livestock judges was much more complicated than hiring rodeo judges. There were many more animals involved in the livestock section. Most complicated of all was the handicraft-fancy work-schools section. But all the various departments had operated for years under standing committees similar to the Stampede Committee without a paid manager.

By midsummer 1932 the Stampede had evolved to a point where it almost ran itself. Jack Dillon had taken over the responsibility for running off all the rodeo events. A cadre of judges had been collected who worked the various events each year with increasing expertise and proportionately decreasing grumbling and protests from contestants.

field, Herman Linder of Cardston, Lee Ferris, "The Canada Kid" of DeWinton, Eddie Bowlen of Calgary, Norman Edge, Dick Cosgrave, Pete LaGrande, the Watrin Brothers—Lee and Slim—Ray Knight, the Indians Pete Bruisehead and Johnny Lefthand, were names that appeared time and again on rodeo trophies, not only in Calgary but in American rodeos as well.

By 1932 it was clear that the Stampede would never have to be concerned about a shortage of cowboy entries, regardless of the size of the purse. So what did the Stampede need with Weadick? More pre-

By the end of the 1920s the Calgary Stampede had developed a group of superstars who could compete successfully anywhere. Herman Linder on Steel Grey was the all around winner at Calgary man times. *Courtesy of Glenbow Archives. Calgary, Alberta.*

Above all, the Calgary Stampede had established a life of its own. Its chuckwagon races had grown to a point where they regularly attracted entries of twenty rigs. All over the West, community stampedes were enabling young riders to sharpen their skills at all the rodeo sports, always with the idea of competing with the best from all over the world at the Calgary Stampede.

In less than a decade, moreover, rodeoing was developing into a major sport with recognizable star performers. Weadick had been solely responsible for bringing in the outstanding American cowboys and cowgirls. But by 1928 Canadian performers were developing so quickly that the Canadians were winning most of the main events on the program. Clem Gardner, who had been the outstanding local performer at the 1912 Stampede, was still riding and roping and driving chuckwagons with reckless abandon. Pete Knight of Cross-

cisely, what did it need with Weadick's $5,400 a year salary? The answer was provided in the letter Richardson wrote to Weadick on August 16, 1932:

At a meeting of the directors held today for the discussion of future plans for the Calgary Exhibition & Stampede, while it is the intention to continue the Stampede feature of the Exhibition, it was decided in the interests of economy, to discontinue the position of Stampede manager. In accordance with this decision you will not be engaged as Stampede manager for the ensuing year. This will constitute notice that the arrangement existing between the company and yourself in the past will not be continued.

(signed E. L. Richardson)

Weadick's reaction was to retain Andrew Naismith and A. L. Smith and sue the

TOM LAUDER
Chuck Wagon Race

PETE BRUISEHEAD
Canadian Calf Roper

PETE KNIGHT
Bucking Horse
Rider

RICHARD MERCHANT
Calf Roper

NORMAN EDGE
Steer
Rider

JACK HILL
Bareback Bucking

company for $100,000 for breach of contract and unfair dismissal. He also asked that the Exhibition Company be restrained from using the word "Stampede" in the name of its show, a suit later abandoned.

The board of directors originally had relied on a straightforward justification for dispensing with Weadick's services. He had been hired on a year to year basis. During the first couple of years, his contract was renewed by letter each year. Then it was decided to dispense with the annual letter and have the contract extend automatically for one year unless Weadick was notified to the contrary prior to December 1. The August letter had been the required notification.

But when the case came to trial before Judge William Ives in 1935, the original defense plan was abandoned. Weadick's drunken behavior was brought into court as justification for his dismissal. Ives found

in fact that Weadick had been drunk at the trophy presentation. But so what? Wasn't he expected to consume some of the Exhibition-bought booze when he was entertaining guests of the company? Ives found there was no grounds for dismissal and awarded Weadick half a year's pay, $2,700 plus $1,700 costs.

The company's attorneys—the firm of Bennett, Might, Nolan and Chambers —was clearly outraged by the verdict and strongly recommended the Exhibition appeal the decision. The advice was rejected in favor of paying the damages, letting the controversy die, and giving the scars time to heal over the wounds.

It would prove a slow and painful process, and almost twenty years would elapse before another administration would feel up to inviting Weadick back to the show, and Weadick would feel up to accepting.

Pete Knight, standing in the center, was a world champion bucking horse rider at the time of his death in California in 1937. *Courtesy of Glenbow Archives, Calgary, Alberta.*

CHAPTER 8

Hockey Booms Again— Sort Of

I f the sponsors of the Calgary Exhibition and Stampede had reason for apprehension about the future of their enterprise in 1932, there was cause for downright panic in 1933. That was not merely a winter of discontent for Calgarians, Albertans, and Canadians, it was a winter of unalloyed doom and gloom.

The Calgary Chamber of Commerce members saw their city being dragged into bankruptcy by the cost of unemployment relief for the city's twenty-seven hundred destitute families and two thousand single unemployed. Yielding to those concerns, the city cut the relief allowance for a family of four from $10 a week to $8.50, cut teachers' salaries and civic wages by a total of twenty percent. Department heads and top administrators were cut thirty percent. When the relief cuts provoked hundreds of married unemployed into going on strike against the make-work projects they were forced to do for their relief, picket line riots occurred. Demonstrations disrupted the soup kitchens for single men the province had established at Victoria Park. These were followed by a noisy mass protest meeting in the livestock pavilion at which three thousand attended.

In the world beyond, Hitler had just come to power in Germany. Stalin was beginning his reign of terror in Russia. President F. D. Roosevelt had ordered the closing of every bank in the United States to end the nationwide runs on the banks by

their panicky depositors. He followed that by taking the country off the gold standard for its currency.

This was the atmosphere in late May, 1933, when Jack Dillon reopened the Stampede office in Victoria Park to begin preparations for the Stampede. It was a move he had been making for five years, or since he had been appointed arena director and general factotum under A. E. Cross and Guy Weadick.

From an earlier ranching life, Dillon had settled comfortably into a livestock commission agency at the Calgary Stockyards during the First World War. When the Exhibition was joined permanently with the Stampede he became what in later years would be called a "Stampede groupie"—he became so fascinated with the show that he simply could not be driven away from the action. Of all the volunteers on whom the Exhibition board could call for assistance, he was the most enthusiastic and reliable.

Back in 1924, Dillon was naturally greeted with open arms by Weadick and Cross and put to work at the jobs nobody

Jack Dillon's successor as arena director was, of course, Dick Cosgrave, the greatest chuckwagon driver of them all, shown here on his palomino gelding, Chief. *Courtesy of the Calgary Stampede.*

else wanted, mainly seeing to the details of the scores of special tasks that were essential to the success of the show. Arrangements had to be completed with a dozen ranchers to trail hundreds of head of horses and cattle from outlying ranches into the Stampede grounds, well in advance of the show. Judges had to be recruited and trained, along with timers and starters. Feed supplies had to be lined up, renovations to the plant undertaken, improvements to procedures worked into the program. Dillon went at it all with such enthusiasm that it was not long before he was appointed arena director and given charge of running off the Stampede events.

The logistics of the Stampede had been fine-tuned over the first decade of the combined operation but 1933 was a whole new ball game. Not only was Weadick gone, but the death of A. E. Cross in March, 1932, had robbed the Stampede committee of its main driving force. Pat Burns had taken over briefly in 1932 as the titular head of the committee, but the de facto working replacement was A. E.'s eldest son, James B.

Like his father, Jim Cross's consuming interest in life was the A7 Ranch where as a boy he had spent his summer holidays as a working cowboy. When he finished high school, he enrolled, as his father had done before him in the agricultural college at Guelph, Ontario. He then did post-graduate work in economics in England to prepare him for succession to his father's multitude of commercial interests. But that young Cross remained a cowboy at heart is evidenced by the fact that he enlisted as an outrider on the Drumheller-McLeary-Cross rig that won the first Stampede chuckwagon race. He returned to outriding year after year whenever the A7 had a wagon in the race.

From acting as a sort of messenger for his father at the beginning he developed over the years into the elder Cross's alter ego, in the operation of the ranch, the Calgary Brewery and in his father's other interests, including the running of the Stampede committee. It was therefore eminently logical for the shareholders of the Calgary Exhibition and Stampede to choose the thirty-year-old Jim Cross to fill his father's place on the board of directors and for the directors to appoint him chairman of the Stampede committee in 1933.

As far as Jack Dillon was concerned, there could not have been any better choice than Jim Cross. Dillon and Cross had worked together to a point where each knew what the other was doing, until they were functionally interchangeable. Despite the impenetrable cloud of gloom that permeated everything in 1933, they determined to place their own stamp on the Stampede. Their first objective was to de-emphasize the Stampede as a spectacle and recast it as an athletic contest.

Until 1933 the chuckwagon races were regarded by the Exhibition board more as a "filler" than as a main event, as an ideal crowd amuser for the hour before the evening grandstand performance and little more. If the winning chuckwagon teams were mentioned at all in the summaries of the day's events, it was as the last item on the list. The twenty-odd rigs that raced each night for ribbons and a final trophy were paid a small fee to cover the expenses of the drivers and outriders, who usually bedded down in the stables with the horses.

In 1933 the subsidies system was abandoned in favor of racing for cash prizes —$100 split five ways in day money for four days and $575 for the final race on Friday night. On that occasion Dick Cosgrave won the $300 first prize; Clem Gardner took $150 second; Jim Ross $75 third; and Scott Hamilton $50 fourth.

Dick Cosgrave, who by 1933 was doubling as Jack Dillon's assistant for six weeks before the show opened, would go on to win no less than ten chuckwagon racing championships. With the wild driving Clem Gardner he might well have shared the title of "father of chuckwagon racing."

Cosgrave, like Gardner opted for thoroughbreds pulling a lighter wagon. But he dominated chuckwagon racing during the 1930s because he concentrated more on driving penalty-free races than on sheer speed. Unlike Gardner, whose driving could only be described as vintage reckless-abandon, Cosgrave developed a genius for getting around the barrels with consumate smoothness and finishing the race with all outriders alongside his wagon. The posting of cash prizes transformed the chuckwagon contests into real horse races and put the crowning touch on the Stampede.

To emphasize the competitive nature of the show, a professional rodeo announcer, Johnny Jordan, was brought in to call each event and keep the audience informed of the standings of the various competitors. Then, as each day's rodeo events were concluded the day's results were summarized for the audience. The whole project was topped on Saturday night when the Calgary *Herald* brought out a special edition, front-paging the final results of all events for the week.

Those results were burial notices for the Weadick notion that Calgary had to depend on American cowboys to headline its shows. Thirty-one Americans did compete in 1933, but they had to take back seat to the performance of the top Canadians. Pete Knight of Crossfield won both the Canadian and North American open saddle bronc competitions. Pat Burton of Claresholm beat three American finalists in the calf roping contest, Frank Sharp of Black Diamond won the Brahma bull riding, and Herman Linder was the best all around cowboy for the third year in a row. The American cowboys kept coming, and they kept winning prizes. But they were no longer essential for the staging of a successful Stampede.

The Calgary Stampedes of 1912 and 1919 had struck responsive chords not only in young Alberta ranch hands. They had infected the civic leaders of most of the important towns in the south country. In some places the annual Stampede had even replaced the annual fair as the outstanding community enterprise. When Jack Dillon organized the Alberta Stampede Directors Association in 1933 he attracted more than twenty participants to his first meeting.

Throughout the summers, one stampede followed hard on the heels of another. As a result the embryo rodeo stars of Alberta could spend their summers honing their roping and riding skills at neighborhood stampedes; serving an apprenticeship that would lead them inevitably to Calgary, and to Cheyenne, Pendleton, and beyond. So

there was never a shortage of cowboys for the Calgary Stampede. And, thanks to the depression, there was never a shortage of the kind of skilled extra help the Stampede needed to function smoothly.

When the cowboys sent in their entries for the Stampede events they were frequently accompanied by urgent appeals for employment on the grounds during the show. The Stampede Committee gave these applications the same positive response the Exhibition department gave to applications for employment for Calgary's unemployed. The poverty-stricken cowboys got jobs feeding, watering, and moving six-hundred head of livestock on the grounds; as chute men, unsaddlers, pick-up men, saddle and halter collectors. Combining working and performing was possible for the cowboys because their performing duties took only a few minutes every other day or so. The unskilled workers were paid $3.50 a day; jobs requiring certain skills were paid slightly more. Top pay of $8 a day went to the pick-up men in the bucking events but to earn that money they had to provide two grain-fed horses with which to ply their trade.

So great was the volume of job applications that the Stampede committee had to establish a system of hiring priorities. First choice went to those who had worked the previous year, and whose performances justified their being rehired. That would fill half the fifty or sixty job openings. The second preference went to the chuckwagon drivers who had to bring in the most horses and who collected the smallest rewards. Then came the persons whose competitive presence was desired, or who had been competitors and were past their prime. Such a person was Tom Three Persons, the saddle bronc champion of 1912, who worked as a pick-up man during the 1930s.

From all this it is clear that it was no trick at all for the Stampede to assemble a full crew of highly skilled extra help to serve its needs, year after year. This was the key to the viability of the Exhibition and Stampede over the years, its ability to mount a year-round operation with a super-skeleton permanent staff, scarcely larger, or more costly, in 1933 than it had been in 1923, or 1913. At the top was E. L. Richardson and his assistant W. N. Gibson. Fred Stanford was the accountant and cashier, Robert Thomson was the livestock superintendent, Robert Spencer was the grounds superintendent. Dillon was on staff for two months, Cosgrave for six weeks. Both Thomson and Spencer had rosters of experienced extra-helpers on whom they could call to flesh out the volunteers supplied by the associations which sponsored the various shows that took place at Victoria Park.

One reason that the cowboys were so eager to be hired for the Stampede was they lacked the funds to pay for their entry fees. These ranged from five to ten dollars for each event. Fully half the entries received came without an accompanying fee. Payment of the fee was not required with the entry but it did have to be paid before the cowboys could compete. Those with jobs could charge their fees against their wages.

With upwards of three-hundred cowboys competing, the odds were stacked against any average cowboy winning any more than enough money to pay his entrance fees. This resulted, in part, because of the way the prize money was split—the big money prizes were reserved for the final championship competitions, the day-money allotments were chicken feed. For example, the four finalists in the North American Saddle Bronc Riding contest split $950 with $500 going to the winner, $300 to second, $100 to third, and $50 to fourth. The open calf roping championship carried a similar prize and split. For the Canadian championships in these events the prizes were just half. But the daily prize totalled only $100 in the open events, half that in the contest for Canadians. Thus a bareback rider could finish in the top four three days in a row and pocket less than $50 in prize money. In addition to the cash awards there were also "trophies" in the form of merchandise—saddles, bridles, blankets, boots, spurs, hats and suits of clothes—which went to the champions. All were readily convertible into cash if the need arose.

For the overwhelming majority of the young cowboys, stampeding was of necessity a fun thing. But for the cream of the crop it was a lot better than working. For his double win in the saddle bronc categories Pete Knight won $140 in day money and $750 for the championship finals, along with $300 worth of merchandise prizes. Cowboys who made the finals would pocket $150 to $200 even if they struck out. Those earnings for a week's work were more in 1933 than most ordinary ranchhands could hope to earn in wages in a year.

As for the aforementioned gloom and doom of 1933, it was banished without a trace in Calgary during Stampede week. The weather was superb throughout the entire show and the crowd of 188,436 exceeded that of 1932 by almost 14,000. Despite cutting the general admission price from fifty cents before 6:00 P.M. to twenty-five cents, gate receipts were up $1,600 over 1932 and the company ended the year with a surplus of $1,064.

What the 1933 show demonstrated was that the Calgary Exhibition and Stampede was becoming almost independent of economic circumstances. If the directors had not come to feel that was true, the 1933 show might have been called off in midstream. Certainly the reception the donation collectors got from Calgary businessmen that spring would have discouraged a lesser breed of men.

Participation in the Stampede parade and in the downtown carnival was encouraged by awarding cash prizes for the best float in various categories; to best dressed cowgirls, cowboys, Indians; for the most imaginative chuckwagon decorations. These prizes were funded by donations from downtown businessmen. Donations had neared $5,000 in 1930 but dwindled almost to the vanishing point to $528 in 1933. Naturally the committee had to drastically cut back on its prize money and it did so with trepidation.

The plain truth, however, was that when it came to community participation in the Calgary Exhibition and Stampede, money did not matter. Despite the cutback in prize money, entries for the 1933 parade broke all records. And did to such an extent that criticisms were heard that it was getting out of hand, that a two-hour parade was putting too great a physical strain on both participants and spectators. On the grounds, the livestock exhibits were as numerous and as high in quality as ever before. The drastic cut back in advertising did not adversely affect attendance because more people came to the show every day than had attended in 1932. Cutting back on the prize list had not reduced the entries for the Stampede events, or dampened the enthusiasm of the competitors. Surviving the worst depression year the country had ever known and making money to boot was all the proof that anyone would need that the continuity of the Calgary Exhibition and Stampede was assured.

Though agricultural Alberta would live through another half decade of drought and depression, *the* Depression ended for the Calgary Exhibition and Stampede in 1933. The following year, the annual report of the directors to the shareholders became downright lyrical.

> . . . Never in the history of the Calgary Exhibition and Stampede have so many complimentary remarks been made about the show as were made regarding the last one. This was due to the excellent co-operation extended to the show by all and to the excellence of several departments. The exhibits in most departments were outstanding, the cattle and horse exhibits increasing by 21% over last year. Anyone who witnessed the livestock parade in front of the grandstand on Friday morning would be convinced of the valuable encouragement being given to the livestock industry through the annual exhibition.

A new Indian Affairs administrator, M. Christianson, ended the Indian near-boycott of the show by instituting instead full participation. Special exhibitions of Indian handicrafts and schoolwork were established, the public was invited into the Indian Village to inspect the interiors of the teepees.

Despite near freezing temperatures on two nights, attendance was up almost 30,000 in 1934 to 214,000, the third highest ever. With increased patronage finances also improved and continued to do so for the balance of the decade.

The Exhibition indeed seemed to acquire a new promotional vigor during the depression. The auto dealers were persuaded to rent the underside of the grandstand in which to stage an auto show. The Canadian General Electric Company was sold on setting up a wave-of-the-future display of electrical wizardry that included room-to-room transmission and reception of television, and a seven-thousand-pound robot that talked, smoked, drank, and answered the telephone.

The art exhibit arranged through the Royal College of Art was augmented by a special presentation by Roland Gissing of a display of his Alberta landscapes. The art exhibit overall was adjudged the most successful in many years, both in the attendance and the quality of the work on display.

In both 1934 and 1935 the Exhibition went in big for historical pageantry. The first was a celebration of Calgary's golden anniversary as a town. Its parade honored three members of the first city government. Col. James Walker was a member of the 1884 school board, I. S. Freeze was a member of the city council, and G. C. King was the postmaster; and a half dozen previous mayors were rounded up. The prime minister, Rt. Hon. R. B. Bennett, came home from Ottawa officially to open the fair.

The next year, 1935, was the sixtieth anniversary of the arrival of the North West Mounted Police at the site of Calgary and the mounties sent their musical ride for a week-long performing visit to the parade and the fair. This was conceded to be a celebration of such importance that some easing up on the purse strings was justified. So an addition of five thousand dollars was allocated to the prize list of which two thousand dollars went to sweetening the cowboys' events. That year Turk Greenough of Red Lodge, Montana, picked up a cheque for one thousand dollars for winning the North American open saddle bronc championship. That was more than any cowboy had ever won in Canada before, more than any would win again for the next decade at least.

After 1935 the prize list went back to normal—about half the 1935 total. The first tentative steps taken in 1934 to "colorize" the Stampede became fixed policy in 1936 when all entrants were notified that the wearing of colorful regalia in the centerfield would be required. Each chuckwagon was also required to adopt its own colors for outriders and driver. All advertising had to be removed from the rigs and only the name of the owners allowed to appear.

Color coding the contestants was a signal for Calgary women to get into the act. Not only did they take to wearing gaudy hand-embroidered silk blouses and decorated split skirts, they began to embroider even more colorful silk shirts for their men folk. Over the next two decades, even Calgarians who had never sat a horse turned up Stampede week in frontier pants, embroidered shirts, and Stetson hats. Then, after the Stampeding duds were packed away until next year the Stetson hats stayed out. The fawn-colored "open road" Stetson became as much the identifying trademark of the people of Calgary as the jet black fedora identified Toronto and Montreal bankers and Ottawa lawyer-lobbyists.

Ultimately of course Gresham's law came into play and the spurious drove out the authentic. But until the bargain basement denims and dime store ties proliferated, the age of elegance in Stampede Week attire was wonderful to behold, and it lasted well into the 1950s!

One of the continuing problems of the Calgary Exhibition, indeed a continuing problem for all exhibitions, was with the midways. The rides were a super attraction, and along with the rides were the so-called games of chance and each year seemed to bring something new to attract the attention of the unwary—new ball throws, roll downs, string pulls, chuck-a-lucks, bingo. All were capable of being rigged to ensure that the "marks" left their money with the operators. They were also, it was discovered much later, capable of being rigged to skim the cream off the top of the gross receipts of the midway before the Exhibition's cut of the gross revenues was calculated.

Floating along with the midways from town to town were a motley gang of sneak thieves, pickpockets, and hustlers. All exhibitions and police departments worked especially hard during Exhibition weeks to keep the game operators within bounds

and the grifters and drifters under control. Indeed Inspector James Melville of the Winnipeg Police Department, who was reputed to know on sight every important carnival pickpocket and thief, followed the prairie circuit each summer to scare off the pickpockets.

Such was the reputation of the carnivals and circuses as early as 1920 that Winnipeg refused to permit any of them to set up within its corporate boundaries. Calgary naturally tried to keep the swindling along the midway to a minimum and when complaints were loud enough the management was frequently persuaded to refund the losses of gullible customers and shut down or run off the operators of the offending games. Over the years Calgary and the other western fairs tried several midways before settling in 1936 for the Royal American shows which seemed, at that time, to be a cut above most of its competition. That was the year, too, when a semi-permanent arrangement was made with the Ernie Young organization of Chicago for a package deal of entertainment for the evening grandstand shows.

In 1937 the first real break in the permanent staff of the company occurred. W. N. Gibson, who had been chief clerk and later assistant manager for thirty years, died after a short illness. His place was taken by Walter Ross, who had been a full-time volunteer and part-time employee since 1929. "Squibb" Ross would serve as assistant manager until 1962.

It was during the 1930s that the educational system reached its widest participation in the annual show. Dr. A. Melville Scott was chairman of the schools committee and there was no aspect of public education that he did not "shoehorn" into the Exhibition. Every phase of school work was entered in competition by both public and separate schools. Music, art, writing, and arithmetic work was all there as were the essays and poetry of the pupils along with an infinite variety of "manual training" exhibits.

The crowning touch was the Grade VIII spelling bees that went on throughout the week and were finalized on the last night of the show as the curtain raiser before the grandstand show. As important for many of the pupils as their exhibits were the jobs

The last thing on the minds of any Calgary Exhibition directors when the Victoria Arena was built was to turn it into a hockey rink. But after Lloyd Turner came onto the scene the Arena became the hot bed of Calgary hockey. The Calgary Canadians won the Canadian junior championship in 1926. *Courtesy of Glenbow Archives, Calgary, Alberta.*

Lloyd Turner's association began with the organization of the Calgary Tigers in 1923 and it ended with his retirement in 1964. He is shown here with Mr. Justice M. M. "Marsh" Porter who was chairman of the finance committee for many years.
Photograph by DeLorme Photography, Calgary. Courtesy of the Calgary Stampede.

they obtained mounting the displays. It took a week before the show to put them up and a week following to take them down. Conscientious kids could earn as much as thirty dollars as exhibit mounters, to say nothing of free passes to the grounds for the duration.

Curiously enough, it was the very nadir of the depression when the game of hockey reached its peak of popularity in southern Alberta. Towns like Strathmore, Okotoks, High River, Turner Valley, Gleichen, all had teams playing in organized leagues. Calgary had a half dozen outdoor rinks operating city-wide pee-wee, midget, and juvenile leagues. At playoff time they all moved into the Arena, along with teams from the commercial league.

Unhappily the most any hockey enthusiast could count on in the Calgary area

was a three-month season at best. Between 1920 and 1935 perhaps a dozen different leagues existed ephemerally in the Arena. The one that came closest to succeeding was the junior league in which the Calgary Canadians went all the way to national champions in 1925–26. Several attempts were made to organize a western professional league, sometimes of Calgary, Edmonton, Saskatoon, and Regina, sometimes of Calgary, Edmonton, Vancouver, Seattle, and Portland. No Calgary franchise was ever able to survive, in any of these leagues, for more than a year or two, regardless of whether the team finished at the top or on the bottom.

Lloyd Turner, who brought hockey to the Arena in 1920, gave the promotion of professional hockey a thorough try before taking off for Minneapolis in 1925. Then

Rosie Helmer became the city's hockey impresario and from time to time coached or managed junior, senior, and professional teams. Jimmy Condon lent his financial support and name—the "Jimmies"—to a number of minor league teams. To accommodate all these efforts the Exhibition board over the years substantially modified the interior of the Arena, cutting back on the length of the surface to provide 1,500 additional seats. Unhappily the 4,500 seating capacity of the building was seldom needed though crowds of 2,500 were frequently attracted to the junior, senior, and professional games.

It was not lack of patronage that killed off the professional leagues so quickly. It was the short season and low admission prices. No professional team, operating on a thirty-six-game schedule and making three trips to Vancouver and Portland, could hope to survive on fifty cents and seventy-five cents admission with crowds averaging between fifteen hundred and twenty-five hundred. Not when the season did not open until late November and was into the playoffs by the end of February. Sometimes the weather even made it necessary to delay opening until December and cancel scheduled games in February.

But as ice permitted, there was a hockey game of some kind almost every night of the week. Indeed, when it was uncommonly cold, there were frequently two and sometimes three games a night. When the hockey schedules permitted, there was public skating to band music for an admission fee of thirty-five cents. In summary, the building was used for a week during the April horse show, for a couple of weeks during the Exhibition, and for a maximum of four months during the winter. Under such circumstances, that it could ever break even on its year's operation was a minor miracle.

What Calgary needed was an artificial ice-making plant like the one installed in the Winnipeg Amphitheatre or in the west coast arenas. That idea surfaced every time a chinook disrupted a hockey schedule, but until Lloyd Turner returned to Calgary in 1933 it was only talk. Turner had managed artificial ice arenas in Minneapolis and Portland and then was the manager of the Seattle hockey team for several years.

On his return to Calgary he tried to convince the Exhibition Board that it should turn the Arena into an artificial ice rink that could operate from October to April. Faced as it was with doubts about its ability to even survive, the board would have nothing to do with any kind of proposal that would commit it to a risk venture of any kind.

Turner then turned his attention to raising enough money from private sources, an estimated $25,000, to install an ice plant in the arena. Here he got caught up in the chicken-egg syndrome—he could not complete a deal for the Arena until he had raised the money and could not raise the money until he had a lease on the Arena. Eventually a way around the dilemma was found and a lease was signed in the winter of 1934–35. The lease would run for nine years, at the end of which the board would purchase the ice plant from Turner for $12,500. Under the terms of the lease, rental was to be:

1/12 of the gross receipt on the first $18,000;

1/3 of the next $5,000 in gross receipts;

2/5 of the next $2,500 in gross receipts;

1/2 of gross receipts in excess of $25,500.

Turner then assigned the lease to the Calgary Artificial Ice Rink Company Limited he had promoted and Calgary was on its way to becoming the hockey capital of Alberta. But for Turner's entrepreneurial skill as a hockey team owner it was another story. His Calgary Tigers team in the Northwestern Hockey League that included Edmonton, Vancouver, Seattle, and Portland was an unmixed disaster. It finished dead last in the league standing in 1935–36 and failed to draw paying crowds at home. The following year both Edmonton and Calgary abandoned professional hockey for participation in the Big Six Senior Amateur League of two Calgary teams, two Edmonton teams and the Drumheller Miners and Olds Elks.

From 1937 onward there was hockey almost every night at the Victoria Arena. There was a junior league, a commercial league that played two games a night, a juvenile league and even a pee-wee league in which the young players adopted, as nicknames, the names of the players who played their positions on the Toronto Maple Leafs, Montreal Canadiens, Boston Bruins. Thus in 1937 Roy "Chapman" Brandreth scored the last-minute goal that gave his New York Americans the league championship over the Toronto Maple Leafs.

Victoria Park by this time was still evolving into the activities center of Calgary. In addition to the horse shows and livestock shows in which the company played a part, areas of the premises were rented out for commercial demonstrations and promotions. Joe Zabow, the grunt and groan impresario, for example, was attracting crowds to his weekly wrestling extravaganzas in the livestock pavilion featuring such performers as "Popeye," Frankenstein, and the "Red Shadow."

The installation of artificial ice, though it turned out to be a profitable investment for the shareholders of the Artificial Ice Rink Company, was less than a bonanza for the Exhibition board, despite the patronage the Arena enjoyed. The explanation lay in the definition in the lease of what constituted the gross income on which its percentage was based. That "gross" income was what was left after the hockey teams had extracted their percentages of the gate.

In April, 1938, the Victoria Arena was the site of the Allan Cup Finals which the Trail Smoke Eaters won in three straight games from Cornwall. The teams drew capacity crowds in excess of 4,500 for each game. The Allan Cup Finals followed a season of near-saturate use of the Arena. Yet the company's rental revenue that year dropped $3,063 from the previous year, of which the rink was responsible for a decline of $1,300. The total income from all rents for the rink, the pavilion, and from race track tack-rooms converted into wintering quarters for horse owners was $5,886.46.

Despite the failure of the Arena to develop a satisfactory cash flow after the installation of artificial ice, the Exhibition and Stampede nevertheless remained in the black for the balance of the depression. Substantially increased expenditures on improvements and repairs were made but it was still able to report a modest surplus each year in the $6,000 to $8,000 range. This was in part attributable to a slow but steady increase in attendance which reached 240,000 in 1939.

More important, as a contributor to the obliteration of red ink from the Stampede books, however, was a development that could be summed up in two words—horse racing. From his first involvement with putting the prairie racing circuit together, R. J. Speers had realized that the long-term interests of horse racing required a thoroughbred breeding industry that would provide an adequate supply of race horses for the race tracks.

By 1931 Speers had sixty days of racing across the Prairies and western bred horses were beginning to come very much to the fore. In that year twenty thoroughbred stallions were in service and western breds won over $75,000 in purses. The leading sire that year was Will Somers whose get took 27 races; James T. Clark sired 21 winners; Riveteer sired 18; Dr. Joe, 14; and Nepperhan, 13.

The sport of kings naturally attracted a motley crowd of commoners during the pioneer era of racing on the Prairies. A Calgary hotel owner, whose light-o'-love operated Calgary's largest brothel, was a successful breeder and racer of thoroughbreds. Kemo Inamasu, a Japanese-Canadian restaurant owner, was the owner and trainer of the great race mare, Duchess of York. The Jacques Brothers, who were the owners of a Calgary upholstery shop, were the owners of the fabulous Joey and a continuing string of other winners. A half dozen directors of the Exhibition were horse owners and Fred Johnston is generally credited with giving Johnny Longden the chance he needed to develop his riding skill on prairie tracks. Such people as W. A. Dutton, Don Grant, Nat Christie, E. D. Adams, K. M. Leach, Tom Burton, Mrs. Ruth Stedman, and Mrs. R. Leavitt all added luster to the sport in its formative decade.

That it could use some luster was obvious from its less than glowing public image, an image improved not at all by the crusade launched in the Alberta Legislature in 1933 by J. J. Bowlen, MLA, for severe laws to interdict the practice of doping race horses. There was an almost universal belief among race horse trainers that a horse's speed and courage could be profit-

On the winning horse is Johnny Longden riding his first winner on May 21, 1929. He would go on to win six thousand more in a forty-year riding career. The jockey on the second horse is Dwight Hurlburt and the other is Alvin Snider both of whom would go on to successful careers on the major tracks of the continent. *Courtesy of Glenbow Archives, Calgary, Alberta.*

One of the wildest promotional ideas of the decade belonged to Tex Austin who decided to stage a rodeo at the White City Stadium, London, England in June 1934 at the very depths of the world depression. Not only that, he persuaded this octet of Alberta cowboys to join the play. Shown here, in May 1934, about to embark on the long journey from Calgary are: Herman Linder, Clark Lund (above), Harry Knight, Pat Burton, Frank McDonald, Jack Streeter, Norman Edge, and Jackie Cooper. *Photo from Norman Edge.*

ably enhanced by the administration of a syringe full of drugs prior to a race. The trick was in formulating the concoction which best suited each individual animal.

Action was already being taken at major American and eastern Canadian tracks to suppress the equine drug traffic so Bowlen was simply one voice of many. Eventually the federal government established a laboratory to analyze the urine of the winning racers for drugs. Calgary, like all the other prairie tracks, then posted notices warning all owners that their horses would be subject to urine analysis. When difficulty was encountered in identifying the culprit who administered the drugs, more stringent measures were taken. Holding stalls were established to which all horses had to be taken ninety minutes before post time.

Incidental to the development of the breeding industry was the quiet appearance over the first decade of racing of a growing army of inveterate, unreconstructible horse players. No exact census was possible, but a fair estimate was that within the Calgary environs by 1935 there existed at least twenty-five hundred hard core horse players who could be counted on to

This is the immortal Joey, "lookin' for more horses and a bigger race track." He died in 1941 but when his shoes were auctioned in 1944 at a Victory Bond rally they raised $40,000. Those of two other race track immortals—Seabiscuit and Whirlaway—brought $10,000 and $6,500 respectively.

rush, lemming like, for the betting wickets whenever the horse races came to town.

The horse players' contributions to the Exhibition income hardly varied from the onset of the depression until the outbreak of the Second World War. The track distributed $17,000 in purses to the horsemen in 1930 and the horse players contributed $21,000 to the company's share of the parimutuel receipts. By 1933 the purses had been cut to just under $15,000 and the net return from the machines dropped to $19,000. By 1939 the purses were back to the 1930 level and the parimutuel income exceeded $23,500.

Based on the above figures alone, horse racing would not seem to have ever been any great bonanza for the Calgary Exhibition and Stampede, though the four-thou-

sand-odd dollars clear profit obtained each year certainly was acceptable. But the twenty-five hundred horse players also had to buy their way into Victoria Park and into the grandstand at a cost of one dollar a day. They went not to savor the excitement of the Stampede, but to bet on the horse races in spite of the Stampede. No credit was ever given to the racing department by the Exhibition board's accountant for the horse players' admissions, a matter of at least fifteen thousand dollars a year during the depression. When the credit is given where credit is due, an argument can certainly be made that the Calgary horse players contributed mightily to the survival of the Calgary Exhibition and Stampede in its hour of greatest need.

As a concomitant of the horse playing there evolved the arcana of punters' folk heroes, equine and human. There was Rochester 11, Magdu Don, McGonigle, Olds Eight, Pagan Knight, Carhan Queen among the horses. And there was Johnny Longden, Red Pollard, Georgie Woolf, Ernie Petzoldt among the humans. All apprenticed on the prairie circuit and went off to fame and fortune at the major American tracks. All were the names of household heroes for those thousands of wagerers of war against the odds in the 1930s.

But most of all there was Joey, everybody's favorite icon.

Joey, the woefully undersized son of Dr. Joe and Eileen Hoey, was born in 1930 on the farm of Arthur Layzell, a Calgary horse dealer. Layzell sold the dam with colt at foot to C. L. Jacques for $185. Nobody expected the little black horse ever to amount to anything. Nevertheless Jacques took him to Winnipeg for the spring meet of 1932 and he won the Winnipeg futurity. He followed that with an easy win in the Calgary futurity and he never looked back. He could run on any kind of track for any distance from half a mile to a mile and won the Speers handicap in 1935 and the Western Canada handicap in 1940. Over a nine-year span he started 187 times, won 41 races, was second 40 times, third 28 times, won $37,000, and was a crowd favorite whenever and wherever he raced. He died in 1941 and was buried in Victoria Park.

CHAPTER 9

The Men at the Top

The death of Colonel James Walker on March 31, 1936, followed in a matter of months by the passing of Senator Patrick Burns, severed two of the main roots of the Calgary Exhibition and Stampede with its beginnings, and with the beginnings of Calgary itself.

It was Colonel, then Major Walker who had presided over the meetings of the first organizing committee in 1884. When the Calgary and District Agricultural Society was born in 1886 he was its first president. It was he who persuaded the federal government to make the grant of Victoria Park to the society. He remained an active director of its succeeding associations for more than forty years and, on his retirement at the age of seventy-nine, in 1928, he was named first life director.

Compared with Walker, who arrived with the original North West Mounted Police expedition in 1875, Burns was a Johnny-come-lately to the Calgary scene in 1890. And as perhaps befitted a man engrossed in building a worldwide meat-packing empire, Burns's involvement with the Exhibition was a sometimes thing. He was a director at the turn of the century but dropped off the board thereafter until he became a permanent fixture in 1924. But as he demonstrated in the financing of the 1912 and 1919 Stampedes, he was always around when he was needed. He joined Walker as a life director in 1932.

The two men are symbolic of the life-time commitments that so many Albertans brought to their associations with the Calgary Exhibition and Stampede. Colonel A. G. Wolley-Dod, who also died in 1937, had maintained an association with the organization from the late 1880s, was a director in 1898 and president in 1899. Fred Johnston, who was president in 1924 and 1925 had been a director for thirty years at his death a few weeks after the passing of Pat Burns. E. D. Adams' association with the company also extended over thirty years, during twenty of which he was chairman of its finance committee. Nat Christie was another who could boast a thirty-year span of service to the company. The names of those who maintained a twenty-year record were legion.

In some cases it was more than a lifetime commitment. At the time of his death in 1932, A. E. Cross had been deeply involved in the affairs of the Exhibition for almost fifty years. With him, it was almost an association on a daily basis. Over this stretch a week seldom passed when he and Richardson were not in conversation about the affairs of the company. There was hardly an aspect of the operation with

Colonel James Walker, the first president, died on March 30, 1936 after a half-century association with the Calgary Exhibition and Stampede. *Courtesy of Glenbow Archives, Calgary, Alberta.*

which he was not familiar from setting the prize lists for the livestock shows, in the early days, to the intricacies of overall financing of the operations. He was the first chairman of the Stampede committee and remained in that post until his death, when of course his son James B. Cross replaced him as chairman of the committee as well as on the board of directors and served as president from 1949 until 1951. Then Donald Cross, A. E.'s grandson, became a director in 1973 and president in 1979.

There were, moreover, those who floated into the orbit of the organization simply by being around. One such was I. S. G. VanWart who came west from Ontario with the railway and became established as one of the largest building supply merchants in Calgary when the boom was rushing toward its frenzied climax. He was elected president of the board of trade, grand master of the masonic order and

lived in one of the showplace homes on Thirteenth Avenue West. He was also what scientists would call a biological "sport" —an indestructible Liberal politician in the Conservative hotbed of Calgary. Those were the days when all politicians played the patronage game with boisterous enthusiasm, and political muscle was meant to be exercised. Thus when Calgarians were threshing around in 1899 in an effort to get their Exhibition restarted it was to Van-Wart they turned for political assistance. It was the two thousand dollars he raised as seed money from Ottawa that got the Exhibition back into business.

When the campaign first began to get the 1908 Dominion Exhibition for Calgary it was recognized that the natural spearhead of that drive had to be someone with political influence in Ottawa. The same person, in fact, that the newly elected Liberal government in Edmonton had appointed the first sheriff of Calgary—I. S. G. VanWart. As president of the Inter-Western Pacific Exhibition, he not only helped get that bonanza for Calgary, he saw it through to triumphant completion and stayed on as president until 1912.

The last two years of VanWart's Calgary career were, however, far from happy. He had been persuaded to accept the nomination of the Liberal party to contest the Calgary West seat in the 1911 general election. He was opposed in that election by R. B. Bennett, who later became Canadian prime minister, from 1930 to 1935, and still later Viscount Bennett of Calgary and Mickelham.

The Liberals' promise of tariff reciprocity with the United States carried the day everywhere in Alberta except in Calgary West where VanWart was badly beaten. The beating, however, would have been easier to take had it not been for a bitter campaign of denigration which the Calgary *Herald* waged against VanWart during the election. In its news columns it ridiculed his platform performances, sneered at his inability to attract crowds. At the same time it devoted column after column to the ecstatic reporting of Bennett's campaign. Still smarting, VanWart shook Calgary's dust from his shoes in 1912 and returned to Toronto where he died in 1918 at the age of sixty-five.

VanWart's successor as president in 1913 was another immigrant from the East who arrived at the turn of the century. E. J. Dewey's interest in the Exhibition derived from the fact that he had been a prominent chicken fancier in Toronto. He took a long look at the quality of the poultry on display in Calgary and decided it could stand improvement. He was promptly elected to the Exhibition's board of directors and appointed chairman of its poultry committee.

As cashier at the Great West Life Insurance Company office, Dewey seemed to have a freewheeling work schedule which made him an ideal type to be elected president of the Exhibition to succeed VanWart. Not that being director, or even president, was all that time-consuming in the VanWart-Dewey era, except for a couple of weeks before and a couple of weeks after the annual show. At all other times Ernie Richardson and his special committees had matters well in hand. Dewey served in almost total anonymity for ten years, from 1913 to 1923, when ill health forced his retirement after presiding at the marriage of the Stampede to the Exhibition in 1923.

With the retirement of Dewey, Fred Johnston succeeded to the presidency. The post might have gone to E. D. Adams who had been first vice-president, but Adams begged off. He much preferred the chairmanship of the finance committee when in 1926 Nat Christie vacated that position to become president. Adams remained in that post for twenty-three years, until he was made an honorary life director in 1949. He was not alone in preferring service on special committees to the presidency. James "Cappy" Smart, the Calgary fire chief, was chairman of the parade committee and grand marshal of the parade from 1903 until two weeks before his death in 1939. A. H. McGuire was chairman of the attractions committee from 1936 until 1946. The same penchant for reelecting experienced chairmen applied to the associate directors as well. Alex Calhoun, the city librarian, was chairman of the arts committee for almost twenty years. Mrs. P. S. Goodhall was chairman of the domestic arts committee from 1930 until her death in 1946.

Once the chairmen settled into their jobs there was a noticeable reluctance on the part of the directors to disturb anything that was working well. The same applied to membership of the various committees. Reliance was on experience which was obviously regarded as a quality to be valued above all others. That attitude came naturally to a group of people who themselves were long on experience and continuity, and always had been.

Of the fifteen directors of the company in 1913, eight were still there in 1923. Of the fifteen members of the board in 1923, eight were still members in 1933, five of the other seven having died in the interval. At other times, and under different circumstances, complaints might have been heard that the Calgary Exhibition and Stampede was a "closed corporation" or a "cronycorp" of lodge brothers. If there was such grumbling in the inter-wars years it had to be very much soto voce. The problem during the depression years was to find people who could afford to devote the time, and the expense, to the cause.

The advantage to the organization of the experience and continuity was the reliance it enabled the board of directors to place on the judgment and the decisions of the volunteer committees. During the depression the executive was forced to curtail expenditures, but it was the special committees which determined how their appropriations should be spent. Thus it was the Stampede committee which decided how that program should be run off, how the prize money was to be allocated among events, how much the judges were to be paid, whether the bucking horses should be bought or rented. The livestock committee apportioned the prize money to the various purebred associations, and among horses, cattle, sheep and swine. It was the breed sub-committees who divided it further.

When all the decisions of the various committees were run past the executive committee of the board of directors, approval was automatic. There is almost no record of the executive committee, or the board of directors, rejecting important recommendations from the standing committees. Continuity provided the directors with an awareness of the background of the recommendations being made, even when the decisions being taken in 1935 were rooted in events of 1929.

If any public disgruntlement had developed with the way things were being run at Victoria Park, it might have been squelched by simple recourse to the record as the basis for this question: what could anybody else have done that would have been any improvement?

Calgary, between 1921 and 1941, was a stuck-in-the-mud place compared with the seams-breaking boomtown of the first decade of the century. Over that twenty-year stretch it lost all its attractiveness for immigrants and was barely able to retain the natural growth of its population. And that despite the Turner Valley gas boom of the 1920s and the more solidly based Royalties oil boom of the late thirties. Yet the popularity of the combined Exhibition and Stampede grew steadily from the twenties; survived the disaster years of 1931, 1932, and 1933; went on to surpass the attendance records established in 1929. So, if a coterie of directors seem on the surface to have made the company their private preserve, the company was not suffering from their ministrations.

But nothing goes on forever and the break came for the Calgary Exhibition and Stampede on a December morning in 1939. Ernie Richardson got the executive committee together and broke the news that he was reaching the end of the line. After thirty-seven years on the job he gave notice of his retirement, to become effective on October 1, 1940. As he explained, he had been in failing health for some years, had been forced to absent himself from the city for several long stretches while recuperating. The organization needed a steadier hand than his and the time had come to take his departure.

Richardson provided the board with a year's notice of his retirement to make the job of selecting his successor less pressing. Indeed he offered to stay on as a part-time employee for an additional year to help the new manager become accustomed to the job. As things turned out, the succession of general managers went off much more smoothly than might have been expected.

J. Charles Yule, everybody's unanimous choice for the job, had been a member of the board of directors since 1929 and president since 1937. He came to the board with a reputation for the superb quality of the Shorthorn cattle he raised on his Carstairs farm. While he was raising Shorthorns he was also building a Canadian and ultimately a world reputation as a showring judge of beef cattle. Unfortunately, his was only one of the many purebred cattle herds that were liquidated by the depression and his appointment as general manager of the Calgary Exhibition and Stampede was a felicitous one for both Yule and the company.

Unhappily for Yule and Richardson, finances were such in 1940 that the directors decided they would have to spread the general manager's already reduced monthly salary over both men. So Richardson was paid $250 a month as consultant and Yule started at $275, plus whatever he took in as secretary-manager of the various livestock associations who had their headquarters in the company offices.

By the time Richardson completed his consultancy and Yule was on his own, Canada's wartime wages and prices ceiling was firmly in place. It took the Stampede board the better part of a year, and a trip by the president to Ottawa, to get government permission to raise Yule's salary to $375 a month, and it took until June, 1946, to get his yearly salary to $7,500 a year.

The change in managers brought a slight veer, a subtle change in the direction, in the emphasis, of the Calgary Exhibition and Stampede. Ernie Richardson, despite his agricultural degree from Guelph, and the farm he owned south of the city, had developed into a promoter's promoter. He had become injected with Weadick's boisterous enthusiasm for show business, for forever pushing into new fields of entertainment.

It was Richardson who brought Weadick back to the Calgary Horse Show, which ultimately led to the union of the Exhibition and Stampede. He was a supporter of one hockey league after another, even taking on the thankless job of commissioner for one league. It was he who pushed deals with Lloyd Turner and Rosie Helmer to keep hockey going at the Arena despite the failure of the leagues to survive. When it came to producing "the greatest show on

Long before the Stampede was even thought of, tenderfooted Calgarians rubbed shoulders with breed-wise ranchers at Calgary's spring sale of purebred bulls. And once the annual sale moved indoors to the Victoria Pavilion, they were joined by buyers from around the world. This is a typical scene, repeated year after year, as the presale judging was completed before the raptly attentive audience. After the judging the ratio of dudes to ranchers increased as Calgarians jammed the seats to watch the ranchers paying thousands of dollars for champion bulls, and even more, sometimes, for specimens that did not catch the judge's eye. *Photograph by Browarny. Courtesy of* **Hereford Digest.**

earth," would P. T. Barnum himself not have boggled at constructing a ski-jumping hill on top of the Victoria Park grandstand? Richardson never batted an eye!

Charles Yule could not have been a director of the Calgary Exhibition and Stampede for a full decade without absorbing some of the Stampede elan. But Yule had been born into the cattle business, beef cattle had been his life, and if that were not enough, he had married into it. His wife was the daughter of Professor W. L. Carlyle, a renowned Shorthorn specialist who became the manager of the E P Ranch for the Prince of Wales, and stocked it with imported Scottish Shorthorns and thoroughbred horses. Under Charles Yule more attention would be paid to the beef cattle industry and the horse

industry. The Calgary Exhibition and Stampede would expand the vital role it had been playing for forty years in the evolution of the livestock industry of southern Alberta and western Canada.

Ironically for Yule, the Canadian and Alberta governments seemed bent on liquidating their support of agricultural exhibitions just as he was settling into the general manager's job. As a wartime economy measure, Ottawa sliced four thousand dollars from its annual contribution to the purebred livestock prize lists for the Exhibition. Edmonton did likewise to the tune of two thousand dollars. As a result Yule had to tell the purebred associations they would face at least a twenty-five percent reduction in the money available for their prize lists. Eventually, however, private donors were located to make up for the government cuts and the prize list was restored.

There were other problems. Wartime material shortages prevented needed improvements being made. The Edmonton Exhibition suspended operations for the duration and left a gaping hole in the Class A fairs circuit. Gasoline rationing prevented long haul tourist traffic. For a while there was deep concern that gas shortages would prevent many regular exhibitors from attending the Calgary events.

Just the opposite happened. The outbreak of the war turned gloom into boom in the livestock industry, and in particular for the purebred livestock breeders. And just about in time! It had been a long, frustrating, and frequently losing battle to persevere with the ideas that had led to the establishment of the purebred livestock organizations in the first place back in 1900.

The annual Calgary purebred bull sale offered the scattering of farmers who were raising purebred cattle a deal they could hardly refuse. For an entry fee of one dollar, plus a two-dollar freight charge from any point within eight hundred miles of Calgary, and a commission of one-half percent on the sale price they could have their bulls sold at auction at Calgary. The entry fee was to cover the cost to the Calgary Exhibition of providing the facilities for holding the sale. The commission would pay the auctioneers and if there was a surplus at the end of the sale it would go not to the Exhibition but to the livestock association.

This was the system and fee structure that would survive at Victoria Park with but a few modifications for the next fifty years. That first bull sale established the principle on which the Calgary Exhibition would operate throughout its ensuing existence. It would serve the farmers and ranchers of Alberta at the bare cost of providing service, not with the intent of making a profit from the operation. That principle applied to everything that followed in the utilization of Victoria Park facilities by all other purebred livestock and farm organizations. The Exhibition provided the facilities, the organizations ran the shows and sales, and took whatever

profit there was in them for themselves.

That first bull sale gave no hint of ever becoming the premier event of its kind in Canada. It attracted just sixty-four entries which were sold for an average of ninety dollars a piece. It was no bonanza but it did attract increased patronage over the next couple of years.

Disaster struck in 1905. A flood of 340 animals hit the sales ring, far more than the market could absorb, and the average price per bull dropped to $70, hardly more than it would have brought as a market steer at the stockyards. For the next several years it was touch and go whether the bull sale could survive. Patronage dropped to an all-time low in 1909 when only 59 bulls were offered for sale. The decline in offerings however helped restore prices to a more attractive level and by 1913 a record average of $200 per bull was established. The Great War kept the average well above $200 until 1920 when the average reached a record $280. Thereafter prices skidded sharply to the $125 range and stayed there for the next ten years.

Regardless of the swings in prices, however, the reputation of the Calgary bull sale increased steadily with the farmers and ranchers. So did its impact on Calgary commercial life. Each year the bull sale brought three or four hundred families to Calgary. Families who could afford to buy purebred bulls could also afford to buy food, clothing, household supplies, and other creature comforts. And the families who sold purebred bulls would also have money to spend, sometimes for other bulls but most often for other things.

By 1918 a record 792 bulls were sold for an aggregate of $121,000, a record that would not be equalled for almost thirty years. It was within that time span that a new industry, the specialized business of raising purebred breeding stock, was born in the sales ring at Victoria Park, under the aegis of the Calgary Exhibition.

The value of raising quality cattle had of course been recognized by the southern Alberta ranchers from the very beginning. The Cochrane, Walrond, Oxley, Quorn ranches, had all imported purebred foundation stock from the United Kingdom. The Canadian Government had stocked its experimental farm at Lacombe with

For many of the purebred livestock exhibitors the Friday morning parade of champions was the highlight of the show. And it was also the highlight for upwards of twenty thousand Calgary youngsters who came, not to ogle the parading champions but to win a pony, a saddle, a bicycle, or maybe a dog. *Photograph by J. Rosettis, Calgary, Alberta. Courtesy of the Calgary Stampede.*

purebred Shorthorn and Aberdeen Angus. The use of Angus bulls fanned out in a widening circle from Lacombe. But the raising of purebred bulls for sale had been much more a sideline with the farmers than a primary occupation, although specialists were evolving. Sam Mace of Pekisko was pioneering with a purebred Hereford farm, as were Baxter Reed of Olds, John Wilson of Innisfail, and W. H. Curtice of Shepard. The Hendersons of Lacombe and F. R. Cathroe were deeply into Angus and there were half a dozen Shorthorn raisers in the Calgary area.

In the beginning, the Shorthorns ruled the roost, both in numbers and prices brought at sales. In the early days of the Calgary bull sale the Shorthorns outnumbered all others combined and in five of the first six years topped the sale in price.

When the Herefords and Aberdeen Angus became involved in the "battle of the breeds" to challenge the Shorthorns is lost to history. But there can be little doubt of the identity of the one man who spearheaded the Hereford drive for a place in the sun. He was Frank Collicutt, a one-time railway candy-butcher cum cattle-buyer for Pat Burns, and a Calgary Exhibition and Stampede director for more than forty years.

Collicutt began the process of converting his Willow Springs ranch into a purebred layout in 1912 when he bought Baxter Reed's herd. This herd of 120 cattle contained three outstanding sires of which Beau Perfection 11 was the most important. It was the half brother of the highest priced bull in American history to that time. Four years later Collicutt attracted wide attention when he purchased the famous imported bull from Missouri, Gay Lad 16, and thirty-five females for $50,000. Then he went off to Missouri and purchased Gay Lad 40, a half brother to Gay Lad 16. By 1930 Collicutt had a purebred herd of over 600 head, one of the largest in the world. It was also one of the best in the world.

In 1931 Collicutt accomplished the seeming impossible by winning the grand championships of the Royal Winter Fair for both Hereford bulls and Hereford cows. The cow, Willow Springs Gay Lass 414, went on to win the grand championship of the Chicago International. Throughout his long life in livestock, Collicutt was always a patron of the Calgary bull sale, on the buying as well as the selling side.

The fledgling purebred livestock industry barely survived the Great Depression but with the outbreak of the Second World War conditions improved substantially. Despite wartime price controls, meat rationing, and the shutting off of the export markets, bull sale prices rose steadily until a peak average of $450 was reached by 1945 when a near record 799 animals were run through the sale. Thereafter the industry never looked back.

Bull sales, fat stock shows, purebred competitions were the passion of Charlie Yule's life and this was reflected in many ways at Victoria Park. During his early years as a director he had promoted an annual camp for farmers' sons and daughters at the livestock exhibitions. The purpose was to expose the teenagers to quality livestock and enable them to develop eyes and fingers for identifying the best that could be produced. As general manager of the operation he encouraged the expansion of this and other youth projects. Similarly he concentrated attention on the promotion of the parades of champions at the Friday morning show for city school children, encouraging them to become familiar with farm animals. And all the while he pushed for the improvement of the livestock facilities in Victoria Park, along with the accommodation for the livestock exhibitors.

Such was the growth of the bull sale patronage, however, that the improvements could not keep pace with the needs.

Not only were the barning facilities for the livestock overcrowded, the crush of humans attracted to the sale became almost impenetrable. Going to the bull sale as spectators, indeed, had become a favorite Calgary pastime during the first week in March. Calgary spectators took up so much room in the sales pavilion that there was a shortage of space for potential buyers.

The influx of farm trucks created such traffic jams on the grounds, particularly in wet weather, that demands for increased parking space became an endless refrain around the directors' gatherings. Each year more space was reclaimed, more gravel spread and more paving done. But it was never enough, never would be enough as a matter of fact.

The overcrowding of men, machines, and farm animals however was never regarded as a negative factor when expansion of activities was under active consideration. Thus in 1941, when the bull sale was beginning to boom, it was decided to add a horse sale as well.

The first of a long succession of successful horse sales was held on the heels of the bull sale. These sales, coupled with the fall cattle, sheep, and swine sale, and the spring fat stock show and sale, plus the spring and summer horse shows, dog shows and poultry shows, emphasized the vital place Victoria Park had come to hold in the life of Alberta agriculture.

The Stampede promotional material could quote with pride the statement of J. C. Treacy of the National Broadcasting Company that the Calgary Stampede was one of the "big three" annual events of the North American continent. (The other two were the World Series of Baseball and the Indianapolis 500 auto race.) But it had also developed into Canada's most important livestock activities-center as well. And as years passed its growth in importance would fully keep pace with the Stampede itself.

As for that Stampede, its wartime life was fraught with problems, some great and some small. The army and air force moved into its vacant buildings and the program committees operated around the tenants.

With the outbreak of the war, the Royal American Show was barred from the

It was not long after the Stampede became a Calgary fixture before the kids got into the act. Scenes like this were repeated a hundred times over the last fifty years—a terrified boy on a plunging steer, scared out of his wits, but afraid to show it! *Photograph by Fred Kobsted. Courtesy of the Calgary Stampede.*

railways and, hence, from the prairie fairs circuit. In its place the fair managers succeeded in bringing in the smaller Paddy Conklin Show from Ontario. In 1942 the Canadian Government changed the celebration of Dominion Day from July 1 to July 5 and sideswiped the Stampede out of three days of horse racing. That change coupled with torrential rains dropped attendance that year by over 30,000 customers. The entry of the United States into the war denuded the grandstand shows of their star attractions. Gasoline rationing reduced the inflow of visitors from the more remote areas.

Despite the dilution in quality of the shows, however, attendance, except for the 1942 disaster, increased steadily to set all-time records. Full employment at improved wages and a moderate increase in farm prices in Alberta attracted new thousands to the show who could never afford to come before. As a result a special visitors' bureau was established as a permanent feature of the annual show. Literally thousands of visitors found sleeping accommodation in Calgary homes each year through this bureau which kept a registry of all the beds that were available during Stampede Week.

As for the rodeo events in wartime, they turned out each year to be better staged and more exciting than the year before. After twenty years, all the important wrinkling had been ironed out of the bucking horse, bull riding, and calf roping events. New chutes had been built and then rebuilt to make the start of all the events more efficiently managed. The rules had been refined and improved. Professional announcers were on the job and the skilled judges who presided over all events were now paid fees that made their attendance worthwhile.

Most important of all, over those twenty years the performers in all events had honed and refined their skills and multiplied their numbers so that competition in all events was keener than it had ever been before. That was particularly true of the chuckwagon races which of everything that happened were most sharply identified as the "spectacular" of the Calgary Stampede.

The tight rein which the directors had been accustomed to holding on Exhibition and Stampede expenditures during the depression was relaxed hardly at all during the war. As a result the reports of the finance chairman were, increasingly, a joy to read. From gross income of $166,921 and a surplus of $7,438 in 1939 revenues soared to a gross income of $300,973 and a surplus of $88,632 in 1945. In addition to the cash surpluses, substantial sums were spent every year on plant improvement and renovations. The buildings in Victoria Park were excessively costly to maintain for they were mainly of frame construction and subjected to hard usage as horse barns, livestock stables. The old Arena was particularly costly to keep in shape and when it was jammed to the rafters for hockey finals, as it was at play-off time, there was fear that one day it might collapse in a heap.

It was undoubtedly the improvement in finances that resulted in the first shot being fired across the bow, the first outbreak of animus toward the Calgary Exhibition and Stampede. It happened in the fall of 1943, when the ten-year lease of Victoria Park came before the city council for renewal. Ordinarily the lease would have been approved automatically. But the motion gave several aldermen a chance to ask questions about the operation of the organization. What was the Stampede doing with all the money it was making, while the city council was battling to balance its budget? Why had the Arena been leased out to the Artificial Ice Rink Company? What right did the Stampede board have to lease Victoria Park from the city for a dollar a year, and then lease the Arena to a private group to run a money-making enterprise? Why shouldn't the Stampede

pay the city at least twenty thousand dollars a year in rental? Better still, why not give the motion to approve a new lease "at least a sixty-year hoist" and have the city council take over the operation?

Instead of approving the lease, the city council referred it to a committee. Ald. W. G. Southern produced a twelve-clause bill raising questions about the operations of the organization. Ultimately the city appointed a firm of independent auditors to prepare a full report on the operation of the company.

While all this was going on one could have cut the cloud of umbrage in the Stampede office with a knife. The kindest sentiments expressed were that the aldermen were a bunch of ingrates without appreciation for the worth of the Stampede to the city. If they wanted information, they had four directors on the board who could supply it! If they were not satisfied, all they had to do was ask! What was the point in making a federal case out of nothing issues? A year later, at the time of the 1944 annual meeting, some of the directors were still stewing over the unappreciative aldermen. In the meantime the firm of Henderson and Waines produced a report that vindicated the company and its directors on every count. It seemed to satisfy even the most critical of the aldermen and the lease was approved.

There were a couple of important modifications that came about as a result of the negotiations between the directors and the city commissioners. The first change insured there would be an infusion of new blood into the board of directors. Once a director served a couple of terms as president he would move on to become a life director. That would create a place for a new member of the board every two years. A second change was that two of the four aldermen who were appointed to the board should be elected to the executive committee which was the de facto operating arm of the executive. In addition, the city council got the right to nominate twenty-five associate directors, a concession which provided all the aldermen with gate passes and preferred grandstand seating for the Stampede.

The issue that seemed to have got the council's back up, aside from the profits the Stampede was making and plowing back into the operation, was the sub-lease of the Arena to the Artificial Ice Rink Company. Disconsolate parents of teenage skaters undoubtedly complained to their aldermen about the lack of facilities for kids' hockey. Although in the nature of things one rink could not begin to supply all the demands, the ice rink company came about as close as was possible to providing Calgarians with a facility at cost. The six-team inter-services league got four two-hour practice sessions a week free of charge. A new three-hundred-boy pee-wee league was slotted into Saturday while junior and senior high school leagues operated in the late afternoons, all without cost to the students. There were also regular junior and senior teams operating in full fledged leagues. On top of everything else the Arena had to find time for pleasure skating which was Calgary's most popular physical recreational activity in winter.

Curiously enough, at the very time when the city aldermen were muttering in their teeth, the Stampede board had all but completed negotiations with the Ice Rink Company to take back the operations of the rink.

Despite the multiple usage of the ice, the arena lease was no road to riches for the Artificial Ice Rink Company. The company also operated a senior team, the Calgary Stampeders, in the Western Canada Hockey League that embraced Calgary, Edmonton, Saskatoon, Regina, and Lethbridge. The salaries paid to the "amateurs" were a rather loosely held secret. Run of the mill players were paid around thirty-five to fifty dollars a week for the November-to-March season plus a year-round job at about the same figure. The top players on the team, the two or three stars around whom the team was built, might command up to seventy-five dollars a week which was also roughly what the team coach and manager were paid. So the team faced a "nut" of about twenty thousand dollars for salaries and expenses, a budget that had to be covered out of the team's share of the thirty-five-cent and fifty-cent admission prices that prevailed throughout the season from fans who seldom more than half-filled the rink.

Under different circumstances a run of victories in the playoffs, which always filled the rinks, might have created a bonanza for the sponsors of winning teams. The circumstance which dictated otherwise was the Canadian Amateur Hockey Association which operated the Canadian hockey monopoly. During ordinary league play from November to February, the teams and the rink operators split the gate receipts, which were seldom much more than enough to pay the bare expenses of both. Once the playoffs en route to the Allan and Memorial cup began in March, and enthusiastic crowds filled the rinks to the rafters, the CAHA stepped in and took over everything. The CAHA bureaucrats did all the deals with the rink owners for use of the rinks, they arranged the playoff schedules, hired all the officials, paid the teams traveling expenses, and pocketed whatever remained of the gate receipts.

Not only did the team owners have to provide a secret cash out-of-season pot to split among the players as an incentive for winning playoff performances, they also had to reimburse the players for their time off work without pay during their extended trips on the road. When the Calgary Stampeders went to the Allan Cup finals in 1940, they were on the road for almost a month. In their western finals with Port Arthur, the series began in Port Arthur, switched to Saskatoon because the horse show had taken over the Calgary Arena, then came to Calgary for a couple of games and wound up the series back in Port Arthur. Unhappily the team that boasted such stars as Art Rice-Jones, Cam Burke, Dave Duchak, Tony Desmarais, Chuck Millman, Pat Hill, Joe Shannon, and Tommy Dewar was blown out of Maple Leaf Gardens by the team from Kirkland Lake. The scores were 8 to 5, 9 to 1, and 7 to 1.

The owners of the team would have been better off financially never to have gone beyond their own league, instead of going all the way to the Allan Cup. So it was hardly surprising that the Ice Rink Company was willing to relinquish its hockey operation to the Calgary Exhibition and Stampede and sell it the ice-making equipment when its lease expired at the end of 1943.

CHAPTER 10

Post-war Progress

I t has been said that a camel is a horse that was designed by a committee. That is just another way of saying too many cooks spoil the broth. But if ever "too many cooks" made up a committee that utterly demolished that notion it was the rink committee of the Calgary Exhibition and Stampede. It was the committee that took charge of the old Arena when the company bought out the Calgary Artificial Ice Rink Company in 1944. It was composed of J. B. Cross, chairman, and H. Gordon Love, Clar Manning, John Moyer, and Ald. Ernie McCullough, all former directors of the Ice Rink Company.

All the committee had to do to be modestly successful was to go on keeping an eye on overall rink operations while Lloyd Turner took care of all the details. The old building was contributing an operating profit of $9,000 a year which satisfied everybody. Instead the committee decided that what Calgary needed most was a senior hockey team in the about-to-be-organized Western Canada Hockey League and it was up to the committee to get one. It proceeded to do so, and to win the Allan Cup in its first full season of operations—1946-47.

Inter-city hockey had all but disappeared during the war and was replaced in large measure by armed services hockey teams competing against each other on a local basis. Calgary had two service leagues, a major league of three teams representing the army, navy, and airforce, and an eight-team minor league of garrison teams. In addition there were the Buffalo Hockey Association teams that embraced leagues from the pee-wees to the juniors who participated in provincial and regional playoffs. The Buffaloes, on which the Calgary Brewery spent from $15,000 to $20,000 a year, played all their games at the Arena, under the direction of two full-time Calgary brewery employees, Dave Duchak and Jack Arbour.

The committee's first idea was to take over the Buffalo junior team and operate it in a western Canadian junior league. When that proved impractical, a deal was done to procure the part-time services of Duchak as manager and Arbour as coach for the Calgary Stampeders club in the Western Canada Senior Amateur Hockey League. The league was to be made up of teams from Calgary, Lethbridge, Edmonton, Saskatoon, and Regina. For personnel, the teams had only to look to the recently

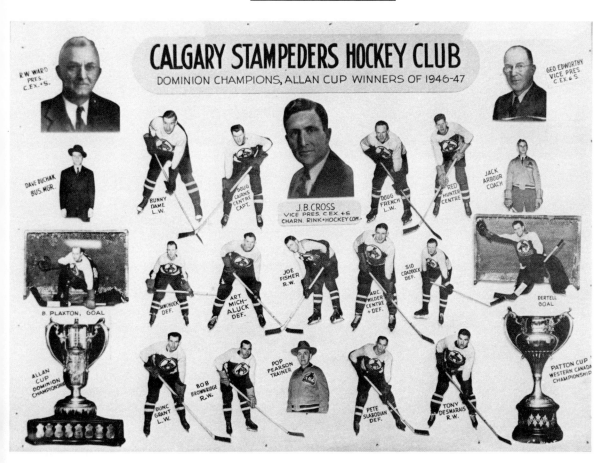

After the Calgary Stampeders began their long campaign for the Allan Cup in the old Arena in 1946–1947, could a brand new hockey rink be far behind? But a new rink called the Stampede Corral? *Courtesy of the Calgary Stampede.*

discharged service players who were not ripe for National Hockey League play, and there were scores of them around looking for jobs. That was the bait that got the signatures on contracts, the undertaking to provide steady jobs, at around $175 a month, plus $40 to $50 a week pay for the hockey season.

The titular heads of the hockey operations were the coach and manager, but the de facto boss was very much the committee, and naturally so. It was the committee members who twisted the arms that got the players their jobs, who arranged for boardinghouses and other living accommodations. They frequently accompanied the team on its games out of town, scrutinized the play and the coaching strategy with occasionally baleful eyes.

Under the aegis of the rink committee the Calgary Stampeders won not only the western championship, but also the only Allan Cup ever won by a Calgary hockey team. They knocked off the Hamilton Tigers four games to one. The 1946 Stampeders were Dertell, Michaluk, Sawchuk, Cairns, Fisher, Dame, Craddock, Wilder, Hunter, Brownridge, Grant, Desmarais, and Slabodian. Five of the players, Dertell, Michaluk, Hunter, Brownridge, and Wilder had played together on the RCAF team; Grant, Desmarais, and Dame played on the army team; and Cairns was recruited from the navy veterans.

Not only did the Stampeders win the Allan Cup, but they filled the Arena for game after game during the season and in the process provided the added impetus that got Calgary's primary post-war project off the ground. That was the need for a new auditorium to replace the aged and decrepit Arena.

As the Second World War moved toward its conclusion there was hardly anyone who was anybody in the Canadian establishment who was not concerned with "post-war objectives." Primarily there were two concerns—how to avoid a repetition of the inflationary spiral that followed the First World War; and how to prevent a return to the mass unemployment that only the war had cured. These concerns led to the compilation of lists of projects that could be undertaken once the war was over. The lists ranged all the way from the private objectives of individual families to the massive projects of the national government. In short, all the way from acquiring Bendex washers, electric refrigerators, and automobiles to the construction of the Trans-Canada Highway and the St. Lawrence Seaway. It was something that the city of Calgary, and the Stampede board was very much caught up in from 1944 onward.

The war was the greatest thing that ever happened to the Stampede, as it was to the Alberta economy. Full employment and military expenditures along with good crops and markets provided the annual Stampede with audiences eager to escape wartime austerity in a week of boisterous fun. The fame of the Stampede was reaching to the farthest corners of the continent long before the war. But wartime travel restriction cut off most of the outside patronage. It was more than made up by the rush of the people of Alberta through the turnstiles. Just as attendance soared, so did the income of the organization.

In 1943 attendance figures were up 30,000 from the previous year and a profit of $76,245 broke all previous records. The next year all attendance, income, and profits records were again shattered and by a wide margin. All records were broken again in 1945.

By 1943, however, the Stampede was already suffering an embarrassment of riches for the evidence was plain that its popularity was outstripping its facilities. The parimutuel booths were habitually so jammed that people had difficulty placing and cashing their bets. The bleachers were scarcely half large enough to serve the crowds. The centerfield facilities for the rodeo events continually required repairs and replacement. The sound system for the grandstand show was inadequate and complaints were legion about "dead spots" in the grandstand. There was a critical shortage of toilet facilities on the grounds. New low spots seemed to develop on the ground each year which turned into quagmires with the inevitable summer thunderstorms.

The space behind the grandstand and bleachers was occupied cheek-to-jowl by canopied outdoor eating places operated by ladies aids, local charities, churches, etc.

The passageway that separated the restaurants from the midway was noon-to-midnight congestion. Both the eateries and the concessions were dust coated from clouds stirred up by marching feet. Paddy Conklin, who ran the wartime midway, offered to pave the strip at his expense in return for a three-year contract. His offer was refused with thanks because the Stampede looked forward to a return of a bigger midway at the end of the war.

Despite wartime gas rationing and the shutting off of new car sales, the inadequacy of parking facilities was a festering sore. The board tried without success to persuade the city to vacate the street car barn, power station, city stores, and pole yard. As the annual show prospered, the worse the overall congestion became, and the more pressing the demands became for more space by the exhibitors and concessionaires.

Even the evolutionary changes taking place in farming practices seemed to be conspiring to embarrass the Stampede board. The development of farm tractors had decimated the heavy horse breeding industry. There was scarcely a farm in southern Alberta that did not have a surplus team or two in pasture retirement. It was in order to restore the depleted treasury of the Horse Breeders Association that the Stampede board, in 1941, inaugurated the annual horse sale to be held alongside the Calgary bull sale. The sale attracted buyers from the fox food, dog food, and cat food processing industries from across the country and provided a market for surplus horses. The farmers took advantage of the market with such enthusiasm that Victoria Park stabling facilities were taxed far beyond capacity.

Finding barn space for the sometimes prickly owners of eight hundred purebred bulls in facilities designed for six hundred was trying enough. Trying, at almost the same time, to fit fifteen hundred horses into stalls for one thousand complicated everything. Three-way shouting matches among cattlemen, horsemen, and grounds superintendents were inevitable.

Early in the war, when efforts were made to expand facilities, they collided with the rigid wartime controls of vital materials and supplies. Eventually in 1944 a special permit was obtained from Ottawa to make a 55 foot by 320 foot extension to the livestock pavilion. That raised the stabling capacity for the bull sale to one thousand stalls, but did nothing for the horses.

This addition did very little to dampen the criticism flowing in from the cattlemen and eventually the board lost patience. It ordered its number one cattle director, W. A. Crawford-Frost, to read the riot act to the complainers. To wit:

The Calgary Bull Sale, for 40 years, was run by the Calgary Exhibition and Stampede for the sole benefit of the cattle producers. The breed associations made the rules that governed the sale, set the fees charged, engaged the auctioneers. The Exhibition Board gave the breeders what amounted to free use of all the Victoria Park facilities charging only enough to cover out of pocket expenses. All the profits earned by the sale went to the livestock association. If the association wanted the Stampede Board to take over the sale, run it its way and pocket the profits, it would be happy to do so. It would also be happy to increase the charges to the sellers so as to pay for needed expansion of the Livestock sales facilities when materials become available.

The cattlemen got the Stampede board's message and the carping dissolved into better understanding.

The cattle problem was no different from the people problem—Victoria Park was never intended to accommodate the vastly increased numbers of either that were descending upon it. That fact, however, never discouraged the Stampede board from embracing new ideas that would increase the attendance of both animals and humans. And it did try to come to grips with the congestion problem. As the money poured in it made what improvements it could to existing facilities, extended the livestock barns, increased the toilet facilities, added day care centers.

As the piecemeal construction went on concern began to mount over the wisdom of the entire operation. Was it not penny-wise and pound-foolish to be forever spending money on obsolete old buildings? Would it not make a lot more sense to tear

From the early 1930s Victoria Park was the showcase for the farming and ranching activities of Alberta's youth. Proud young exhibitors at the Calgary Spring Stock Show, 1947. *Photograph by Rosettis Studio. Courtesy of the Calgary Stampede.*

everything out and start over with brand new modern facilities? A case in point which focused attention sharply on that question was a fire in the Arena boiler room in late March, 1943. Fortunately quick action confined the fire to the furnace room and resulted only in a short postponement of the spring horse show. But it raised concern over what might have happened if such a fire had got out of hand while the Arena was full of hockey fans.

Most important, the fire focused attention on two tinder box horse barns that had been carpentered onto the north and south sides of the Arena. These barns were used mainly to house the overflow from the regular stables. For most of the year they stood idle, frequently littered with dried out straw bedding. If the fire had spread into the barns the entire Victoria Park plant might have gone up in smoke. The horse barns would have to go. Removing them, however, became tangled up with the repairs of the fire damage which was in turn tangled up with negotiations of the lease extension with the city hall. It was during that hiatus that the Stampede took over the ownership of the artificial ice plant in the Arena.

For some years the chinook-plagued

Calgary curlers had been trying to persuade the Artificial Ice Rink Company to convert the Arena ice into a curling rink between hockey games. The idea never got much beyond the "why don't we?" stage until the Stampede board took over. Then the curlers began button-holing directors and talking up the curling rink idea for the horse barns that were so handy to the ice-making plant. There was room in the two barns for twelve sheets of curling ice! If 300 curlers paid $25 a year for the use thereof that would produce $7,500 for the season for the Arena! The more the directors listened the better they liked the idea and eventually, midway through 1944, a deal was done with the curlers.

Before that project was completed, however, the board was to discover the gap that separated original cost estimates from the price of finished projects. The original idea was to extend the Arena ice-making equipment into the horse barns. That was the basis for the deal with the curlers. Instead it turned out that a whole new ice plant would have to be installed. Then the twelve sheets of curling ice had to be cut to eight. The number of Calgarians prepared to pay twenty-five dollars a season to curl on artificial ice dropped from three hundred to two hundred. The cost of the project zoomed from near nothing to twenty-five thousand dollars.

Curling, nevertheless, was a financial success from the start. It netted the company $4,800 for the half-season of 1944–45 and encouraged the further expenditure of $2,400 to acquire 64 sets of matched curling rocks. Not only that. It encouraged the launching of a campaign to bring the Macdonald Brier National curling championship tournament to Calgary in 1948.

As the curling ice machinery was being installed, and the fire damage to the Arena was being repaired everybody concerned with Victoria Park was taking critical looks at the old building. Its front wall was a couple of feet out of plumb. Its roof was forever needing repairs. Its walls shed paint like dogs shed hair. The city engineer put the installation of ceiling sprinklers in the congested areas at the top of his list of priorities. Even with sprinklers it would still be a fire hazard.

With the company piling up reserves the way it had been doing lately, why not replace the Arena with a modern fireproof rink? That would be the perfect post-war job-creating project. It would be the frontispiece for the bigger and better Exhibition and Stampede everybody wanted for post-war Calgary.

Why not indeed! And not only a new Arena. How about a restructured grandstand to increase spectator accommodation? And a new parimutuel facility to take care of the increased popularity of horse racing? At the onset of the war a deal had been done with the owners of Chinook Park Racing Association to rent their charter and transfer the racing dates from Chinook to Victoria Park. That gave Victoria Park two weeks additional racing. Arrangements were made with the R. J. Speers Corporation to supply the horses and manage two weeks racing in the spring and another week in late summer. By 1944 the horse racing operation was producing better than $54,000 a year, double the figure for five years earlier.

The first step on the long road to the construction of the new arena was taken in July 1945 immediately after the conclusion of the Exhibition and Stampede. That year convinced everybody that reconstruction and expansion of facilities for handling the crowds was imperative. Charles Yule was sent on an idea collecting tour of other facilities, including the Ottawa, Toronto, and Quebec City Exhibitions and a half dozen State Fairs south of the line. What impressed Yule most was the Quebec Coliseum, a multipurpose edifice of 7,500 seating capacity. He was also impressed with the acres and acres of paved grounds that contrasted with Calgary's crushed stone, crushed brick and shavings mixture. And he saw a half dozen models of cattle barns Calgary might well adopt.

By July 1946 the new arena project had reached the stage where the board proposed to the city that a 10,000 seat building could be constructed at a cost of $750,000. If the city would put up $500,000, the Stampede board would contribute $250,000. The proposal was rejected by city hall on the grounds that (a) a by-law for that amount would have to get approval of the ratepayers and (b) the way the ratepayers were acting, they'd never approve it. An alternative was suggested: have the legislature amend the company's charter so that it could borrow $500,000. The legislature obliged in 1947 and the project was off and running. Walking? Crawling? For the next two years it moved like the plot of a radio soap opera.

The word that Edmonton had approved the charter change arrived simultaneously with the victory of the Stampeders in the 1947 western hockey final and the celebration in the Stampeders hockey club dressing room that night became doubly exuberant. Along toward dawn the company president, Art McGuire, who was general manager of the Canada Cement Company, mounted a bench to announce that he would personally undertake to see that all the cement required would be made immediately available.

To the cheers of the assemblage a shovel was procured and the crowd moved outside for a token turning of the first sod for the new arena. Apprised of his promise the next day, McGuire was horrified. "My God," he cried, "if I have to do that I can only do it by stealing the cement allotments for two churches and a cathedral!"

The episode is illustrative of the problems that confronted all construction projects in the post-war era. Housing projects ground to a halt for shortages of nails, or lathing mesh. Contractors lined up at building supply warehouses waiting for cement to arrive. Even getting plans drawn for new projects encountered endless delays. As for the new arena, an architect, G. G. Reid, was located in Toronto who had some already-drafted plans for an arena. He was hired to provide the Stampede board with a set of plans. However, when his plans eventually arrived the city engineer found them riddled with faults. Ultimately Reid was fired and J. M. Stevenson, the Calgary architect, was hired to design something less grandiose, with a capacity of 7,500 instead of 10,000.

The real sod-breaking for the new rink was set back from 1947, to 1948 and finally 1949 when the contract was awarded to Bird Construction Company for $1,109,000. The ultimate cost, when it was completed in December 1950, was $1,350,000.

At the directors' meeting which awarded

the contract the name of the new rink was formally selected. It was to be "The Coliseum." Between the contract letting and the official opening of the new rink, however, the directors began to have second thoughts about the unimaginative name they had chosen for the new building. What was needed, really, was a name that more closely identified the building with the Calgary Stampede. This sentiment was heightened by the company's recent involvement with the Calgary Stampeders Football team.

When the football Stampeders won the western championship in 1948 a spontaneous movement sprung up to take a train load of colorfully clad Calgarians to Toronto to cheer for the team in the Grey Cup final, along with a couple of carloads of western riding horses. Bill Herron and Archie Currie, who spearheaded the drive for the trainload of supporters, were also moving spirits in the Calgary Western Riders who favored the use of western saddles and bridles, cowboy boots, frontier pants and gaily colored western shirts and cowboy hats instead of the traditional "English" saddlery and costumes. The Calgary Exhibition and Stampede kicked in one thousand dollars to pay the freight on the horses and when the Grey Cup special wound up with a deficit of nine hundred dollars the company took care of that as well.

The rationale for these subsidies was that a group of rambunctious Calgarians in gaudy western costumes riding in western saddles in a football parade in Toronto would be easily identified with the Calgary Stampede. Such identification was super advertising. So, while some such a label as "the Coliseum" might have been appropriate for such benighted places as Winnipeg, Regina, or Chicago, it would be decidedly inappropriate for a building on what was now officially the Exhibition grounds. At the annual meeting of the directors on January 5, 1950, George Edworthy said it had been suggested to him that the new rink should be more appropriately named "The Corral." The first impression of the board was highly favorable, but it was agreed that further consideration should be given.

Along about the middle of April the

name question was again raised and by a show of hands "The Corral" was again favored. But still the final decision was delayed. Finally, as the completion of the edifice was looming ahead a choice had to be made between "The Corral," "The Coliseum," and "Fort Calgary." The latter was a late starter, stemming from the fact that a replica of the original Fort Calgary was being built on the grounds behind a new stockade type fence and entrance.

When put to a vote of the directors, "The Corral" was the near unanimous choice. But instead of making it official with a formal announcement, it was decided quietly to noise the selection abroad and see how the public reacted. That set non-cowboying Calgary on its collective ear. To the citified mind, "corral" conjured up visions of horse manure, cow droppings, litter, mud, and saddle bums. To wish such a name on so beautiful a new building bordered on sacrilege in the eyes of these Calgarians.

The selection of the name was certainly a public relations goof. It stemmed, in all probability, from the discovery that San Francisco had named its elegant new Exhibition arena "The Cow Palace," and obtained widespread public acceptance. The majority of the board was committed to "The Corral" from the beginning, but clearly, from its hesitation in announcing the choice, had some doubts about how Calgary would accept it. Or perhaps it was only waiting for an inspired public relation gambit with which to sell the title. The procedure ultimately chosen could hardly have been worse.

Everything else about the new arena was just what the doctor ordered. The grand opening public dance party brought more than 7,000 to the combined square-dance, ballroom dancing shindig. Then it formally opened it with a hockey game between the Calgary Stampeders and the Edmonton Flyers on Boxing Day 1950. At this game five thousand ballots were distributed to obtain the public's choice of names among five suggested possibilities. These were:

The Coliseum
The Corral
Stampede Gardens
The Stampedium
The Teepee

No particular secret was made of the public choice as the ballots were being counted. The newspapers and radio all announced that the overwhelming public choice was "Stampede Gardens." That, in the public mind at least, settled the issue. A capacity crowd that filled every last standing room slot for the next game eagerly awaited the announcement that would make the name official. Instead, the name that came over the public address system was "The Stampede Corral."

The sonic boom of boos and catcalls which the announcement precipitated rivalled the volume that tumbled the walls of Jericho. The next day angry Calgarians were ringing the phones off walls in newspaper sports departments and in the Stampede office itself. All the columnists and commentators took pens in hand and shifted tonsils into high gear. Fred Kennedy of the *Herald*, who had had a running feud going with the Stampede management for three decades, attributed the choice to the fact that the Stampede board was composed of Calgary businessmen utterly unfamiliar with the blood-stained muck and excised parts that were the marks of a real corral!

Among the directors that year, giving lie to Kennedy, were W. A. Crawford-Frost, George Edworthy, I. V. Parslow, J. B. Cross, P. J. Rock, Frank Collicutt, Angus McKinnon, and Charles Yule!

If the word "corral" impinged on the sensitivities of the cognoscenti like Fred Kennedy, then the juxtapositioning of the words "stampede" and "gardens" should have done the same for gardeners. Why then, the uproar over the rejection of "Stampede Gardens"? The reaction was not so much to the rejection of the insipid "Stampede Gardens" as to the selection of "Stampede Corral." In any event the Stampede board toughened out the public discontent as outrage softened over the months to mere muttering in the beer. That muttering however went on far longer than expected. The *Albertan* sports department refused to accept the name and throughout 1950 persisted in referring to it as "the new Arena." Ken Foss, the Foster Hewitt of Calgary hockey broadcasting, did the same in his radio broadcasts until the Corral management threatened suspension of his privileges unless he changed his ways. He changed.

In some ways the event might have been regarded as a rather fitting finish to 1950. It had been that kind of year, one in which Murphy's Law took over and anything that could go wrong did go wrong. And in a year in which everything began on so high a note!

This was the seventy-fifth anniversary of the birth of Calgary, of the arrival of the first detachment of the North West Mounted Police at the confluence of the Bow and Elbow in 1875. The Exhibition and Stampede was always big on recognizing special anniversaries. For Calgary's seventy-fifth anniversary it went all out in spades. It invited Prime Minister L. S. St. Laurent to be the grand marshal of the parade and official opener of the Stampede. It invited Viscount Alexander of Tunis, the governor-general, to preside at the closing ceremonies. It invited the lieutenant-governor of Alberta, the Hon. J. J. Bowlen and Premier E. C. Manning, the mayor of Edmonton, the mayor of Toronto, three members of the federal cabinet, the leaders of the opposition parties in Parliament. It got acceptance from all of them.

The beautiful weather of June continued into July and convinced everybody that Calgary's Seventy-fifth Anniversary Exhibition and Stampede would be the greatest ever. On the Saturday afternoon before the grand opening there was a line-up half a block long before the accommodations booth on Ninth Avenue. The Kinsmen had opened the booth with a list of one thousand rooms in private homes for rent to Stampede visitors. By late Sunday there was some doubt that these would be sufficient.

The weather, indeed, had been so good for so long that concern was spreading that another drought of historic proportions was building within the Palliser Triangle. Memories of the Dirty Thirties were evoked when Don S. Johnston of Regina turned up in Calgary with a gadget he called the "universcope" with which he claimed to be able to make rain, if anybody would pay his fee. Nobody would, so he left for parts unknown.

A cold front moved in on Saturday night, dropped temperatures sharply, and rain threatened the opening of the parade Monday morning. However, the clouds thinned out and the rain held off and the Stampede got under way without a hitch on Monday afternoon. The chuckwagon races were run off that evening and the decks were cleared for the official opening. President Jim Cross had just finished introducing the platform guests when the first hail stones of a deluge began beating down.

Mayor Don Mackay introduced the prime minister, who made a rain-shortened official opening speech and stepped back. Then as the rain scattered the standees in front of the stage, Alderman William Hawrelak brought greetings, and a specially baked cake, from Edmonton. The greetings took the form of the text of a formal speech which Hawrelak insisted on reading in its entirety while the clouds burst over the grandstand and soaked the platform party to their skins. By the time he was through the grandstand enclosure and bleachers were deserted.

As the first hailstones pelted down the five thousand occupants of the bleachers had fled to the concourse under the grandstand. They were joined later by the people from the unprotected section of the grandstand seats. As the people poured into the concourse from both ends and the front, the crush in the center became threatening to lives and limbs. Fortunately, the occupants of the grandstand seats that were protected by the roof stayed put. Mayor Mackay's last words to them were—hang tough, the show will go on when the shower passes. When, two hours later, the shower had all the appearance of an all-night rain, the show was called off, and the crowd gave up and went home.

That set the tone for the 1950 Calgary Exhibition and Stampede; and everything went downhill from there. On Tuesday afternoon the rains closed the Royal American Shows midway but cleared up for the evening show. The weather cleared on Wednesday but the storm returned on Thursday to force cancellation of another grandstand show. To accommodate the rained-out patrons a special show was scheduled for ten o'clock Friday night. As the crowd from the first show was clearing the grandstand, the deluge returned and the special show was cancelled.

The incessant rain turned the rodeo and race track into a sea of mud. Midway through the week a spectacular spill in a chuckwagon race resulted in the death of one of the horses and injuries to several others and set up a demand the races be outlawed.

On top of everything else there was trouble with the Indians, who had been a fixture at every Exhibition and Stampede from the beginning. Curiously enough, the trouble arose from the efforts of the Indian Committee to solve one of the Indians' more vexing problems—intrusive strangers. For the better part of twenty years the Indians had been a special project of the Exhibition and Stampede. A special Indian section of the exhibition was established to display the school work and the handicrafts of the Indians. Cash prizes and certificates of merit were awarded to winners of competitions. The three tribes in the Calgary area, the Blackfoot, Sarcee, and Stoney brought in ten teepees apiece and camped in an area set aside for them just inside the main gates of Victoria Park.

Here they lived, eight, ten or twelve to a teepee for the duration of the Stampede. They drew their food from a commissary set up in the Stampede office—flour, frozen meat, bread, tea—and cooked their meals in their teepees. Cash prizes were awarded for the most attractive, best kept teepees. The Indians were free to wander the grounds, take in the grandstand events from special bleachers set up for them. They won cash prizes for participation in the parade and for taking part in the downtown festivities. In between times they could sit in front of their teepees and be photographed, for a small fee, with the children of the tourists.

All this was done with the amicable cooperation of the tribal councils, Indian Affairs, and the individual Indians. The problem was with the non-participating Indians who turned up in increasing numbers every year from other Alberta reserves, mainly the Blood, Peigan, and Hobbema. They too wandered freely through the turnstiles and around the grounds. They also got drunk and tried to move into the teepees with the cooperating Indians. As beggars they made nuisances of themselves on the grounds and on the streets.

Because to white eyes one Indian looked very much like every other Indian, the behavior of the uninvited gave all Indians a bad name. That of course, was not difficult because racism was still rampant in white society and in that regard Indians were near the bottom of the pecking order. The very word "Indian" was a pejorative epithet. For example, "Indian giver" meant someone without honor, "Indian summerfallow" described a slipshod farmer, a white drunk stoned out of his mind behaved like "a drunken Indian."

It so happened that Ed C. Hall and his son Tom, who together made up the Indian committee of the Calgary Exhibition and Stampede, had a real empathy with the Indians. The elder Hall had picked up a working knowledge of the language through serving Indians in his hardware store over forty years and was known and welcomed on the reserves. So the Halls decided to do something about the nuisance Indians. With the approval and cooperation, they thought, of the participating Indians, they persuaded the board of directors to restrict free entry to the grounds to the Indians who camped on the grounds and participated in the parade and downtown festivities. All Indians from other reserves would have to pay their way into the grounds like everybody else. That, it was believed, would at least protect the teepee village from intrusion of outsiders, cut down the nuisance in other areas of the grounds.

Unhappily the Stoney tribe either did not get the message or it lost something in translation. They assumed they too would have to pay their way into the grounds and boycotted the 1950 Stampede. Whether they would have been missed if it had not been for the rain is doubtful for there were twenty teepees of Sarcees and Blackfoot in residence on the grounds. They each took an extra day downtown to fill the gaps left by the Stoneys. But a reporter for the Calgary *Albertan*, in his report on the rain and hail storm, wondered in print whether the disgruntled Stoneys might have hired the Regina rainmaker, Don Johnston, to bring the torrents down on the Stampede.

One of the worst moments at the Calgary Exhibition and Stampede involved the command performance of the Stampede staged for Princess Elizabeth and Prince Philip, October 18, 1951. An overnight blizzard had dropped the temperature to near zero and coated the downtown streets and the Stampede infield with ice. However, the command performance went off as scheduled, while 7,500 Calgarians shivered and shook in the grandstand and the royal visitors watched bundled in blankets and furs. *Photograph by Harry Befus and Jack DeLorme. Courtesy of the Calgary Herald.*

Out of that casual piece of whole cloth was manufactured the myth of the Stoney Indians staging a rain dance to ruin the Stampede. It became one of the enduring myths of the Calgary Stampede as the radio reporters picked up the rain dance idea, converted it to fact, and broadcast variations on it throughout the week. And throughout the week there were plenty of instances to report of Indians who refused to buy tickets being turned away from the gates, often after the policemen on duty were called to intervene. So there were angry letters to the newspapers about the Indians as well as protests over the way the cancellation of the evening performances were handled.

While in many ways the 1950 show was a public relations disaster, it was far from the financial disaster it might have been. Attendance was only down 34,800 from the all time record of 407,954 established in 1949. Gross income was also down, from $554,172 to $524,678 but the surplus carried forward was within $10,000 of 1949, $99,072 versus $109,648.

Over the long term, the Stoney boycott of 1950 probably did more good than harm. It provided the Halls with an opportunity to persuade the board of directors that improvements were long overdue in relations with the Indians. The area where the Indian village was located was a notorious low spot that had once been a sunken garden. By the middle of the week some of the teepees were standing in a foot of water and their occupants had to be moved into the Arena to dry out. Sufficient fill was brought in to bring the ground up to street level and the whole area was regrassed.

The prize list for all Indian events was gone over and the budget doubled. Moreover the practice was abandoned of dumping the Indians' food into flour sacks, a practice that went back to the way in which starving Indians were given famine relief in the first days of the North West Mounted Police. In its place a system was installed for providing the Indians with specially prepared and packaged hampers containing food that made for a varied and balanced diet.

A footnote of sorts might be added to the myth of the Stoney rain dance causing the rain disruptions of the 1950 Stampede. Over the following months relations with the Stoneys were restored to mutual understanding and respect. The Stoneys accepted the wisdom of insulating the Indian village from the non-participating intruders and were back in full force for the start of the 1951 celebration.

And into another rhubarb! Sometime during the night before the 1951 parade the rains came back with a vengeance and fell with such force that for a while it was debatable whether the parade would have to be cancelled. But when the decision was made to carry on with the parade the Indians balked at participating in full native dress. The rain would ruin their beadwork and doeskin jackets! Eventually a compromise was worked out. The men would wear their feathered headgear but wear their ordinary clothes under hastily provided slickers to protect them from the rain.

Then tragedy struck. As Ed Hall was preparing to mount his horse to lead the Indians into the Stampede parade for the twenty-fifth time, he dropped dead on the street in front of the Mewata Armories. The Indian chiefs attended his funeral in their full regalia two days later.

The parade itself went off on schedule, before a crowd that lined the streets three and four deep over its entire route. Soaked to the skin in their fancy Stampeding shirts, pants and boots, somewhere between thirty and forty thousand Calgarians thus expressed their solidarity with Stampede directors, cowboys, old timers, Indians, visiting dignitaries, riding clubs, bands, and float riders. All ignored the worst rain soaking the Stampede parade had ever experienced, ever would experience. Only after the parade was long completed did the skies clear, and stay reasonably clear for the rest of the week.

Until, that is, the crowd was filing in for the final performance of the evening show which included the finals of the chuckwagon races. Then, between 6:30 and 7:00 P.M., Victoria Park was hit by the granddaddy of all hail, wind, and rainstorms. Within a matter of minutes the carnival midway was a foot deep in water. Spectators who sought shelter in the canvas topped eateries were doused when the

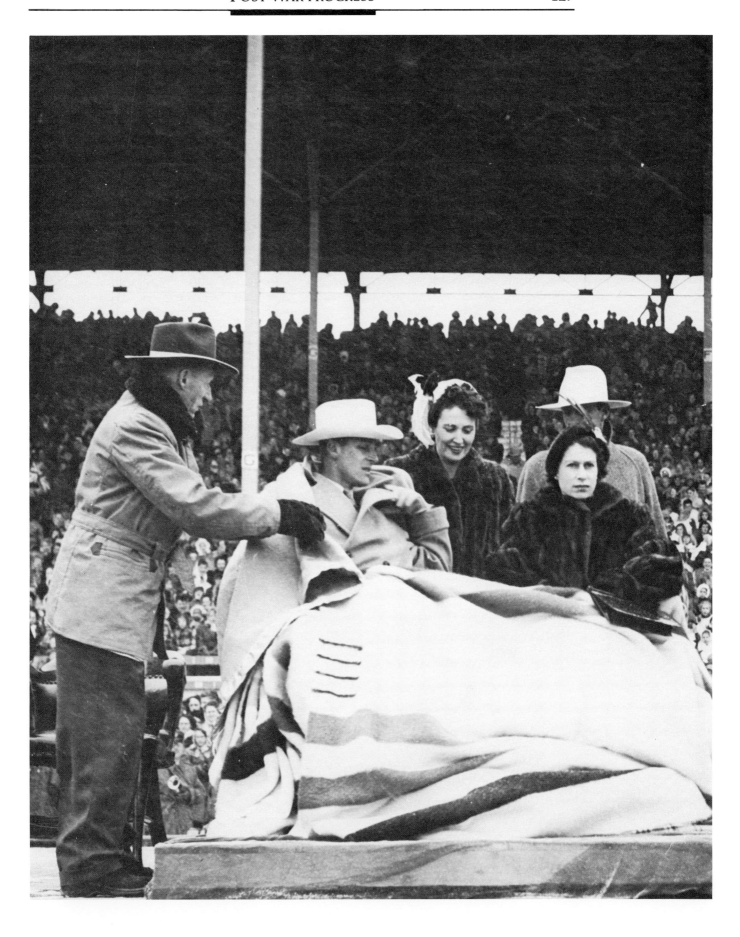

gusting winds blew the tops away.

And then, as if all this had not been enough, the perverse gods of the weather leaned back and waited for the chance to show the Calgary Exhibition and Stampede what could happen when they really got angry. That chance came in the second week of October on the eve of the visit of Princess Elizabeth and the Duke of Edinburgh to Calgary.

For this festive occasion the Stampede board had volunteered to stage an authentic Stampede program for the royal couple. To that end a couple of dozen of the best bucking horse riders, calf ropers, and steer decorators in the country were rounded up, along with all the necessary livestock. The Indians from all the southern Alberta reserves were invited to pitch their teepees on the Exhibition grounds. All the fixings were prepared for a super-barbeque luncheon for a couple of thousand in the Stampede Corral. The stage was all set to give the royal couple the most exciting afternoon on their entire tour.

All this was to happen on Thursday, October 18. On the night previous a blizzard blew across the Calgary area from the north, dumping several inches of snow on the city and coating the streets with ice.

Then it got worse and stayed worse. When the royal party arrived Thursday morning the temperature was hovering around the ten above zero mark at parade time. Instead of standing sedately on the sidewalk and cheering, the bone-chilled crowds engulfed the royal car and ran along beside it to keep warm. The princess had wisely come prepared for Calgary weather for she had brought along the full length mink coat Canada had given her as a wedding present four years before.

While the royal couple huddled under layers of blankets in the royal box, the performers outdid themselves to provide an exciting full dress stampede. They decorated steers, roped calves, staged a wild horse race, rode both saddle broncs and bareback, and crowned it all with a four-rig chuckwagon race.

There was one important constructive result of the 1950–52 rainstorms and blizzard. The directors were convinced that nothing was as important as paving the walkways and parking lots on the Exhibition grounds. That, and construction of proper sewers to carry off the water from the storms that seemed to have become a Calgary fact of life. The paving projects began in earnest in 1952.

CHAPTER 11

The Golden Age of the Stampede

Tastes differ and fashions change. But there is a French aphorism that holds the more things change the more they remain the same. As Canada reached midcentury, the traditional time for looking back and looking ahead, the Calgary Exhibition and Stampede gave point to that aphorism.

For example, any spectator who turned up for an afternoon show after a twenty-five-year absence would have felt perfectly at home, on two counts at least. Josh Henshorn was still announcing the grandstand events in the same tone of voice over the electric microphone he had once used with a handheld megaphone. And he was still using, and getting laughs with, the longest running joke in Christendom. It went like this: "If the Rev. Mr. Albert Ramsbottom is within the sound of my voice will he please go at once to the check room under the Grandstand. (long pause) Your valise is leaking."

The joke had its origin in the prohibition era when scoflawing travelers carried their booze with them. Forty years later sections of the crowd would beat Josh to the punchline by shouting it back at him as he was getting it out.

In the centerfield, Warren Cooper was still announcing the infield events with a tone of voice which, when the wind was right, could be heard at the outer limits of Okotoks.

The game in the infield was still very much the same, though the players had changed. The champions of the 1920s were now ensconced in chairs in the judges' stands, working the timers' watches, opening and shutting gates and picking cowboys off bucking horses. Jack Dillon was gone from the key role as Arena director to be replaced by Dick Cosgrave. The most noticeable change was the smoothness with which the events overlapped with the thoroughbreds encircling the race track. At night the chuckwagon races had evolved into the super attraction of the week, had undergone many refinements of equipment, and had evolved much stricter running rules.

One change that was expected at once did not come for more than ten years. That was the abandoning of the old Arena once the Stampede Corral was in place and operating.

The Arena was built primarily as a horse show facility but quickly developed into a multi-purpose livestock building. When it was being used for cattle and sheep, it was the Livestock Arena. When the horse shows were there it was the Horse Show

Arena. When in later years it was site for hockey games, it was the Hockey Arena. The terms were interchangeable. But in connection with the hockey operation there was an important distinction.

The horse shows and livestock shows and sales were operated by the Exhibition company on behalf of the appropriate livestock association. Hockey was always operated by outside interests under a lease of the premises from the board.

And so it was, when the board bought out the Calgary Artificial Ice Rink Company in 1944, and organized the Calgary Stampeders Hockey Club, it was breaking new ground. It was veering off from its raison d'être—serving the mutual interests of the farming and livestock industries of southern Alberta. It was this change in direction, minor as it obviously was, that led in part at least to the departure of Charles Yule as general manager in 1951.

In his facilities tour in 1945, Yule had seen a half dozen fair grounds coliseums that would have served as models to replace the Arena. He had also seen several two-storey livestock barns that would have been ideal for Victoria Park. For one thing, they would have halved the ground-space needed for livestock barns and freed up space for other areas. While the directors quickly moved to embrace the idea of a new coliseum, nobody wanted to listen when he brought up the double-decker barn for discussion.

There is no record of Yule being opposed to the construction of the new arena in principle and he saw to its construction with his usual flair. But there was clearly some doubt in his mind about the board's priorities and he reacted vigorously from time to time to the way Lloyd Turner and the rink committee were running things. Decisions, he complained, were too frequently taken without consulting him, from such small things as buying supplies for the hockey team without proper paperwork, to booking events in the Arena without notifying him.

Matters came to a head in January, 1951, when Yule angrily told the executive committee if it did not take steps to bring the rink under his jurisdiction, he would resign effective April 1. Yule, who was then sixty-five, had been in failing health off

and on for a couple of years. The executive managed to smooth ruffled feathers all around and suggested that after the Stampede ended he should take a couple of months vacation in an effort to restore his health. Instead, in late July, he insisted on tendering his resignation, effective September 30, 1951.

Regretfully, the directors accepted after voting Yule a full year's salary—$10,000—as a retiring allowance and insisted that he, as a former president, take a permanent place on the board of directors. The search for a new general manager got as far as Maurice E. Hartnett, the deputy minister of agriculture in Saskatchewan, and went no further. After graduation from the University of Saskatchewan, Hartnett had served previously as agricultural editor of the *Western Producer*, was widely regarded as a livestock judge and, on top of everything else, had the enthusiastic endorsement of Charles Yule as his successor.

Here and there around the edges of the Exhibition operation some questions were then raised as to why the job had not gone to W. L. "Squibb" Ross, the assistant general manager who was widely recognized as "the guy who keeps all the balls in the air." Ross was minutely familiar with every aspect of the operation, was always the person people went to to get things done. The directors, however, had opted for a much younger man—Hartnett was forty-six—and one with much wider experience in riding herd on the sort of expansion everybody had in mind for the Exhibition grounds. Ross was reappointed assistant general manager with a seventy-five dollars a month salary increase. I. W. Parsons, the secretary of the company, and D. T. McKillop, the accountant, got fifty dollars a month raises.

Long before the Hartnett era, long even before Charlie Yule had come on the scene, the Exhibition directors and the other wealthy Calgarians had converted their stables to garages and junked their buggies and democrats. The horse as any kind of a beast of burden had clearly seen his day on Calgary streets. Ironically, it was only after all this had happened that the horse came into his own in Calgary at midcentury and the old cowtown image faded while the horse-town image bloomed. Calgary became a city of horse fanciers, and the fancier the better. More, it became a city of female horse fanciers.

Wherever there are horses there are, of course, people with eyes for conformation quality and performance. That was certainly true of the arrival of the Mounted Police who began at once to look around for additions and replacements for their herd. The importation of blooded equine stock began with the beginning of Calgary. But it was well into the waning years of the half century before the proliferation of the breeds became apparent at the Calgary Spring Horse Show.

Pat Burns was always partial to the Morgans and was breeding them on his ranches prior to the First World War. The Palominos were brought into the country in the 1920s by cowboys coming to the rodeos and stampedes but it was not until 1944 that they were sufficiently established to be recognized as a breed. Joe Fulkerth of Didsbury began importing Kentucky-bred fore-runners of the American Saddlebred three gaited and five gaited show horses in the 1920s and had three five gaited "Kentucky" on display at the 1932 horse show. A decade later there were enough breeders in the Calgary area to form a Saddlebred Association. Among them were R. M. Spence, the shoe merchant who imported the double registered Palomino Saddlebred "Ronald Lee Rose," a popular stud for many years; Jerry Puckett, H. R. McConachie, and Mary Anderson.

Quarterhorses were being imported into

Palomino horses of exquisite beauty abounded in the 1950s. Here is Nan Graham on one of them—Rusty Denver—which was eventually purchased by the New York Police Department. *Courtesy of the Calgary Stampede.*

One of the outstanding features of the Calgary horse shows was always the Arabian Costume Class. This is Kay Dench on one of the prize Arabians her family imported. *Photograph by Jack DeLorme. Courtesy of the Calgary Stampede.*

Alberta as working cow horses long before they were recognized as a separate breed. During the depression C. C. Matthews of the Highland Stockfarm shipped Aberdeen Angus breeding stock to Montana and brought back Quarterhorses in exchange. Farther south, the Streeter brothers of Stavely and the Burtons at Claresholm established Quarterhorse herds.

It was George Cheatham, however, a "pig-iron peddlar from Oklahoma," as he defined himself, who put the Quarterhorse on the Alberta horse map. Cheatham came to Calgary in 1948 after the Leduc oil discovery as the manager of an American oilfield supply company. But his waking-sleeping passion was the Quarterhorse in a Texas style cutting horse contest. In short order he persuaded the Calgary Horse Show to stage a cutting horse exhibition with Quarterhorses cutting calves out of

herds in simulated ranching conditions. Thereafter the cutting horse contest became a featured attraction at the Calgary horse shows, and at all the other shows where calves and horses were available.

Another popular "using" horse was the Appaloosa which Jim Wyatt of High River introduced to challenge the quarter horses in the cutting contests. Bill Herron pioneered the pinto horses. He imported the celebrated American parade horse "Pride's Diamond" with which the glamour classes were introduced and popularized at the horse shows.

The first Arabian in Alberta was Aldebar which the Prince of Wales sent out to his E P Ranch in the 1920s. In the Calgary area the first of the breed was imported as a foal in 1942 by Mrs. Edith Stevens who lived near the Stockyards. She kept the stallion Ahmur in her backyard,

rode him over to the Stockyards to perform his services. Col. J. F. Scott, C. O. Dench, Dr. John Duffin, and Stan and Lenora Wilson were also importers. In 1951 Kay and Connie Dench created a mild sensation at the horse show by appearing on their Arabians in diaphanous harem costumes in the first "Arabian costume class."

So popular did the Arabian become so quickly in Alberta that, ten years after the Dench girls' performance, the Arabian Horse Association was able to take over the Stampede Corral to stage its first national championship. The show ran for three days and attracted more than two hundred entries from all over the continent. Thereafter the Arabian Horse Show was an annual event in Calgary in August. The traditional Arab costume class, which became one of the features of the Calgary Spring Horse Show, bore no resemblance

to those of the Dench girls. What the Dench girls did in 1951 was provide an added dimension to other performance classes and to emphasize the increasing domination of the horse shows by women riders.

Then well into his seventies, Clem Gardner was still riding over the jumps at the Calgary Show and his daughters Audrey and Joan were matching him stride for stride. Except for competing in the high jumps, they were among the women who were into everything else. Among them were Joy Cardell, Nan Graham, Doris Littlewood, Gloria Klaver, Demaris Batch, Joyce Cheshire, Kay Dunford, Delores and Kay Bowlen, Donna Christie, Peggy Robertson, Madeline Herron, Marion McMahon, Marjory Upper, Joy Patterson, Sidney Smith, Edith Rodie, Diana Cross. When horse show stake races evolved into girls'

Bridging the gap between the generations were Mrs. Henderson, Gloria Klaver, Madeline Herron, Joy Patterson, Mae Cooke, and Nan Graham. Mrs. Herron, more than any other Calgarian, was responsible for the super-colorful embroidered shirts so popular with both sexes in Calgary in the post-war decade. *Courtesy of the Calgary Stampede.*

barrel racing the sport became so popular all over Alberta that a special saddle had to be invented to accommodate the girl racers.

There had always been more than enough saddle horses and hunter types to fill out the Calgary Horse Show classes. But the rapid expansion in the varieties and numbers at midcentury, coupled with increased female participation, added new variety to the show. That was particularly true in the western pleasure classes where so many entries ultimately led to the holding of preliminary culling.

The burgeoning popularity of the pleasure horse population also added variety to the Stampede parade. More and more space had to be allotted to the saddle clubs. One result was the stretching of the parade from around an hour to almost two hours. That gave rise in turn to a lot of grumbling about the tiresome length of the parade.

As for the annual Stampede itself it would again demonstrate in 1952 that it had reached a substantial degree of immunity from buffeting from business cycles and downturns in economy. That was the year in which disaster, in the form of an outbreak of foot-and-mouth disease, struck the cattle business. It was identified on a farm south of Regina in late February and took weeks to bring under control. Before it ran its course more than two thousand cattle were destroyed. But the slaughter of the farm animals was nothing compared to the panic that swept the continent when the epidemic was confirmed.

The United States government immediately closed its border to *all* Canadian livestock. British Columbia, Ontario, and Quebec immediately imposed an embargo on shipments into those provinces from Alberta as well as Saskatchewan. Why Alberta? Nobody could think of a logical answer at the time. The epidemic was declared under control in August, 1952, but it took the United States until the following March to reopen its door to Canadian livestock. But it would take the Alberta cattle business more than a decade to recover the ground it had lost.

Before the epidemic prime steers were bringing $33 a hundred pounds at the Calgary stockyards. Indeed, for the previous year the cattlemen had been worrying aloud over whether the high price was discouraging consumer spending on the red meats. The epidemic ended that worry, for almost overnight the price of prime steers dropped from $33 to $21 per hundred pounds. The federal government stepped in and established a $22.50 floor price for the duration of the emergency.

The emergency had arisen, moreover, smack in the middle of preparing for what was expected would be the greatest Calgary bull sale in history. The previous year 729 animals had been sold for $816,000 for an average of $1,100. That average was almost double the best previous record. The impact of foot-and-mouth dropped the average by almost forty percent to $725, and signalled the onset of a ten-year depression for the cattle industry. Twenty years would pass before livestock prices would fully recover from that disaster.

Yet in face of what was happening to its most important constituency, the 1952 Calgary Exhibition and Stampede broke every record that mattered! More people, 433,000, passed through the gates than ever before and contributed more to the company coffers than ever before. Out of total revenues of $754,000 the company had net operating revenue of $334,565.

Behind those figures lay some extraneous facts that would profoundly change the character of the city. The development of the Leduc oilfield and the discoveries of Redwater, Golden Spike, and a half dozen other important oilfields had transformed Calgary into the oil capital of Canada. Immigrants poured in in such numbers from the United States that by 1952 the city was bursting at the seams as it had not done since 1912. Between 1949 and 1951 Calgary's population jumped from 100,000 to 129,000 and then to 180,000 during the next five years.

The "quality," for want of a better word, of the immigrant army was as important as its numbers. It was composed mainly of managerial types whose salary level as "foreign service" employees of American companies far exceeded the Calgary level. They came in the main from the south and southwest of the United States and hence were thoroughly familiar with rodeo as an entertainment medium. And anyway most

Three of the winners of the top four events at the 1954 Calgary Stampede went on to win the Canadian championships of the Cowboys Protective Association. They were Hank Willard, left, the chuckwagon winner; Cliff Vandergrift, third from left, the calf-roper; and Marty Wood, fourth from left, the bronc riding winner. Gordon Earl, second from left, yielded the Stampede decorating title to Francis Manywounds. *Photograph by Jack DeLorme. Courtesy of the Calgary Stampede.*

of them had already heard of the Calgary Stampede. Not only was there immediate immersion of all concerned in the Stampede week ethos, there was an invitation-writing binge to all their friends and relations in the States to put the Calgary Stampede on their vacation calendars for the following year.

The American influx had other profound influences upon midcentury Calgary. They came from an era where outdoor living had become an intrenched way of life, at just about the time when the portable metal barbecue grill was becoming popular. In short order Stampede Week became the time when the aroma of cooking steaks began to emanate from Calgary backyards. Family barbecues, neighborhood barbecues, company barbecues, all became preludes or postscripts to attendance at the Calgary Exhibition and Stampede. So while it would take more than a decade for the cattle industry to begin to recover, the 1950s would become the golden age of the Calgary Stampede.

What had happened was that Calgary

had stumbled on, or otherwise came to have, a surefire formula for outdoor entertainment and wisely held fast to it. Cattle country people came naturally to a rodeo so that every year Calgary could count on drawing between seventy-five and eighty percent of its attendance from southern Alberta. Sitting for hours on end in the hot sun watching cowboys being thrown from bucking horses, roping steers, and riding Brahma bulls was not everybody's cup of tea. But as time passed rodeo sports developed the same sort of fans that existed for baseball, football, and hockey—people who appreciated the fine points of the sport had their favorite performers, and were quick to demonstrate their feelings.

One of the most emotional such demonstrations was Marty Wood's spectacular ride in the saddle bronc championship of 1955. The first native Calgarian to win the North American Saddle event, Wood burst upon the scene in 1954. The following year he again made the finals and the wildness of his Saturday performance was greeted

Casey Tibbs was unquestionably one of the all-time greats of North American rodeo, on account of both sheer ability and colorful lifestyle. His checkered shirts and purple chaps made him instantly recognizable at the Calgary Stampede. This is a typical shot of his utterly uninhibited riding style. *Courtesy of the Calgary Stampede.*

with deafening applause. On the other hand Deb Copenhaver, the American cowboy, did not seem to be trying nearly as hard. When Copenhaver was awarded the championship and Wood placed only in a tie for third, the crowd erupted in a sustained chorus of boos and catcalls seldom heard at a rodeo performance.

From that ride Wood went on to win bronc riding championships all over North America, including four more at the Calgary Stampede. Fred Kennedy called him the greatest bronc rider since Pete Knight. As a sporting contest the Calgary Stampede over the years developed an imposing roster of athletic superstars to match the Babe Ruths, Joe DiMaggios, Bobbie Orrs, Gordie Howes, Jackie Parkers, and Fritzie Hansons.

Probably the most famous cowboy of them all was Pete Knight of Crossfield who

won the IRA world's saddle bronc riding championship four times and the Calgary open championship three times. Everybody's choice for the all time Canadian all around cowboy would be Herman Linder of Cardston, who practically "owned" the Calgary Stampede from 1929 to 1939. He competed in three or four events. He won with a saddle and riding bareback. He won the calf roping. He won the Canadian all around championship seven times, and the North American championship five times in a row. The Babe Ruth of the chuckwagon drivers was of course Dick Cosgrave who won the championship ten times before retiring to become the arena director in 1949. The Joe DiMaggio of the calf ropers was undoubtedly Pat Burton of Claresholm who won eight roping championships between 1932 and 1940.

As with other sports, as some stars were

fading others were appearing to take their places and to become household words to the Stampede fans. One of the greatest of all time performers and favorites with the fans was Casey Tibbs, the kid from South Dakota who was prepared to ride anything that moved. He won his first North American Saddle Bronc championship in Calgary in 1949 and returned the following year to win both the saddle and bareback titles. Then Marty Wood displaced Tibbs in the crowds' affections. Winston Bruce in 1959 completed one of the wildest rides ever seen in Calgary when he moved from seventh place to win the saddle bronc championship, and became a great favorite of Stampede fans.

Among the score of other star performers like Bob Robinson, Keith Hyland, Wilf Gerlitz, Reg Kesler, and Wally Lindstrom, was Cliff Vandergrift who won no less than

five wild horse races, four wild cow milking contests, and two calf roping championships. With Dick Cosgrave retired, Ronnie Glass dominated the chuckwagon races for a while, then Hank Willard came to the fore to run up a five championship skein of wins.

It was clear long before midcentury that the Calgary Exhibition and Stampede had developed a winning formula for its annual show. All it had to do to keep breaking attendance records, as Calgary's population zoomed, was to conform to the formula and keep up the quality. This it did by steadily, though modestly, increasing the prize money offered the cowboy contestants, and by bringing in the best acts it could find as special crowd attracters. This latter was achieved by having teams of directors fan out across the United States after each show to see what was pleasing

No rider got his spurs higher on a bronco's shoulders than Winston Bruce who won many saddle bronc championships before retiring to become Stampede Rodeo Manager. *Courtesy of the Calgary Stampede.*

Charles Beil began his art studies in Helena, Montana, under the guidance of Charlie Russell, but his mastery of the sculptor's art was developed at his studio in Banff. Though his trophies for calf roping, steer decorating, bull riding, and bronc riding were highly prized, his finest piece was his bronze trophy for the chuckwagon races. Two of the proudest winners of that trophy were Hank Willard and Dale Flett who drove the Peter Bawden rig. *Courtesy of Glenbow Archives, Calgary, Alberta.*

the crowds in the biggest shows south of the line.

This search turned up Slim Pickens, the cowboy movie actor, and Buddy Heaton, as the best one-two combination of clowns for the rodeo arena. Monty Montana and the Hendricks family repeatedly thrilled the crowds with their specialty acts. Other acts ranged all the way from trained sheep dogs and performing buffalo to a hanging-by-the-heels-from-a-helicopter super dazzler.

It was only when it tried to mesh the Corral facilities with its outdoor show that the record was less than a howling success. It brought in the Sonja Henie ice show and filled the rink. Then it brought in another highly rated ice show and it bombed. So did a water show. The Polock Brothers Circus was a hit one year and a flop the next. So was a Mexican Village that played under a huge canvas tent.

The Polock Brothers Circus was important, however, for another reason. It brought Duncan Renaldo and Leo Carillo, "The Cisco Kid," and "Pancho" of movie, radio, and television fame, to the city for the first time. They both came back again and again as goodwill ambassadors. They went everywhere, glad-handed everybody in sight, particularly inmates in children's hospitals and old folks homes and turned up at four or five functions a day. Out of their performance an idea was born. Why not bring in other Hollywood stars as special guests of the Stampede and have them do the same thing? As things turned out it was not one of the brightest ideas the promotions committee ever had. Some of the special guests did everything asked of them; others were crashing, temperamental bores.

Despite its disabilities as a Stampede Week facility, the Corral was nevertheless

Facing Page
In the 1950s the square dancing boom reached its peak during Stampede week when there was dancing at every intersection on Eighth Avenue. *Courtesy of Glenbow-Alberta Institute, Calgary, Alberta.*

The trouble was that the Corral was a superb hockey facility and not much good for any other type of entertainment. In 1952 a spring performance of the Minneapolis Symphony Orchestra proved the acoustics were impossible, a fact that was later confirmed by visits by Louis Armstrong and Spike Jones. Many efforts were made over the years to improve the sound quality of the Corral without notable success. One idea was to hang huge sets of drapes from the rafters. Another was to wrap all the girders and pipes in layers of burlap.

responsible for turning the Exhibition into the sports center of Calgary. It had been assumed too, particularly by all the horse show exhibitors, that the spring and summer horse shows would move into the Corral. The first year there was so much concern over what piling dirt a foot deep would do to the polished concrete floor of the Corral that the horse show was relegated to the Arena, the dismantling of which would remain a "next year" project for the next decade. Hard on that decision came another, to lease the Arena to the Buffalo Athletic Association for minor league

hockey for the winter. That did not work out so the next year the curlers persuaded the company to turn the Arena into a fourteen-sheet curling rink cum horse show. The horsemen grumbled but the curlers were delighted. Curling quickly became Calgary's most popular winter sport, for both men and women, and the Arena ice was occupied from morning until night.

One of the best promotions of the Stampede board, in the eyes of its farming and ranching supporters, was the expanded youth activities program it embarked upon in 1952. That came about almost by accident.

Except for parimutuel betting, church basement bingo, and charitable raffles, gambling of all kinds was strictly forbidden in Canada. From time to time various service clubs had approached the Stampede with suggestions of raffles that could be run during Stampede Week. Nothing came of them until the Kinsmen proposed that a new car be raffled to support a youth program.

It was a tremendous success. The Kinsmen and the Stampede split a $10,000 profit and the car raffle became a permanent feature. This led to a beefing up of junior activities under the aegis of the newly created junior agriculture committee headed by Charles Kennedy. In cooperation with the district 4-H clubs, judging competitions for cattle and sheep were held along with calf clubs and livestock shows and sales for juniors. In addition, there was enough revenue for increased support of minor league sports in Calgary, particularly hockey.

So popular did the car raffles become that they were expanded from one car a week to one car a night. Then the Young Men's Section of the Board of Trade undertook the promotion of a "dream house" raffle and that was followed by a "pot o' gold" raffle. All were great money makers for both the service clubs and the Stampede.

In 1953-54 the management for the first time kept track of attendance for all events on the grounds. It discovered that more people went through the Corral turnstiles than attended the Stampede and horse races combined. The figures were:

Stampede Corral	708,663
Arena	109,039
Pavilion	143,163
Exhibition & Races	568,926
Sundry	49,643
	1,579,440

That was the year of the hockey Stampeders' miraculous recovery time from its disastrous entry into the Western Hockey League composed of Calgary, Edmonton, Saskatoon and the four-team Pacific Coast Professional League. Six teams made the playoffs but Calgary was not one of them. The next year the rink committee arranged an affiliation with the Chicago Black Hawks who helped strengthen the team and it did better. In 1953-54 Frank Currie was hired as coach and general manager and he took the Stampeders to the league championship and then to defeat the Quebec Aces four games to one in the first year of the Edinburgh Trophy competition.

Building the Stampede Corral, and in particular the size of the debt assumed as a consequence, was an important watershed in the lives of the directors. For one thing they were continually aware of the need to put the building to use, and hence they became more promotion minded. And they got rid of the make-do, patch-it-up, add-onto thinking that economic conditions had engendered. From midcentury on "thinking big" became the order of the day.

How much of this drive derived from Maurice Hartnett, how much was an offshoot of the new optimism that had engulfed Calgary, and how much was spontaneously combusted by the board itself would be impossible to determine. Hartnett was a driving force. As a deputy minister of a rapidly expanding department, he had mastered the art of getting along with cabinet ministers, of knowing when to push, and when to fall back and let his superiors think what was being advocated was their idea. And certainly in "Red" Dutton, Cliff Cross, Jack Grogan, George Edworthy, Clar Manning, and Marsh Porter, the perennial chairman of the finance committee, the board had a full complement of pushers and doers.

In any event, the 1950s became the

building years for the Calgary Exhibition and Stampede when neither the size of a project or its costs were regarded as valid excuses for not getting on with it. The first indication of all this was the decision in 1951 to spend $137,000 on the installation of a new parimutuel plant. It was not the size of the project that mattered. It was spending that much money on a facility that was generally regarded as a very minor aspect of the company's operation.

Hard upon the completion of the horse racing facility, it was decided to go back to the beginning and start over in attempting to solve the increasingly vexing problem of draining the Stampede grounds. This ninety-four-acre tract drained, generally, to the Elbow River on the south and east. But the spotting of buildings here, there, and everywhere without regard to the lay of the land created innumerable hillocks and hollows that became instant disaster areas every time it rained. And the rapid expansion of paved areas merely confounded the problem.

The grandstand frontal area sloped toward the race track. The race track sloped toward and drained into the center-field. Ad hoc repairs and changes severely damaged the race track. By 1954 the company embarked on a costly and extensive rebuilding of the race track and the installation of a whole network of storm sewers. At the same time a drive was intensified to persuade the city to remove the city-owned structures that cluttered the east side of the grounds. Successive boards for fifteen years had been pleading for the removal of the street car barns, the city stores, the City Hydro pole yard, an electrical sub-station. Not even the offer of $50,000 moved the city commissioners to move out.

These city facilities occupied fifteen acres desperately needed for parking and horse barns. Eventually, but only after the entire city council, the city commissioners, and department heads became associate directors, a deal was done. For $100,000 payable at $10,000 a year for ten years, the city agreed to get out. The power plant was turned into a stable for the chuckwagon horses and the other buildings either dismantled or turned to Stampede use. Simultaneously the decision was taken

to double the size of the livestock pavilion at a cost of $300,000. Efforts to pry grants from the federal and provincial governments delayed the project for several years to a point where its estimated costs approached $600,000. When the grants did come through it was decided to double the size and add a second story, all of which ran the cost to $900,000.

As the crowds kept breaking new records every year, the space available for exhibitors shrank and shrank. With the livestock pavilion out of the way a decision was taken to proceed with a new million-dollar combination curling rink and exhibitors' building.

To everybody's surprise, the conversion of the old arena to a curling facility had been extremely profitable. Revenue from it provided, as it were, the down payment on what would be known as the Big Four Building, named for the sponsors of the original Stampede. And by turning the main floor into a twenty-four-sheet curling rink the directors were confident that the building would ultimately be able to pay for itself.

The construction of the Big Four Building in 1959 necessitated the removal from the site of the Bessborough exhibits building to the race barn area where it was converted into winter quarters for race horses. The Willingdon building was removed to the newly acquired Sunshine Auto Court property east of the Elbow and converted into a general storage facility.

It was during this period of expansion in all directions of the physical plant, of yearly record-breaking attendance, and growth in income and profits, that the growing pains naturally became most severe. Parking problems intensified despite expansion of parking areas. Nothing caused more grumbling than the annual hassle over the allotment of grandstand tickets.

Nobody, seemingly, was ever able to get the number of seats they wanted in the areas they wanted to sit. Because, went the litany, "after the directors have grabbed off all the good seats for themselves and their friends there are no decent seats left."

By this time the company had over two hundred patrons, life directors, honorary directors, and associate directors along

A prime factor in the development of curling into Calgary's favorite indoor winter sport was the construction in 1957 of the Big Four Building. *Courtesy of Glenbow-Alberta Institute, Calgary, Alberta.*

with a couple of hundred volunteers who provided the labor essential to the success of the annual parade and show. All were entitled to buy seats for themselves and their families but only for one evening and one afternoon performance. The notion that there was a good-seat-freeze-out, however, was a baseless canard. There were still good seats available long after the mail orders were filled in February each

year. Over the years all kinds of changes were made to the system of ticket disposal. Blocks of seats were withheld from early sale to be available for incoming tourists. Various deadlines were established for the receipt of applications. Nothing, however, substantially reduced the grumbling over seat distribution. Given the 200,000 increase in patronage between 1949 and 1959 it was a problem without a solution.

CHAPTER 12

From Record Breaking Gates to Disaster

An American horse player known as "Titanic" Thompson has been credited with popularizing the phrase. In reply to a question about how he had done at the track, on a day he had done nothing but lose, the gambler, with a Trudeauean shrug of the shoulders and an up-spreading of palms replied: "You win some, you lose some."

The Calgary Exhibition began in 1959, in a small way, what would become a decade-long experience with "win some and lose some." Its experience with bringing in American movie and television stars as special guests had proved such an outstanding success with Leo Carillo and Duncan Renaldo that it decided to make similar appearances an annual feature of the Stampede. In 1959 it brought in Gene Barry, then star of a television horse opera called *Bat Masterson*. Barry began as a winner and ended as a dead loss, not to say an embarrassment.

As a counter to Barry, Bing Crosby turned up uninvited on the Sunday before the show as a guest of Max Bell, became the honorary parade marshal, stayed for most of the week playing golf, attending barbecues, and endearing himself to the entire population.

That was the year of the royal visit and Queen Elizabeth and Prince Philip's second go-round at the Calgary Stampede. This time the Queen and Prince Philip watched an evening of chuckwagon racing in glorious summer weather and enjoyed

every minute of it. The visit was credited with being an important factor in breaking the all-time attendance record in 1959. The attendance that year topped 591,715, some 42,000 more than had ever jammed into Exhibition Park before.

Unhappily, there was little enjoyment for the Queen, or for anybody else, in her visit to the Indian village. The Indians had counted on a private audience with Her Majesty and planned for the occasion for weeks. They brought their best buffalo robes to the Indian village and used them as a walkway for the Queen and Prince Philip. The robes were trampled and strewn with cigarette butts by an army of photographers who descended on the village in the wake of the royal couple. Then the Indian audience with the Queen was nullified by a horde of reporters, guards, and officials eavesdropping on what was said. As Chief Black Bull of the Blackfoot Tribe wrote in a bitter letter to the Calgary *Herald*:

The newspapermen pushed and shoved the Indians and blocked Her Majesty's way, taking pictures right in Her Ma-

From the royal family to international statesmen, the Calgary Stampede never lacked for celebrities. Duncan Renaldo, "The Cisco Kid," spent days on end entertaining shut-in children. *Courtesy of Glenbow-Alberta Institute, Calgary, Alberta.*

assault on holy writ. Not since the naming of the Stampede Corral had there been such a reaction.

In an effort to water down the criticism, steps were taken which in the long run would prove successful with the patrons. Free entertainment began on the grounds. Bands were hired to perform on special stages. A champion American tree climber was brought in to race up and down a one-hundred-foot pole. There was also an animal act from a circus which performed three times a day. Thereafter, the free outdoor show became a regular feature of the Stampede.

Inside the Corral, that was the year that management was convinced that it would strike it rich. It had succeeded in booking the most popular State Fair act in the United States—Roy Rogers, Dale Evans, and the Sons of the Pioneers. A couple of weeks before the show opened Rogers cancelled out. In substitution it was arranged to split the week into two segments—world championship wrestling for two nights and a country music jubilee for four nights, Johnny Cash on two and Red Foley on the other two. Cash, pleading throat trouble, was a no show. For the Corral and the Stampede management, that was the week that wasn't!

Those were the losses. In the win column was a visit by Prime Minister Diefenbaker to open the show, the medals presentations by Sir Neil Ritchie, onetime commander of the British Eighth Army. The parade that year was the loudest ever heard in Calgary and perhaps anywhere else. It contained military massed bands along with thirty marching bands from all over the continent. And perhaps most felicitous of all, Bing Crosby not only came back for a second look, but he also brought Phil Harris and Alice Faye with him. The famous American band leader was the Stampede Parade Marshal of 1960.

In 1958 the livestock committee had hit upon the idea of the various breed associations having their national championship shows at the Stampede on succeeding years. The first breed to accept was the Shorthorn and its 1958 show drew entries from eastern Canada and the United States and helped swell all livestock entries to record proportions. It was followed by the

jesty's face. His Royal Highness even commented on it.

The Blood Indian Chief came many miles to be able to at least shake the hand of his great Queen, and he was not even introduced to her by the Stampede officials.

Faced as it was with keeping up payments on its new $2,300,000 Big Four Building, on the Stampede Corral, and other improvements it had been making, the board decided in 1960 that the time had come to raise admission prices—from twenty-five cents to fifty cents. All the other western fairs had long since gone to that figure and the state fairs below the border were up to one dollar in some places. Nevertheless, Calgary's vocal minority reacted to the increase as they might have reacted to an

CHARLES A. BEIL
THROUGH HIS SCULPTURE & PAINTINGS,
HIS WORK HAS BECOME WORLD FAMOUS.

CHARLES RUSSELL
ARTIST OF THE FAMOUS RUSSELL PICTURES.
A COMPLETE COLLECTION OF RUSSELL PICTURES IN CONCOURSE

THESE TWO FINE GENTLEMEN WERE CLOSE PERSONAL FRIENDS.

This is a copy of the framed reproduction of portraits of Beil and Russell that has graced the rotunda of the Stampede Corral for a quarter of a century. Like Russell, Beil was a master of oils and watercolor painting. One of his finest murals covers an entire wall of the main dining room of the Palliser Hotel. Others are in the offices of the president and the general manager of the Stampede. Beil's fame, however, rests solidly on his sculpture of men and horses in action. Below is one of the Beil trophies for which cowboys have competed at the Calgary Stampede. *Courtesy of the Calgary Stampede.*

Holstein breed, then by the Ayrshires, Jersey, and Aberdeen-Angus.

The success of the national shows swamped the livestock facilities, despite the steady expansion of stall space that had been taking place. It was not long before a conveyor-belt-like system had to be adopted, with one group moving out of the grounds as soon as judging was completed to make room for a new group preparing for judging.

One livestock group that was increasing in popularity, almost with each passing day, was the racing horse. The construction of a mezzanine floor for the horse players under the grandstand, coupled with the installation of television monitors for viewing the races, sent the betting volume into orbit, reaching a record $6,340,000 in 1960. The following year the Stampede Futurity Stakes for two year olds was established with a purse of $8,000.00. The first winner was Silent Sandra, owned by the M and D Stables and trained by G. Pederson. Johnny Longden came up from Los Angeles to make the presentations.

Also making presentations that year was one of the most eminent of western artists.

He was Charles Beil whose liaison with the Calgary Exhibition and Stampede went back to 1939. Assisting him was Mr. Justice M. M. Porter who that year was named Imperial Potentate of the Shrine Lodge of America. The only Canadian ever to achieve that honor, he had been a director of the Exhibition and Stampede for fifteen

years, chairman of its finance committee for ten.

A protege of C. W. Russell, the famous Montana cowboy artist, Beil put down his roots in Banff after the First World War and during the depression, on pack trips into the Rockies, his path crossed that of G. H. Gaherty, president of Calgary Power. Beil was then refining his skills as a sculptor and suggested to Gaherty that a piece of his work would make a suitable trophy for the Calgary Stampede. Gaherty agreed and Calgary Power supplied the trophy for the saddle bronc champion of 1939.

It was not long before a host of other Calgary firms were following Calgary

Power's example and providing Beil trophies for the winners of all the other rodeo events. Beil's outstanding sculpture, a magnificent representation of a chuckwagon in full flight, was the Canadian Western Natural Gas trophy that went to three-time winners of the Chuckwagon Championship.

For thirty-two years Charles Beil did the Stampede up in bronze. When he eventually retired from the field in 1972, the board commissioned five other Alberta artists to supply the trophies. They were Gina McDougal, Malcolm Mackenzie, Douglas Stephens, Richard Roenisch, and Gerald Tailfeathers.

While the rodeo crew under Jack Dillon

and then under Dick Cosgrave had acquired great expertise over the years in putting their show together, and running it off on time, keeping the show supplied with livestock was a long running headache. When the bucking horses and Brahma bulls failed to perform up to expectations there were protests from the cowboys and demands for rerides. The management first tackled the problem by renting stock from local ranchers. Then Brahma bulls and bucking horses were purchased. Then private stock contractors became suppliers. Then combinations of all the above.

No matter what system was followed it became increasingly difficult to maintain the bucking qualities of the horses. Horses that had wildly bucked one year frequently became excessively docile when returned the following year. There were hassles with the owners over rental payments and these disagreements were frequently fumigated in Fred Kennedy's column in the Calgary *Herald*. Over the years the Stampede committee had become pretty well convinced that the course of wisdom would be to set up a ranch of its own and breed its own bucking stock.

In the summer of 1961 J. B. Cross, George Edworthy, Stuart McRae, and Tom Hall drove out to Dick Cosgrave's ranch at Rosebud to reconnoiter the country in search of an available ranch, preferably one of five or six sections of deeded land with another ten thousand acres of lease that could be bought cheaply. They piled in Cosgrave's car and went driving across the prairie, which at this time of the year was tinder dry.

They found several suitable spreads and were on the point of going back to Calgary to get a real estate agent to start dickering with the owners. One of the passengers, happening to glance backward was astounded to see a trail of smoke behind the car. Cosgrave's overheated tail pipe, touching the dry grass, had started a prairie fire!

Suddenly, the Prairies were filled with ranchers who came from all directions to fight the blaze. They discovered the Stampede directors, began wondering aloud what had brought them into the short grass country of eastern Alberta. When they reached the correct conclusions, the price

of Hanna area range land took a sharp jump in price. In the end the company did acquire Johnny Van Wezel's seventeen-thousand-acre spread, stocked it with a hundred-horse basic herd and started its breeding program.

In 1959 the Stampede board, always big on anniversaries, celebrated the fiftieth anniversary of manned flight in heavier-than-air aircraft in Canada and had J. A. D. McCurdy, the man who made the flight, come up from Nova Scotia to open the show. In 1962 it had a truly authentic anniversary to celebrate—the fiftieth anniversary of Guy Weadick's first Calgary Stampede, and it did the celebration up brown.

Its raffles of cars and dream homes had been such successful money raisers that it was decided that the centerpiece of its Golden Jubilee Celebration should be the raffling of a $50,000 gold ingot. The official release noted that the gold bar weighed 89.3 pounds worth $35 an ounce. (The arithmetic did not work out, gold being weighed on the troy scale at 12 ounces to the pound, but nobody noticed the difference.) The winners all took their winnings as cheques for $50,000. If any of them had taken the gold, kept it for twenty years, they would have become certifiable millionaires.

To get in tune with the times, H. Gordon Love, who became president in 1962, had his tailor conjure up a frontier suit of clothes made out of ten carat gold cloth. As Love joyously repeated, "It weighs a ton, but it sure stands out in a crowd!"

As befitting such an anniversary, the 1962 show was easily the most successful ever staged to that time. Roy Rogers and his troupe finally made it to the Corral for ten performances and sold the place out for most of the time. The wife of the president of Mexico, Senora Eva de Lopez Mateos, headed a troupe of seventy of Mexico's finest singers and dancers and stayed for the entire week.

Curling had been so successful during its first winter in the new Big Four Building that it was decided to double the size of the available ice. An additional twenty-four sheets were installed on the second floor. For the Jubilee Show the ice-making machine was turned on and the Big Four

Building became a superbly air conditioned haven for refugees from the sun-baked midway.

The Jubilee year marked the swansong of the Calgary Stampeders as a professional hockey team. They finished the 1961–62 season on the top of the eastern division and beat Seattle in the playoffs before losing to Edmonton in the finals. But the crowds that winter were off substantially compared with previous years and fell off drastically in 1962–63. When the team failed to make the playoffs the rink committee decided it was time to take a sabbatical from professional hockey and reassess its involvement. The ultimate decision was to disband the team, sell off the players, and leave hockey to whoever wanted to take the responsibility of running a team.

Nobody did for a couple of years. Then Ron Butlin headed a group of hockey buffs and decided Calgary needed a senior amateur team to compete for the Allan Cup. Bert Olmstead, the former Toronto star, was hired as coach and the nameless wonders played exhibition games in the Corral, before crowds of four and five hundred until the Allan Cup playdowns. Then as the Calgary Spurs, they won some games, the crowds came back by the thousands, and a brand new six-team prairie league was organized the next year. The Spurs won the league rather handily the next year, and the next, and Corral attendance zoomed back to the levels achieved in the heyday of the Western Canada League. Then, when the senior league deteriorated, the Junior League moved into the Corral to take up the slack.

As hockey interest declined the popularity of curling, following the installation of the forty-eight sheets of ice in the Big Four Building, increased sharply. Indeed it had been increasing ever since the Macdonald Brier finals in the Corral in 1961 attracted an attendance of 51,000, an attendance matched three years later when the world championship of curling, Air Canada's Scotch cup, was staged in Calgary. The cup was won that year by Earl Dagg of Vancouver.

Perhaps the most important change in 1962 was the decision to hold the finals for all rodeo competitions on Saturday afternoon. It was a natural progression to the two go-rounds during the week, and it filled the grandstand to capacity. New daily attendance records were established for Thursday and Saturday and the overall figure for the week of 585,667 was only 6,000 shy of the all time 1959 record. The show had finally recovered the 80,000 attendance drop that followed from the ticket price increase of 1960.

It had always been assumed that, when the board got rid of the city of Calgary car barns and other buildings, there would be all the room on the grounds the Stampede would ever need. That and the razing of the old arena after the Big Four Building was completed. But so rapidly had the attendance been rising since the war that the congestion increased rather than diminished. By 1962 thought was being given to ways of expanding the outer limits of old Victoria Park.

When rumors began to surface that the Canadian National Railways was considering shutting down its Calgary operation, expansion ideas moved front and center. The railway trackage, right-of-way, and station facilities on the other side of the Elbow River from the Exhibition grounds became the focus of everybody's attention. In 1963 the board unveiled an artist's concept of what could be done to improve things by rerouting the Elbow River and attaching the CNR property to the Stampede Grounds, if, as and when the CNR ever decided to move out and seven million dollars became available. The CNR kept its plans to itself and after a brief flurry of interest the proposal was quietly put on hold.

Expansion plans did not stay on hold for long, however, mainly because of developments on the political front arising from the election of Harry Hays to parliament in 1963 and his appointment as minister of agriculture in the first Pearson administration.

Harry Hays was literally born into the livestock industry at Carstairs where his father operated a large dairy farm. The Hays farm was eventually moved to the southern edge of Calgary and from it Hays developed into one of Canada's most successful and wide-ranging livestock auc-

tioneers. He was a director of the Calgary Exhibition and Stampede when he was elected mayor of Calgary in 1959 to succeed the colorful Mayor Don Mackay. As an ex-officio director during his terms as mayor, Hays was well aware of the congestion at Exhibition Park and of the expansion plans of the company. The consensus is that it was Harry Hays, as minister of agriculture, who focused the attention of

the Stampede on Lincoln Park as an alternative site for the Stampede.

Soon after Hays was settled in Ottawa, the War Assets Disposal Board got cabinet approval to sell off the 426-acre Lincoln Park air base on the southwest corner of Calgary. The property consisted of unused landing strips and a dozen huge hangars that had housed the training planes that flew out of Lincoln Park during the war.

Wall to wall and bumper to bumper congestion. That was Stampede Park in the 1960s. *Photo by Jack DeLorme. Courtesy of the Calgary Stampede.*

The property was bounded on the north by the Currie army establishment, on the east by Twenty-fourth Street, on the west by Thirty-seventh Street, and on the south by the new Glenmore Trail. Beyond the Glenmore was the moderately posh new Lakeview residential development and the Earl Grey Golf Course. Southwest of Lincoln Park was the Sarcee military establishment and a lot of wide open prairie. There was some housing development on the northwest. On the east new housing construction was edging toward Lincoln Park.

In September 1964 the *Herald* carried a two-paragraph story that the city commissioners had approved a proposal of the Stampede Board to purchase Lincoln Park for $750,000. On September 17, city council endorsed the proposal and fired off the offer to Ottawa. Then, when the residents of the general area reacted unfavorably to the idea of having the Calgary Exhibition and Stampede on their doorsteps, the city council backed away from immediate approval of the proposal. Instead it referred the relocation idea back to the commissioners for further study, and the city planners got into the act.

Meanwhile, the Stampede board had called in its architects to get planning started for the new park. These activities were intensified when word came back on November 7 that the Federal Government had accepted the city's bid. That word evoked a lot of other activity. Mount Royal College stepped in with the suggestion that Lincoln Park would make an ideal campus for a new and vastly expanded college. The Baptists proposed putting a theological college on the site. Carma developers offered to swap 280 acres it owned at the intersection of #1 and #2 highways for Lincoln Park, arguing that that was a much more suitable site for the new Stampede grounds. Other developers came forward with proposals for a $24,000,000 shopping center on the site. Atco Industries offered to lease all the hangar area and transfer its expanding trailer manufacturing business to Lincoln Park.

Beset as it was by rivals on all sides, the board nevertheless stuck to its guns. Don Matthews, its president, was the owner of one of Alberta's largest Aberdeen-Angus ranches seven miles west of Calgary, and

traversed Lincoln Park almost daily en route to and from the city. He led groups of directors out into the communities to try to persuade the residents to support the Stampede board's proposal.

It was a hopeless battle. An answer to one question evoked two others. Even when concerns about smells, flies, manure, and noise were satisfied, there were worries about the bums and footpads who would appear all around the place, about the traffic congestion and traffic noise. And not only during Stampede week. How about all the rest of the year with all the things that would be going on?

The complete Stampede plan for the grounds was released at last on March 25, 1965. The main entrance would be on Glenmore Trail. A race track would be in the north center of the tract, surrounded by livestock barns and other facilities. There would be access to the grounds from both Twenty-fourth Street and Thirty-seventh Street. All the plan did was crystallize and intensify the public opposition against moving the Stampede to Lincoln Park. In an effort to counter the criticism, Don Matthews and the directors in May went on a two-hour television phone-in show, the first of its kind in Calgary, to publicize and defend the new plan. The proposal did make an awful lot of sense to an awful lot of people. But none of them lived anywhere near Lincoln Park, and as time passed fewer and fewer were denizens of the city hall either.

When the Calgary city planners unwrapped their Lincoln Park scheme that June, the Calgary Exhibition and Stampede plan was sunk without a trace. The city plan was all things to all men. It included leasing the hangar complex to Atco Industries plus the establishment of a light manufacturing complex within the hangar area. A place was made for Mount Royal College and sites were set aside for a religious college, churches, and schools. What space was left would be divided between high rise apartment complexes, single family residences, and libraries. Most of all, it would bring in millions of new taxes while the Stampede would be a non-taxpayer.

The rush of the Calgary aldermen for the planner's bandwagon was instanta-

Another stroke of genius was the collaboration of Randy Avery and Margot Gooder McDermott in the development of the Young Canadians. *Courtesy of the Calgary Stampede.*

neous and unanimous. Contemplating the divisions within Calgary which their Lincoln Park proposal had caused, the Stampede directors retired to the Exhibition grounds to contemplate their future.

Obviously more space was urgently required. The CNR acreage south of the Elbow was unavailable. There was only the property north of Seventeenth Avenue between Second Street and the Elbow River. So in the fall of 1965 a site planning committee was set up composed of James Kerr, Ed O'Connor, J. B. Cross, George Hill, and Dudley Batchelor, with John Stevenson as architectural consultant. That winter, at the suggestion of Mayor Jack Leslie, a number of informal meetings were held with city aldermen and commissioners to canvass possibilities.

Out of these meetings a rough plan was agreed upon. The Stampede board proposed that the land between Seventeenth Avenue and Eleventh Avenue be made a part of the downtown redevelopment project. Council unanimously approved, but put the northward limits at Fourteenth Avenue. Unrest among Victoria Park residents delayed the implementation of the scheme and it was eventually declared ineligible for inclusion in urban renewal. Ultimately, however, approval by the majority of Victoria Park residents was obtained but only after seemingly endless delays.

In the meantime, on the front burners, the program chairmen were concentrating on getting everybody's mind off Lincoln Park and back on the show itself. The Friday morning children's show, which was started in 1931, had caught on with a vengeance and thirty thousand and more children regularly turned out for their special show. The Saturday morning roundup, which began almost as something to pick up loose ends from the regular rodeo events, grew into a show of consolation contests for cowboys who had failed to make the prize lists during the week. There were enough chuckwagons now competing to fill four or five races on Saturday morning. The Saturday morning performers, being less expert than the stars who made the finals often put on more exciting rides. Soon the Saturday morning show began to attract its own thousands of devotees.

The idea of bringing in celebrities as special guests or parade marshals was enthusiastically continued. Bing Crosby, Phil Harris, and Alice Faye were followed by Bob Hope, Walter Disney, and Senator Robert Kennedy. When the directors began to hear rumblings of discontent over their leaning toward Americans, Gordie Howe, Nancy Green, and Marty Wood, who had become a world class rodeo star, became featured invitees and parade marshals. They were followed in short order by the Earl Mountbatten of Burma, one of Britain's most revered war heroes, and the Duke and Duchess of Kent.

The truth was that over the years the Calgary Exhibition and Stampede had so intensified its promotional efforts in all directions that it had truly become the world's most famous show of its kind. Never hesitating to invite the highest and mightiest to become its guests, it drew enthusiastic acceptances just as at the close of each year it was able to gather up, in bushel baskets, all the newspaper clippings from around the world that publicized the show.

The maturity reached by the organization may best be illustrated by reference to the smoothness of the transition in the change in management in 1965. Maurice Hartnett had told the board several years before that he proposed to retire at sixty and turn his attention to managing his modest livestock interests in Alberta and British Columbia. He confirmed that intention in 1964 when he made it official by tendering his resignation to become effective March 1, 1965.

Under Hartnett the assets of the company had grown from $1,500,000 to more than $8,790,000. Attendance during Stampede week had increased by fifty percent, roughly from 400,000 to 600,000. And while the organization still relied mainly on volunteers to put the show on and over the top each year, the administration had also doubled in size. It had proved its worth during the latter years of Hartnett's tenure when ill health frequently kept him from functioning at top efficiency.

On Hartnett's retirement Irven Parsons, who had been moved up from secretary to assistant general manager in 1952, moved comfortably into Hartnett's job. Tom Hall, who had been manager of plant operations became assistant general manager. Wilf Baker became secretary. The other key personnel in 1965 were: W. D. Tidball, C.A., chief accountant; D. T. McKillop, manager of the Corral and Big Four Buildings; Dick Cosgrave, Stampede arena director; John Foster, buildings engineer; Charles Duncan, grounds superintendent; Duncan Grant, assistant manager Corral and Big Four Buildings; William Marshall, buildings and maintenance superintendent; Ken Greenway, livestock superintendent; Don Welden, publicity director; Jim Hays, electronics supervisor. By this time there were thirty-two standing committees, manned by enough associate directors to fill a page and a half in the annual reports.

In one respect Parsons had an advantage over Hartnett. He would not have to listen to the nattering of the seemingly thousands of self-elected theatrical and drama critics who infested the Calgary scene, and lived in anticipation of another "inferior" grandstand show.

Generally speaking the quality of the show put on every year would have compared at least favorably with that of any state fair below the line. But it did not compare with the best of the supershows on television which was then devouring theatric talent at a horrendous rate. And for a simple reason. It could not afford the kind of fees that Ed Sullivan and other shows could offer. And these were the norms by which the critics judged the Calgary show. The basic trouble was—it was not the Calgary show. It was the show that toured Calgary and all the other western Canadian fairs. Each of the other fairs had a voice in the selection and as time passed a painful gap developed between what Regina, Brandon, and Saskatoon could afford to pay for a week's entertainment package and what Calgary could afford. So Calgary was forced to settle for less than the best that could have been obtained.

Over the years, Randolph Avery of the Barnes-Carruthers Theatrical Agency in Chicago had put many of the show pack-

The Lincoln Park wartime air base was an island of emptiness on the west side of Calgary. *Courtesy of Glenbow Archives, Calgary, Alberta.*

This was how the Stampede proposed to fill the void by moving its entire establishment to Lincoln Park. *Courtesy of the Calgary Stampede.*

ages together for the western Canadian fairs. In 1964 the board decided to invite Avery to come to Calgary and put a locally produced grandstand show together. Thus ended its association with the other western fairs. The show featured the Canadian singer Juliette, Seth Riggs of New York, the Chaine dancers and a raft of vaudeville turns along with the superb ensembles of local dancers under the direction of Margot Gooder McDermott. Using the local "Kidettes" as a nucleus, she began putting her people into rehearsal in March and by opening night the youngsters could have danced their steps in their sleep. From this beginning evolved the Young Canadians who became a star attraction at the grandstand show. The whole performance was judged so successful that Avery was lured to Calgary as the permanent director of the grandstand show.

One surprising development that helped to take the sting out of the Lincoln Park experience was the appearance out of nowhere of a group of Calgary oilmen with a proposal for the staging of an oil show at the 1966 Stampede. They were Jerry D'Arcy, James K. Gray, and K. W. Germond. It would be Calgary's salute to the oil industry and would feature millions of dollars worth of equipment put on display to acquaint the public with the size and variety used in the industry.

The oil show idea first surfaced back in 1964 when Jim Gray, a young Calgary geologist, approached President Bert Baker with the suggestion. When Baker took the proposal to the directors the very size and scope of it scared them off for it would entail demolition of half a dozen old barns, sequestering several acres of already scarce parking space and a substantial financial outlay. Over the next year, however, enough support developed to persuade the directors to change their minds. The directors agreed to clear out the old barns to make room for the erection of a drilling rig which actually was put to work during Stampede week. The Corral, and 200,000 square feet of Exhibition grounds space, was filled with equipment, with 2,000 oil company personnel taking turns manning the rig. During the show Sammy Kaye brought in his band to provide the musical interludes.

The oil show helped to turn the 1966 show into the greatest ever held in Calgary. More than 200,000 attended the oil show itself. Attendance records were broken every day and the overall attendance, 654,000, exceeded the previous record of 1959 by more than 62,000.

The long-range effects of the show were even more important. It brought upwards of six hundred new volunteers into the annual Stampede and many of these stayed on in the years to come. When it was over the opinion was unanimous that Flare Square should remain as a permanent installation. It also was decided that each Stampede thereafter would have a special theme, beginning, of course, with the "100 years of Progress" theme for the 1967 Canadian centennial.

One of the invited guests to the 1966 Stampede was Robert Shaw, the deputy chief commissioner of Montreal Expo. He was so impressed with the show that he invited the Stampede to stage a Calgary Day at Expo. Along with the couple of carloads of chuckwagons, saddles, and equipment, the Stampede took dozens of square dancers, cowboys, Indians in regalia, and sundry citizens in western costumes to the famous Montreal celebration. It turned out to be a public relations coup of the first magnitude for Calgary and the Stampede.

In 1966 success brought the problem of breathing space to the forefront again. Not only was the congestion on the grounds reaching people saturation point, animal congestion passed the point of no return. Over recent years, while new livestock accommodation had been provided, a lot of old barns and stalls were removed. So in 1966 the heavy horse judging had to be run off before the show actually opened in order to clear the barn space for the race horses.

As a temporary solution to the congestion the directors decided after the 1966 show to expand to nine days. It would begin on Thursday, break over Sunday, and run for the following week. More important than that, though it went unrecognized at the time, was the decision to bring Calgary Transit into the parking congestion problem. A shuttle-bus service was established between the North Hill

shopping center and the Exhibition grounds. Motorists who had previously driven to the Stampede were encouraged to park and take the bus. The service caught on and the following year pick-up points were provided for express buses at a half dozen strategic centers across the city. The success of the shuttle buses dropped Exhibition grounds parking off the list of management priorities.

The 1967 Canadian Centenary show, though it had to compete for tourists with Expo, attracted 798,000 patrons during the nine-day show. The daily average of 88,000 was down 20,000 from the oil show peak, but the consensus was that stretching it out to nine days was a good idea. That, however, did not in any way diminish the argument that the institution needed more space if it was to continue to attract the

Not all the ideas of the 1960s turned as sour as Lincoln Park. One of the super successes was Flare Square and the International Oil Exposition. *Courtesy of James Mathieson, Calgary, Alberta.*

body of tourists to the city that Calgary deemed desirable.

In April 1968 the city council decided to provide some assistance in the form of a $4,000,000 grant spread over ten years. This would provide the board with $400,000 a year with which to buy out the property owners from Exhibition Park north to Fourteenth Avenue, a total of about eight city blocks. It looked like a sensible approach. Most of the homes in the area were of pre-World-War-One vintage, many of them modest cottages on thirty-foot lots, many in the hands of absentee owners. The cottages could be picked up as they came on the market and when a string of them were collected the lots could be cleared to make way for Stampede expansion.

It looked like a good idea at the time and eventually proved to be so, but it was a public relations kiss of death. It became a festering sore in the organization's side, suppurating for months stretching into years. The first complaints to surface were that the board was not moving fast enough in making offers. Then it was not paying enough. Then it was trying to drive people out of their homes, undermine the viability of the neighborhood. Then, inevitably, some civic politicians got into the act for there were votes to be harvested by sniping at the Stampede.

Worst of all, the city planners became involved and demanded that plans for Victoria Park and the Exhibition grounds be integrated with the city's urban renewal. When that could not be done because of the uproar in Victoria Park, hopes for a $12,000,000 racetrack and grandstand replacement had to be scrapped. The planners even succeeded in blocking the construction of a new horse barn on the property because of lack of a regional development plan.

Insult was finally added to injury in 1970, when under Mayor Rod Sykes, the city council voted to rescind the earlier $400,000 a year buy-out arrangement and proposed that the city buy back all the Victoria Park land the Stampede had purchased and use it to "rehabilitate" the Victoria Park neighborhood. The situation reached the point where Alderman Roy Farran accused the city council of waging guerrilla warfare against the Stampede.

Curiously enough, while all this was going on, the board was having some serious second thoughts about its own collective personality. The concern first came to a head at the annual meeting for 1967. In his retiring speech President A. T. Baker strongly urged the board to give serious and urgent attention to finding a way of bringing more younger Calgarians onto the board of directors and into more active participation in the direction of the institution. It was not that the ordinary directors themselves were overly aged. But when the honorary directors were added, the scales were tilted to those growing somewhat long in the tooth.

The following year Charles Kennedy, who succeeded Baker as president, set up a special committee headed by Neil Harvie to do a sort of royal commission job on the organization. It spent a lot of time on the problem and eventually, in 1969, brought in a series of recommendations: one to raise the number of directors to twenty-four; another to place an age limit of sixty-three years on membership on the active board; others to make substantial changes in the form and substance of the main committees; to reduce the number of chairmanships allotted to board members; to increase the importance of the non-board volunteers.

On one item, however, there was no difference of opinion. That was that the Stampede would stay in Exhibition Park and that expansion of the premises was to remain the primary goal of the Stampede organization.

CHAPTER 13

A Booming Stampede Park

Between 1949 and 1979, Calgary's population increased from 105,000 to 530,000 and attendance at the annual Calgary Exhibition and Stampede grew from 408,000 to close to 1,000,000. However, if Stampede attendance had kept pace with population growth, it would have touched 1,000,000 in patronage in 1969 and exceeded 2,100,000 by 1979. To put it another way, average daily attendance in 1949 was equal to sixty-five percent of the city's population. By 1979 it had dropped to twenty percent.

Over this particular thirty-year stretch, Stampede attendance failed to keep pace with the city's growth for two very good reasons. The first was the congestion within the Exhibition grounds (renamed Stampede Park in 1975). The second was the radical demographic change taking place within the population of Calgary and southern Alberta.

The congestion on the Stampede grounds during Stampede week had become horrendous by the mid-fifties, particularly on Fridays and Saturdays. And as the management each year increased its efforts to attract more visitors, the congestion became more confounded. The Flare Square and the free entertainment were cases in point. The entertainment brought in more people and the space needed for the free shows shrunk the standing and walking space. As time passed and the crowds grew, Calgarians naturally began to plan their visits to avoid the crowds, and

caused congestion where none had previously existed.

The idea of stretching the show to ten days had surfaced in the 1950s but nobody could figure out how to get around the dead-in-the-middle Sunday. Certainly the idea of running the show through Sunday would have been anathema to the citizenry of the Prairies in those days. True, the retreat from a stiff-necked, straightlaced society had begun, but changes were evolving at something less than breakneck speed.

By 1969 the law of diminishing returns had taken hold and the Stampede had no alternative but to move to a nine-day week. It opened on Thursday, ran full tilt Friday and Saturday, closed Sunday, restarted on Monday with the Stampede Parade, ran until Saturday night. The idea of running the horse races, midway, rodeo, and chuckwagons on Sunday was not even considered. It was only after a change in

Free entertainment in the sylvan setting of Suntree Park was the magnet for the footsore refugees from the midway.

government brought a more relaxed attitude toward the Lord's Day Act that the show was allowed to run wide open—horse races, parimutuels, midway, and all from a Friday start through two Sundays.

Within the Stampede board itself, there was little inclination to be identified with the forces of social change. For example, Alberta was a half-decade into the cocktail bar era before the board, in 1967, got around to adding a drinking lounge to its Big Four dining room. That change was over two years in the making and one into which it tippy-toed gingerly rather than with all publicity guns firing. In adding alcoholic beverages, its motivation ironically was not to increase its restaurant profits but to arrest the decline in patronage of the curling rink. Patronage had dropped sharply when other curling rinks around town began providing liquor service for after curling relaxation. By meeting the competition, the Big Four curling rink was able to recapture its lost patrons.

The attitude of the administration toward its new liquor facility was illustrated by the fact that during the first year of operation it shut down the lounge during Stampede week. The next year it decided to keep the lounge open, but not to advertise that liquor was available. Curiously enough, by this time public opinion in Calgary had moved so far that the evening show was competing for patronage with the wassailing in the downtown hotels that was turning Calgary during Stampede week into a massive pub crawl.

Demographic change within Calgary and southern Alberta was also a significant factor. The farms were doubling and redoubling in size while the farm population was declining. Calgary was evolving from the farm and ranch capital of southern Alberta into the oil capital of Canada. It was expanding its boundaries in all directions, making noises about becoming the financial capital of the West. In the process its office space became as congested as the Exhibition grounds and by 1968, building permits hit $180,000,000 on the way, a decade later, to the billion dollar level. The

Turning the ground floor of the Big Four Building into a gambling casino attracted new thousands to the Stampede in 1969. *Courtesy of Jack DeLorme Photography Ltd., Calgary.*

inflowing populace which would take up the expanding office space would profoundly change the Calgary Exhibition and Stampede's constituency.

It would become a constituency less orientated toward bucking horse riding and rodeoing than toward rock and roll music. True, the thousands of new Calgarians from Saskatchewan to Newfoundland could react as boisterously to the excitement of the chuckwagon races as the Calgarians from Tulsa, or Nanton. But the percentage of the audience that could tell the difference between a poor ride and a good ride on a bucking horse dwindled and shrank.

The urbanization of Calgarians can be seen in the conscious swing of the Calgary newspapers away from publication of news with an agricultural slant. In the 1950s the Calgary bull sale, as one example, was always the subject of extensive daily reportage. By 1970 the coverage was belated and reduced to filler dimension. This, moreover, was but a reflection of an areawide trend. In 1950 there were five

major publications covering the farm and ranch news of western Canada. By 1970 four had ceased publication.

But if the rapid change in the population was mirrored in the Stampede audience, and it was of course, the Stampede maintained the uniqueness of the entertainment it provided. None of the other major exhibitions, Klondike Days, Ottawa National, Toronto Ex, Red River Ex, or Pacific Ex at Vancouver offered what Calgary could offer. Only the Stampede with its rodeo events, chuckwagon races, and grandstand offered entertainment unobtainable anywhere else. In essence, therefore, the unending concern with setting new attendance records every year was a will-o'-the-wisp. Its irrelevancy was surely demonstrated by the dawn of the 1970s when worldwide recognition of the show's unique quality was reaching its peak.

As the "Greatest Outdoor Show On Earth," the Calgary Stampede no longer had to fight for acceptance. It became the cynosure of that blatant, boisterous new entertainment medium, television. The

CBC and CTV networks, vying to broadcast the Stampede parade, the rodeo and the chuckwagon races, had to make room for British and German television and such American network shows as *Arthur Godfrey's* and the *Wide World of Sport.* The Stampede press office regularly accredited up to three hundred correspondents from all over the world.

It was the thrill of the rodeo and chuckwagon races that captured world attention. And it was the time of the Calgary Stampede that brought the "celebrities" in droves whenever the signal went up. Thus, in 1971, Prime Minister Pierre Elliott Trudeau, then at the peak of his popularity, was the Stampede Parade Grand Marshal and Bobby Orr was the official opener of the show. Among those who turned up in Flare Square for the Salute to Sport were Gordie Howe and Ken Dryden from hockey, Al Balding and George Knudson from golf, figure skaters Karen Magnusson and Don Jackson, and Beverly Boys, the diving champion.

All the while, the directors had their sights set on (a) elevating the quality of the grandstand show, (b) finding new ways of attracting the influx of uninitiated newcomers to Calgary's oldest institution, and (c) turning the Stampede grounds into the year-round center of Calgary entertainment. On the first count, Randy Avery was honing his Young Canadians into an accomplished group of young performers that rivalled even the famous Radio City Music Hall Rockettes. Following the 1970 performance they became the featured entertainment at the Ottawa Exhibition and the Michigan State Fair. So enthusiastic did the directors become that they tore up Avery's contract and gave him a new one with a fifty percent increase in pay.

The evening grandstand show provided ninety minutes of fast moving and crowd-pleasing variety acts interspersed with the Young Canadians. The quality may be judged by the reviews of Jamie Portman, the entertainment editor of the Calgary *Herald,* who on three successive years, wrote that the production was the best ever seen at the Stampede.

On the second count, Calgary turned to Edmonton for an inspirational ten-strike. In 1969 Edmonton obtained permission from the government to operate a Las Vegas type gambling concession at its Klondike Days. Not only did the experiment run off without a single untoward incident, but it turned a whopping profit. Calgary, watching from the sidelines, shouted, "Hey, me too!" and rushed to clear out the ground floor of the Big Four Building in 1969 and turn it into a blackjack, roulette, and crown and anchor casino. It went farther. It decided to stage a $100,000 Sweepstakes on the 1970 running of the Calgary Futurity Horse Race. It was fashioned after the Irish Hospitals Sweepstakes which for forty years had been a popular, if illegal, gambling pastime for hundreds of thousands of Canadians.

To operate its Sweepstakes, the Stampede went into a partnership with forty province-wide charities which sold tickets on a commission basis. The winners split a $100,000 prize on the results of the running of the Calgary Futurity for two year olds on September 5. To milk the event of the last drop of excitement, the board arranged to draw twenty-five tickets on the Wednesday before the race. On race day, Saturday, eight of these tickets were drawn for the eight horses in the race. Appropriately, the Saturday draw was made by Mrs. Mary English, the Calgary hospital worker who had run a nation-wide, one-woman crusade for the legalization of hospital lotteries in Canada similar to the Irish Sweepstakes.

The race was won by Brandy Magic, a 13 to 1 shot, owned by R. J. Bennett, a son of Hon. W. A. C. Bennett, premier of British Columbia. It enriched Harold Tooth, a Medicine Hat welder, by $60,000. Second prize was $15,000, third was $7,000, and fifty lesser amounts were awarded. After distributing $100,000 to the charities in sales commissions and $46,000 for expenses, the Stampede earned a whopping $254,000 profit on the event, enabling it to double the prize money in 1971. The Sweepstakes continued to pour increasing profits into the Stampede coffers until 1976 when it was superseded by the Western Express.

On the year-round utilization of the facilities, the management had reached the point where it was prepared to try anything once. It brought in rock and roll bands, established a rodeo college headed by Winston Bruce, staged an annual indoor rodeo—Rodeo Royal. One of its greatest successes ever was the staging of the World Figure Skating Championships in 1972.

Night harness racing was introduced. The thoroughbred racing season was extended. Although Calgary hockey fans never suffered losers gladly, the Corral filled up whenever junior or senior hockey teams put extended skeins of winning games together. Between hockey games, the Corral hosted the Ice Capades, the Russian and Shrine Circuses, Boy Scout Jamborees, and International Arabian and light horse shows.

After watching the promotional gyrations of the World Hockey Association from afar for several years, the board made a deal with Jim Pattison to bring the Vancouver Blazers, née the Philadelphia Blazers, to the Corral for the 1975–76 season. The renamed Calgary Cowboys managed to attract crowds of between four to five thousand but with highly inflated salaries and a killing schedule, the Cowboys never began to break even and were disbanded after a couple of seasons.

Back in 1970 the Kinsmen Club, which had been operating the car lotteries at the Stampede, decided to plow some of its income back into the show. It sponsored the construction of the $500,000 Kinsmen Youth Center. Over the next decade, it would prove a well-used facility during the Stampede and in the year-round activities. It became the home of the Dinner Theatre which Randy Avery pioneered in Calgary and which enjoyed considerable success during the early 1970s. Contributing to that success was the new Food Service Department which the Stampede set up after the death of Roy Beavers in 1968. Beavers had operated the food concessions from the early days of the old Arena and had served as an associate director for more than forty years.

Once the management got the hang of running a food catering business, it expanded in all directions. For almost fifty years the race track concession had been farmed out to the Marks family of Winnipeg. It too was taken over and became part of the food services department. From a net income of $95,137 in 1969, the first full year of operations, the department earned a profit of $165,437 in 1971 and $483,460 in 1979, at the end of its first decade of operations. Gross sales increased from $1,366,081 in 1971 to $3,320,318. Most of the credit for the profit bonanza derived from the expansion of food and liquor sales in the new grandstand facility. Eventually it was the grandstand profits on food and liquor that converted red ink into black ink on the horse racing books. In 1979, to take one example, the combined loss on the thoroughbred and harness racing operations was $263,871 while the net concession income from the racing department exceeded $274,000.

To compete with the downtown hotels during Stampede week for the beer drinking trade, the Stampede opened the "Prairie Schooner" in the Big Four Building in 1971. It was such a successful moneymaker that it was moved into the Corral the next year and billed as "the world's largest saloon." On opening day, it attracted 4,600 patrons who consumed 1,725 dozen beer. The following year "the world's largest saloon" had nothing but trouble and it was ultimately closed in favor of an expanded exhibition of arts, crafts, and homemaking demonstrations.

Beer, however, continued to figure largely in the operation. In 1971 Oktoberfest was launched with 150 Bavarian performers imported from Germany, tables laden with German food and copious quantities of Canadian beer. Oktoberfest played to better than 24,700 during a six-day run and became a regular fall feature until 1976.

Except for the Kinsmen Center and a new horse barn, the Stampede's expansion plans had been pretty much on hold since the Lincoln Park trouble. But the land purchasing program in Victoria Park had been going forward steadily and work was proceeding on a master plan to incorporate the property north of Seventeenth Avenue into the Stampede Park operation. On September 9, 1971, President Ed O'Connor and Vice-President George Crawford, unveiled a $20,000,000 master plan. It called for a new race track and grandstand to be completed by 1975; a trade center and arts center north of the Corral; and an agricul-

The completion of the new grandstand provided improved accommodation for Stampede patrons and racing fans, including restaurant facilities and a glassed-in area making year-round operation possible. It also made it possible to move the Indian Village to more commodious quarters across the Elbow River in a parklike setting. *Courtesy of the Calgary Stampede.*

tural complex on the northeast corner of the property.

Aside from the opposition from the city planners, the master plan received widespread approval. Construction, of course, would have to await the raising of necessary finances. The financial hurdle was partly cleared in 1972 as follows: a low interest loan was obtained from the Canadian government for $4,000,000. Alberta guaranteed a further loan from the Bank of Montreal for $6,000,000 and the balance of $2,500,000 would come from Stampede earnings. This $12,500,000, later raised to $14,000,000, would buy a new five-eighths-mile race track, a new barn to house 624 horses and—

The grandstand, beneath its graceful, cable suspended roof will feature an unobstructed view for 16,000 patrons, escalator service to all floors, excellent lounge and restaurant facilities, large parimutuel areas and an exciting stepped restaurant for race fans who wish a full view of the track while dining. The grandstand in its final stage will offer a glass enclosed clubhouse and air conditioning for year round comfort.

By the time the actual expansion plans were moved front and center, some important changes had taken place at the administration level. Irven Parsons moved from general manager to executive vice-presi-

dent, prior to his departure to become chairman of the Alberta Racing Commission. Bill Pratt took over as general manager and Tom Hall remained as assistant general manager. Prior to joining the Stampede organization in 1968, Pratt had been a project manager for Burns and Dutton-Standard Gravel and had supervised the construction of the Chinook Shopping Center, Heritage Park, and other large projects. The directors were convinced his experience would be invaluable in ramming through the construction of the new race track complex between one Stampede and the next.

Eleven months, almost to the day, after the conclusion of the 1973 Stampede, the new grandstand and racing plant were finished, a tremendous accomplishment, given the shortage of skilled tradesmen then developing in Calgary. On the Sunday before the 1974 show, the directors proudly opened the new facility for public inspection and almost 50,000 Calgarians turned out for the occasion. The public response to what Jim Coleman called Calgary Stampede's Taj Mahal was overwhelming and similar enthusiasm greeted the construction of the Kinsmen Elbow River Park on the south bank of the Elbow and the Sun Tree free entertainment center near the main entrance gate.

Four rainy days and an intruding federal election kept the 1974 attendance from matching the 1973 record of 993,000 by a mere 20,000 but 1974 on all other counts was the best show ever. The honorary parade marshals were famed the world over. Douglas Bader, the legless British Air Force hero of World War II rubbed shoulders with Punch Dickens, the Canadian ace from World War I and pioneer developer of northern aviation, and Eugene Cernan, the American astronaut and last man to walk on the surface of the moon. A prime attraction in the Flare Square "Salute to Aviation" was a number of artifacts of the United States space program. Also featured in the aviation exhibit was a model of the Silver Dart in which J. A. McCurdy made the first heavier-than-air flight in Canada in 1909. The RCAF Snowbirds acrobatic team contributed a spectacular salute to aviation to emphasize the theme of the year.

Across the tarmac from Flare Square in the Livestock Pavilion, records were being broken almost by the hour in the first ever Exotic Cattle Show and Sale. At the Canadian International Simmental sale, seventy-one cattle sold for a cool $1,000,000. Later in the week at the eighth world sale of Charolais cattle, a breeder paid John Rudiger of Calgary $81,000 for a quarter interest for six months of the year in his bull named Cadet Roussel. That would have put the value of the bull at $648,000. The sale of forty-two head of Limousin cattle grossed $350,000 while seventy-three Maine-Anjou animals grossed $988,950.

The official opening of the new facility as a thoroughbred racing complex, was celebrated on July 1 although racing actually began on June 20. The official ceremonies featured Canada's preeminent racing patron, E. P. Taylor of Toronto. Fittingly, the feature race of the day, the Calgary Maturity Stakes, was won by Charlie Bowlen's four year old, Ace Return. Bowlen, a former Rocky Mountain guide and outfitter, had long been a participant at Calgary horse shows and Stampedes.

The Stampede officials had, of course, expected there would be problems of ironing out the inevitable wrinkles that would become apparent in a facility of such magnitude built in so short a time. None was prepared for the shower of brickbats that flew from the horse players and horse owners; and flew, and flew, and flew!

The horse owners and horse players naturally had assumed that the race track and club house had been designed with them in mind. Both were instantly disabused of any such notion.

The most expensive seats in the house for afternoon events—six dollars—were in the clubhouse where there were no parimutuel wickets. So the horse players had to fight their way down to the floor below to place their bets, back up to their seats to watch the races, then down again to cash their bets. Worse, there were wickets for two dollar bettors and five dollar players but none anywhere for fifty dollar bettors, and the delays at the two dollar wickets were horrendous. To exacerbate the frustration of the punters, the parimutuel odds board was infested with gremlins, kept

posting odds that had no relationship to what the winning horses paid.

The complaints of the thoroughbred owners were more fundamental and were concerned with almost everything about the race track. Built as it was hard by the Elbow River, drainage problems were inevitable because of the high water table. To solve these problems, the English architect who designed the track specified that a course of loose rock and gravel be spread below the surface loam to carry away excessive moisture. Rain would then filter down from the surface and away through the gravel bed. Nobody explained to the English architect what every farm boy in western Canada knew from infancy: alternate freezing and thawing brings stones to the surface. Upwardly mobile stones became an instant threat to the tender soles of thoroughbred feet.

The five-eighth-mile oval was fitted with an extension chute on the northwest turn. In theory it would permit the running of seven furlong races, a popular distance. Unhappily, the location of the chute caused a funnelling effect as the horses were forced to head for the center of the track from both the inside and outside stalls of the starting gate. In addition to the ever-present threat to life and limb of jockeys and horses, the funnelling prevented the horses from running true to form, which angered horse players and horse owners alike.

That was only the beginning. The saddling paddock, in any case too small, was enclosed by a concrete wall against which horses could be injured. Finally, the winners circle was placed around the corner of the grandstand where it was hidden from the view of the horse players.

The introduction of the so-called "exotic breeds" from Europe changed the cattle industry of the West. One of the breeds that had the greatest impact was the Charolais. One of the super-Charolais was the bull Cadet Roussel owned by Mr. and Mrs. John Rudiger on the right who sold an interest in Cadet for six months of the year to Mr. and Mrs. R. Vandekerkhove of Burnaby, B.C. in 1974. *Photograph by Browarny. Courtesy of Rudiger Ranches Ltd.*

When all these deficiencies were called to the management's attention at a pre-opening press conference, Bill Pratt refused to concede anything on the grounds that the "administration's interest first, last and always was the Stampede" and that "the horse races are strictly of secondary consideration."

When the horse players among the directors got into the act, wholesale changes were ordered. A dozen betting windows were installed on the club house floor as well as outside the grandstand. The winner's circle was moved to the front of the grandstand. The saddling paddock was doubled in size. But of the seven furlong chute, there was nothing to be done. The jockeys refused to ride in seven furlong races. As for the track surface itself, it would remain a bone of contention for years to come as the freezing-thawing kept bringing stones to the surface.

The disenchantment with the new facility spread to the general public when they discovered the scale of admission prices for the reserved seats in the grandstand ranged from three dollars for the poorest seats in the afternoon to seventeen dollars for the best clubhouse seats at night. General admission to the grandstand enclosure for standing room only was two dollars. The scale evoked a comment from Mayor Rod Sykes, an inveterate, in-season-and-out critic of the Stampede Board, that the Stampede had grown far too expensive and commercial.

Below the surface that week, it seemed that Murphy's Law was coming into play, that anything that could go wrong would go wrong. It started with the grandstand odds board, then five casino employees were arrested for cheating. A flare from a stunting airplane fell on the nearby city pole yard and ignited a fifty-thousand-dollar fire. A spectacular pile-up on the rollercoaster on the midway injured half a dozen people.

Despite these vicissitudes, however, 1974 broke all previous financial records. Gross receipts soared to $12,013,000 compared with the $9,485,000 in 1973. Net operating income reached $2,598,723 compared with $2,446,000. Stampede attendance came within 20,000 of equalling the all-time gate record of 993,000 in 1973,

when the attendance of Queen Elizabeth and the Duke of Edinburgh helped break the previous record by 100,000.

Unhappily, some of the gloss on the profit and loss statement was dulled by the inclusion of a couple of other items for the first time: interest payments of $388,736 and depreciation of $872,624. When administration costs of $631,994 and maintenance and promotion costs were taken into account, net income from operations shrank to $100,926.

In his annual report for 1974, President Jerry D'Arcy took particular pains to point out that, with the construction of the new facilities, the institution was leaving one era behind and entering one that was new and fraught with hazards:

In a few short years our gross revenue has increased four times to an all time high in 1974 of almost $12 million. Without any debt factor we would be probably the healthiest organization of our kind in the world. However, facilities so dearly needed cost money. The type of facilities required are of such magnitude, for example, our new grandstand, that they must be financed on a long term basis. This financing must be tied on a long term basis on our ability to pay through the funds generated on our year-round operations. It is for this reason that future Boards of Directors, Committee Chairmen, our staff and Finance Committee must all share in the future responsibility of living within our financial resources.

The days when the organization could finance its expansion out of earnings were long gone. But it is doubtful that the prophesying president had even the foggiest notion of the impact skyrocketing interest rates would have upon the company finances within a decade.

Meanwhile, with at least one eye focused on the debt and interest problem, the general admission price was raised to $1.50 from $1.00 for the 1975 show. Marking the centennial of the arrival of the North West Mounted Police and the birth of Fort Calgary, its Flare Square theme was "Building Together" and featured a superb historical exhibition and display. Composer Allen Rae choreographed a special ballet presentation for the Kinsmen Center. A children's show *Ready, Steady, Go!* achieved the ultimate in artistic compliments when it was invited to perform at the Stratford Festival.

Not only was 1975 an artistic high water mark, it was a financial success as well, largely because in that year the institution reached maturity as a year-round entertainment center. Gross income soared to $15,597,000 from all sources of which only $4,571,000 was generated by the Stampede. Thoroughbred racing grossed $3,431,000 and harness racing $891,000. Food and liquor service brought in $2,126,000, the Corral grossed $912,000, and the Big Four Building $373,000.

Traffic into the park for all events exceeded 3,000,000 of which 600,000 attended the Big Four Building, 582,000 the Corral and 566,000 went to the races. But when net income was examined, it was still the Stampede itself which turned the greatest profit—$1,747,000—and subsidized much of the other activity. The $3,431,000 gross from the thoroughbreds melted to a net of only $138,000 while the harness races actually lost $127,000.

One interesting aspect of the evolving operation was the way in which it was coming more and more to rely on its gambling profits. Thus in 1975, the casino and lotteries netted $646,289 and the midway revenue totalled $208,933. Together they exceeded the $795,000 net income from general admissions. These facts became germane to the 1975 show because, a week after it closed, the RCMP moved in on the Royal American Shows at the Edmonton Klondike Days and seized all its books and records, on suspicion of tax fraud. That marked the end of the Canadian operation of the Royal American Shows, which had been a fixture on the western fair circuit for over thirty years. Ultimately the show was convicted in Regina of income tax evasion and heavily fined.

In its place, the western fair circuit, including Calgary, chose an Ontario carnival company owned by the Conklin family of Brantford. That change led to a spectacular improvement in the Stampede's share of the midway revenue. From $208,000 in 1975 it jumped to $502,000 in 1976, an indication surely that something

more than mere tax juggling had been taking place in the Royal American Shows' counting house. But, because of the multiplicity of its other activities in the gambling area, midway profit was no longer as vital to the financial health of the operation as it had once been.

Though it really was a super show, the 1975 Stampede was a disappointment of sorts when the attendance fell almost 100,000 below the 1973 peak after it was fully expected that with the new $15,000,000 grandstand in place, it would exceed a million and do it with plenty to spare. In the inevitable post-mortems along the Eighth Avenue Mall, a public consensus developed that "what the Stampede needs is more big names."

The directors were not convinced but they decided to go along with the consensus. And with a vengeance! Helen Reddy, then at the peak of her fame—known around the world for her "I am Woman" song—was booked for two shows on Monday of Stampede week 1976. Bob Hope was brought in, for $25,000 plus a piece of the gross, on Tuesday. On Wednesday Bobby Vinton was in for two shows and Charlie Rich, the biggest name in country music, filled the bill on Thursday. Hope sold the Corral for one performance and picked up a cheque for $33,000. Helen Reddy played two performances to a half-empty Corral. At one of Vinton's two shows, barely 1,000 customers showed up. Charlie Rich, despite the size of his name, drew only 3,100. Obviously, while Calgarians talked big about big names, they could take them or leave them, mostly the latter.

Perhaps the hardest cut of all for the directors was the coming to a head of the horse owners' antagonism toward racing at the Stampede, even with the expensive new facility being provided. The pent-up antagonism burst into flame one afternoon in 1975 when an angry Brahma bull jumped the barricade that separated the rodeo infield from the race track, just as the horses were entering the starting gate for the fifth race. Radio broadcaster, Joe Carbury saw what had happened, grabbed the public address microphone, and screamed to the race starter to hold the gate. If the race had started with the

One of the best buckers, over a period of several years, was Arsenic and on this occasion he was meeting his match in one of the all-time stars of the Stampede infield events, Larry Mahan. Arsenic's status was such that he rated his own fancy halter with his name inscribed. *Courtesy of the Calgary Stampede.*

rampaging bull on the track, injury or death would have awaited horses and jockeys when they sped toward the enraged animal. Fortunately, the starting gate was kept shut until the bull was herded to safety.

That event got the horsemen putting together a bill of particulars and threatening to boycott the Stampede. The track, they claimed, was seriously damaged by the chuckwagons. The events in the centerfield frightened the race horses. So, they said, did the noise of the fireworks at night. So did the inability of the administration to

keep the spectators off the track. The presence of the Brahma bull was the last vexation.

In the end, the Stampede board had to listen and after the 1976 season, the thoroughbred races were dropped from the annual Stampede. And therein lay another reason why the attendance failed to keep pace with population growth. From both the decline in the afternoon attendance following the dropping of the races, and the attendance at the races themselves, this fact emerged: day in and day out, there were between three and four thousand

inveterate horse players in Calgary who over the years had gone to the Stampede to bet on the races, not to watch wild cows being milked or bulls being wrestled. Indeed, most horse players completely ignored the infield events and probably shared the horse owners' antipathy toward the combination program. With the dropping of the horse races, they had no reason to attend and thirty to forty thousand paid admissions were lost over the ten days of the Stampede.

Still, the eight-race horse race card interspersed with the rodeo events un-questionably added zest to the afternoon entertainment for the ordinary spectators, even though the races of themselves did not bring many non-addicts into the grandstand enclosure. The presence of the horse races was another feature which made the Stampede unique entertainment.

The departure of the horse races from the Stampede and the completion of the larger grandstand had another unfavorable impact on attendance. In order to assure themselves an adequate supply of good seats, Calgarians for years had reserved their seats early. This frequently resulted

How it all began—with wild horses and determined cowboys. *Courtesy of the Calgary Stampede.*

in many business firms ending up with unused tickets. As it became general knowledge that the "famine factor" no longer applied, sell-outs became less and less frequent either for the afternoon or evening shows, and eventually became a rarity.

Divorced from the afternoon rodeo, thoroughbred racing was combined with harness racing and turned into a year-round sport for Albertans, with half a year in Calgary and the other half in Edmonton. Though the harness races never equalled the runners in either attendance or betting volume, wagering on both became quickly reflective of the inflationary spiral then beginning to grip Calgary. While the daily average attendance at the thoroughbred races remained constant, wagering increased by thirty percent over a four-year stretch; the harness racing betting average rose by seventy percent.

And that was about par for the growth of Calgary expectations, including those of the Calgary Stampede directors. As the city population was nudging the 500,000 mark, the city council laid plans to accommodate a city of 1,000,000. The modifications of the new grandstand were hardly completed before the directors were setting their sights on their next megaproject. The urgent need to improve the facilities for livestock shows and sales had come to a head with the holding of the World Hereford Congress at the 1976 Stampede. Hereford breeders from all over the world held a convention at Banff and then staged their show during the Stampede. That demonstrated how unsatisfactory the Corral was for such a show.

As the board of directors grew over the years from a dozen members to fifteen, to twenty to twenty four, the representation of the farming-ranching community diminished while that of Calgary business and professional circles increased. This shift might have been a factor in the discussion which occurred during the early 1970s about dropping the livestock shows from the Stampede. Or it may have been a reaction to the complaining of the livestock exhibitors about the congestion they had to contend with at the Stampede. In any event, whether livestock continued to be included, or was dropped, something had

to be done. So in the spring of 1977, the Stanford Research Foundation of California was hired by the board to supply $75,000 worth of proposals of how to proceed "to re-establish Stampede Park as the showcase of agricultural leadership of Western Canada."

While the Stanford experts were probing and pondering, the 1977 show went on with the usual format. The Stampede Parade was moved from Monday to Friday, starting day of the show. The theme of 1977 honored the Alberta Indians on the hundredth anniversary of the signing of Treaty Seven. Prince Charles and Prince Andrew came out to visit the Indian reserves, lead seven major chiefs in all their regalia in the parade, and officially opened the show. In their new Indian village south of the river, the Indians pitched twice as many teepees as ever before. The Arts Alive exhibition featured Indian women's work and demonstrations of the kind of enterprise being fostered on the reserves. These included mobile home construction, golf course development, and garment manufacturing by the Bloods, Peigans, and Sarcees.

Most of all there was Midnight Madness. As a salute to youth, it was decided to offer a night-long, go-on-as-many-rides-as-you-like deal for a flat fee of five dollars. Anticipating a crowd of perhaps five or ten thousand, nobody was prepared for the fifty-eight thousand that stormed the gates and jammed the ride entry points ten deep until dawn. For those who could not get to the rides, rock and roll bands played themselves into exhaustion.

The report of the Stanford researchers was unveiled in December 1977 and it confirmed what everybody had known—the facilities were inadequate for many of the primary purposes of the Calgary Exhibition and Stampede. The Big Four Building, for example, was built primarily as an exhibits building, but was seldom available for major exhibitions when it was needed. The main recommendation was to build a combination agricultural building and exhibits building for a cost of about $14,000,000. A 15,000-seat hockey arena might be made part of a master plan for later construction at a cost of $33,000,000 though it was felt an NHL franchise could be obtained with 11,000 seating capacity.

The board of directors opted immediately for the agriculture complex and mounted a campaign to pry money to pay for it out of the government of Alberta. That proved to be easier than anyone had expected because with skyrocketing oil prices, as a result of the Israeli-Egyptian war, a torrent of money was pouring into Alberta's Heritage Resources Trust Fund. The government made subsidization of the agricomplex part of a $40,000,000 gift to southern Alberta exhibitions. It donated $7,250,000 outright, agreed to guarantee a loan for half the balance, and offered a gift of 1.5 percent of the mutuel play to help the Stampede board pay off the loan.

While the architects were designing the new building, the board dropped the agri-cultural exhibits from the 1978 show in favor of a separate March "Round-Up '78," designed as a sort of springtime cross between the Toronto Royal Winter Fair and the Regina Agribition. It began with the annual bull sale, swung into a week-long agricultural show and machinery exhibition, and concluded with the Rodeo Royal which had now become a regular spring feature at Stampede Park.

Round-up '78 was an unmixed financial disaster and cost the board $278,000. The spring was obviously the wrong time for a livestock show. The exhibitors of machinery and farm supplies were too busy getting ready for spring selling to have time for exhibitions and Calgarians stayed away in droves. It was only when the Round-Up was later moved to October that its potential was fully realized.

General Managers of the Calgary Stampede 1907-1985

E. L. Richardson, 1907–1940

J. Charles Yule, 1940–1951

Maurice Hartnett, 1951–1965

I. W. Parsons, 1965–1970

Wm. Pratt, 1970–1979

Don Jacques, 1980–

CHAPTER 14

Toward the Twenty-first Century

I n the summer of 1978 Casey Tibbs returned to the Calgary Stampede after an absence of twenty years. The one-time king of the bronc riders came back, however, not with his riding gear but with an idea. He was promoting a new concept in rodeoing—team rodeo. The contests would no longer be between individual performers vying against each other but between teams representing cities or areas in organized leagues.

Tibbs was trying to do for the rodeo sport what had already been done for baseball, football, tennis, hockey, basketball—put professional franchises together in an organized league. Tibbs collided with the Canadian Rodeo Cowboys' Association who wanted no part of his proposal and he returned to the States empty-handed.

Or did he? In February, 1979, the Stampede issued a press release to announce a change in the format of the Stampede. It was going to adopt the team concept for the 1979 show! Behind that decision, however, was not the promotional drum-beating of Casey Tibbs but the coming to a head of the new aggressiveness of the cowboy's union, the aforementioned Canadian Rodeo Cowboys' Association. This aggressiveness, moreover, was in turn a part of a trend among athletes generally of demanding a greater say in how entertainment box office receipts were shared

between entrepreneurs and those providing the attraction.

In the United States the development of baseball, football, and basketball players' unions with high-priced and skilled negotiators had led to soaring athletic salaries. In Canada the impact had been upon hockey players' salaries with the organization of the World Hockey League which lured superstar Bobby Hull away from the Chicago Black Hawks with a million-dollar subsidy.

In rodeo there were two notable trends. The sport was making great strides in popularity and in the star quality of its top performers.

The day when the rodeo performers learned the rudiments of bronc riding and steer roping as ordinary ranch hands was long gone. In the southern states, rodeo riding was gaining a place on physical education programs in the colleges. In

A historic moment in the history of the Calgary Bull Sale is captured in the spacious new Roundup Centre. The bull in the sales ring is lot #424, the Leisen and Klein contribution that sold for $280,000. *Photograph by Browarny. Courtesy of Hereford Digest.*

addition, there were rodeo riding schools at which ambitious riders could gain instruction from veterans of the professional circuits, like the one established in Calgary by Winston Bruce.

As the sport spread in popularity, and the performers became more skilled, competition became keener. It became a frequent occurrence for some of the top riders to compete in two rodeos simultaneously, flying from one to the other between go-arounds. As a result of all this, while the prize money being offered rose steadily, the cost of competing, for the cowboys, rose even faster. And in no area was the cost squeeze as acute as it was for the chuckwagon competitors.

The chuckwagon sport boomed in popularity, while the length of the competing season increased. From three or four rodeos a year they were now on the road most of the summer and working a dozen or more events. That fact alone sent their costs through the roof. As the competition became keener, faster and faster horses were needed, which meant costlier and costlier horses. Their higher tensioned thoroughbreds, which alone could stand the gaff, were prone to all the injuries to which the race horses were heir. A chuckwagon outfit which started the season with eight horses in top form might run through twenty-five or thirty animals before the season ended.

Throughout the 1970s the inevitable result of all this was mounting agitation for increased purses and to have the amount of purse money offered tied to gate receipts. In this the cowboys were not alone. The thoroughbred owners were also on the prowl for more purse money and in 1974 staged a ten-day strike to enforce their demands. After a three-year freeze on rodeo purses the board approved an increase of five percent in 1977 and an additional eight percent in 1978. Neither increase came within a country mile of the kind of boost the cowboys wanted.

In 1978, when the riders and drivers checked what the situation was in other fields, they became more disenchanted than ever. In the World Hockey Association, then floundering toward financial

disaster, player salaries absorbed eighty-five percent of the gate receipts. In Canadian football the players got up to fifty percent of the gate receipts. In the National Hockey League in 1977 players' salaries absorbed fifty-three percent of gross revenues, compared with only thirty-two percent five years before.

In 1978 the rodeo cowboys decided that they wanted purses tied to gate receipts. For the 1979 season they demanded twenty-nine percent of the afternoon grandstand gate and thirty-three percent of the grandstand gate for the evening performances. On the basis of the 1978 receipts, that would have meant a total of $197,583 for the rodeo events and $255,243 for the

chuckwagons. Not only that, the cowboys insisted that they should also have a voice in setting the admission prices to the events in which they were the attraction.

During the bargaining the Stampede board came up with a proposal that would both regularize the sponsorship of wagons and add substantially, it was hoped, to the income of the chuckwagon owners. For many years prominent businessmen had "rented the canvas" on the rigs of the most prominent drivers. Johnny Phelan of Red Deer and Cliff Cross and Peter Bawden of Calgary were pioneers in that activity. It was however a hit-or-miss, winner-take-all proposition for the drivers. The top drivers could get sponsorship while the others could not. The board proposed that the rights to putting names on the chuck-wagons should be auctioned off to the highest bidders. When the auction was introduced in 1979 bids ranged from $1,550 to $3,400 and averaged $2,036 for the nineteen rigs which eventually participated. The rig auction idea, however, despite the substantial sum it would raise, was very much a minor issue as far as the cowboys were concerned.

By Christmas, 1978, the attitude of both sides had so hardened that a strike by the CRCA seemed inevitable. Before it came, an agreement was signed with the North American Finals Rodeo Commission to supply competitors for the rodeo events and the chuckwagon races. The cowboys made arrangements to stage a rodeo of

The Stampede Marching Band, under the direction of Robert Eklund, has become a featured grandstand attraction at the annual Stampede. It also provides more than seventy-five young Calgarians with a year-round outlet for their musical talents. *Courtesy of the Calgary Stampede.*

A sometimes added attraction, when the buffalo are available and the Indian boys are eager, is the buffalo riding championship. The lumbering one-time monarchs of the plains don't buck like Brahma bulls, but every now and then one of them puts on a real bucking exhibition, like the one in the middle. *Courtesy of the Calgary Stampede.*

Of all the Stampede events, none puts a greater premium on physical strength and muscular coordination than Brahma bull riding. Nor does any event exceed it in the danger it poses to the participants. This superb ride by Cody Snyder helped him win the World's Bull Riding Championship of 1983. *Courtesy of the Calgary Stampede.*

their own in High River in competition with Calgary for about a quarter of the purse money offered in Calgary.

The residue of bitterness that flowed from the strike undoubtedly affected attendance at the 1979 show. It was down forty thousand compared with 1978. As for the change in Stampede format, a survey conducted over three days seemed to indicate that the team format was acceptable to the majority of the rodeo fans. Those who liked the format outnumbered those who did not by 55 percent to 22 percent. As for the rodeo events, 48 percent gave the overall performance a grade of excellent, 34 percent marked them good, and only 10 percent gave them a marking of fair.

The collision of the cowboys and the Stampede management probably could not have been avoided, given the context of the times. Having the former stars of the Calgary Stampede running their own bush-league rodeo in High River in competition with the Stampede was hardly a public relations triumph for either. Nevertheless 1980 saw a repetition of the previous year and then a sort of Mexican stand-off was arranged in 1981.

In that year there were two separate rodeos at the Calgary Stampede, one with $150,400 in purses, including entry fees, for the NARC cowboys and the other with $123,000 in purses and fees for the CPRA cowboys. There were also $28,340 in prizes for cross entries in minor events. Perma-

A feat of strength in the wild horse race. *Photograph by Jack DeLorme, Courtesy of the Calgary Stampede.*

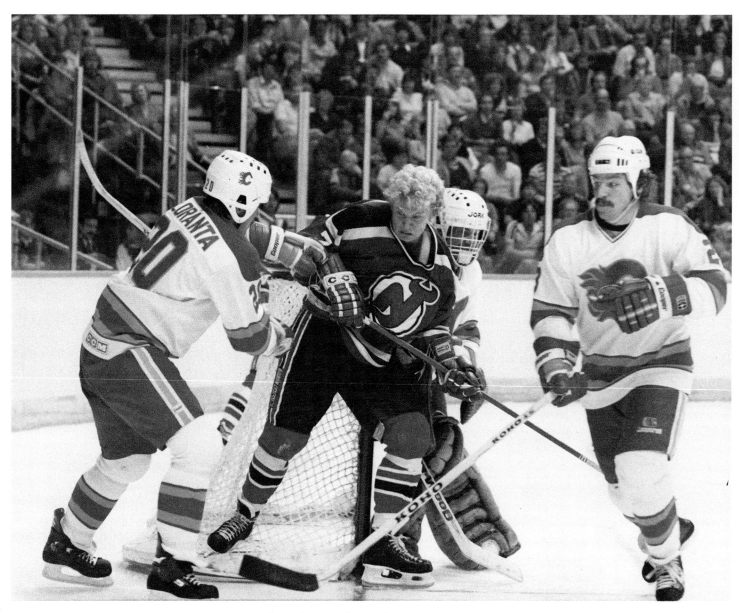

The Flames come home to the Saddledome. *Courtesy of the Calgary Stampede.*

nent peace returned to Stampede Park in 1982 when the total purse of $500,000 was offered to the CPRA cowboys. Nor was that all. The auctioning of advertising space on the chuckwagon canvas covers was turning into a fabulous bonanza for the top outfits. The auction grossed $245,000 in addition to the $175,000 in purses offered for chuckwagon races alone.

But all this is ahead of the story.

The strike and the attendant bitterness aside, 1979 was indeed a vintage year for the Calgary Exhibition and Stampede. An all-time record for gross revenue was established at $23,965,478 while net operating income was $1,918,119. The latter figure represented an improvement of

$176,000 over 1978.

As the decade of the 1970s wound down, the greatest boom in Calgary history was zooming toward its peak. Almost overnight, the central core of the city was being transformed into a thicket of twenty-five and thirty-storey skyscrapers. Not to be outdone, the Stampede board was putting the finishing touches on its own plans for a king-sized exhibits building which would become the focus for its agricultural activities. This Roundup Centre quickly became the center for a cluster of other construction, including a plus-fifteen entry from the LRT to the Corral and eventually to the Saddledome.

Of equal importance to the future of

The Saddledome in perspective. The summer of 1983 saw a frantic scramble to complete the Olympic Saddledome in time for the 1983–84 National Hockey League season. The finishing touches to the exterior and landscaping were still being added a year later. On the left of the Saddledome is the Stampede Corral with the new Roundup Centre beyond. On the center right is the Victoria Park residential district, one of the city's earliest residential developments going back to the turn of the century. Beyond is the downtown concentration of skyscrapers of which only the Calgary Tower in the center is more than twenty years old as most of the construction took place in the 1970s. *ABL Photograph. Courtesy of the Calgary Stampede.*

Calgary and the Calgary Stampede were a number of seemingly unrelated incidents that were occurring while the Roundup Centre was going up. To wit:

(A) In far off Atlanta, Georgia, one Tom Cousans was involved in an on-again, off-again effort to find a buyer, or a new home for, his Atlanta Flames National Hockey League team;

(B) Frank King and Robert Nevin, doodling on a tablecloth during a Booster Club luncheon in the fall of 1978, were wondering if it was not about time to resuscitate the long dormant Calgary Olympic Development Committee and make a run to bring the 1988 Winter Olympics to Calgary;

(C) Darryl K. (Doc) Seaman, in the upper levels of a Bow Valley Industries executive suite, was trying to hatch an idea. An incurable hockey buff (he was a governor of the first Hockey Canada Foundation that Charles Hay had established years before), Seaman wanted to put some sort of foundation together to bring a National Hockey League team to Calgary and use part of the profits to subsidize the Olympic team as well as amateur hockey in Calgary; and

(D) The Calgary Sports Advisory Committee was polishing up its arrangements for building a 17,000-seat hockey facility in Calgary to accommodate the 1988 Winter Olympics, if, as, and when . . .

The completion of the new grandstand and the construction of the Saddledome necessitated another movement of the Indian Village, this time across the Elbow into the commodious and parklike setting on the south side of the river. *Courtesy of the Calgary Stampede.*

Everything came together with a bang in 1979. The campaign to bring the Winter Olympics to Calgary in 1988 was launched and carried through to ultimate success. The construction of a new seventeen-thousand-seat hockey rink, to be financed jointly by the city, the province, and the federal government was approved. Doc Seaman and his brother B. J. filtered their NHL team proposal through Peter Lougheed's ear and got his stamp of approval. It was that they would buy an NHL team, move it to Calgary, and for the next ten years allocate half the profits to the Olympic team and amateur hockey in Calgary. With a green light and pat on the back from the government, the Seamans set off to buy the Atlanta Flames, a team that could be moved to Calgary without having to get prior approval from the NHL Board of Governors.

Tom Cousans turned out to be a horse-trader of the old school, adept at playing one buyer against another, even when there was no "other." The Seamans several times came almost to the point of concluding a deal when Cousans would back off and demand a better offer. Before the Seamans hove into view, Cousans had never heard of Calgary. But when he did, he sent emissaries north where they discovered the Stampede Corral and the Calgary Exhibition and Stampede.

While Cousans was negotiating in Atlanta to sell the Flames to the Seamans, his agents in Calgary were negotiating a lease for the Corral so he could retain ownership of the team. When rumors of the possibility of the Flames coming to Calgary reached the local media, public pressure mounted on the Stampede board to land the Flames at any cost. The result was that substantial concessions not common to other such deals were offered to Cousans for the Flames.

Then, at the eleventh hour of negotiations, a brand new player parachuted into the action. Apprised of the fact that a new king-sized hockey rink was in the works for Calgary, Nelson Skalbania decided to bring his promotional genius to bear on getting an NHL hockey team for Calgary. First, before he approached Cousans, he did a deal with the Molson Brewery to sell it the television rights to the Flames' Calgary home games for $600,000 a year for ten years, payable in advance. Thus loaded, he flew to Atlanta and bought the Flames from under the noses of the Seaman brothers. Then he arrived at Stampede Park to sign the lease on the Corral which the Flames' previous owner had negotiated with the Calgary Stampede.

Negotiating with Skalbania was a wall-climbing experience for the Stampede executives, but eventually a deal was struck and the contract signed on May 22, 1980.

The contract was full of concessions to make it possible for the team to operate in the 6,500-seat Corral. The board agreed to rent at a flat rate rather than on a percentage of gate receipts. The Stampede got no share of television revenue, undertook to spend $150,000 on improvements. Skalbania, meanwhile had contacted the Seaman brothers and sold them a forty-nine percent interest in the Flames. Then he discovered that the trust deed for the new rink would contain a restriction on how the profits were to be split between the professional team's owners and amateur hockey. Skalbania's interest in Calgary hockey evaporated and he sold his fifty-one percent interest to a joint venture composed of the Seaman brothers, Ralph Scurfield, Norman Green, Harley Hotchkiss, and Norman Kwong.

After the senior authorities selected the design of the rink, named it the Saddledome, and ordered its construction on the Stampede grounds, there remained only the awarding of the contract to manage the Saddledome to the Calgary Exhibition and Stampede. This was done on November 16, 1982 after the Stampede directors agreed to spend $2,600,000 on lounge and restaurant facilities and another $1,200,000 on its scoreboards.

The Saddledome gave the Stampede a second centerpiece to the Roundup Centre/Corral Complex. The Roundup

Centre focused attention on the service it could render to Alberta agriculture; the Saddledome would do the same for its other constituency—the people of Calgary. In particular, after hockey, the new center would enable management to bring musical and other attractions to Calgary that had previously bypassed the city. The ink was barely dry on the management contract before a drive was on to bring in Vera Lynn, the world-famous British songstress, for an emotional, nostalgia-packed evening before a sold-out house. By this time, of course, the Calgary Flames were moved in for a sold-out 1983–84 season.

But all this again is ahead of the story. The 1970s cannot be left without noting the importance of the improvements to the facilities which came about in that decade from goodwill gestures of Calgary business and community groups.

In addition to the Kinsmen Center, which provided a facility for year-round use, the Kinsmen Club provided $300,000 to finance the improvement of the Elbow River banks and completion of the river park. The Calgary Samaritan Club sponsored the Suntree Park, the center for the free attractions on the grounds. The Revelstoke Company sponsored an outdoor show ring. With the completion of the new grandstand the Jaycees provided $475,000 to build the centerfield children's playground and picnic area. Imasco Ltd. donated $250,000 to help landscape the south side of Fourteenth Avenue from the Macleod Trail to Fifth Street East. Burns Meats Ltd. assisted the board in the construction of Weadickville. The Coca Cola Company contributed $300,000 to a children's playground which, unfortunately, had to be dismantled, along with the Kinsmen Center and Revelstoke Acres, to make way for the Saddledome.

The effect of the landscaping and tree planting and the expansion and improvement of the Indian village, was substantially to improve the aesthetics of Stampede Park. To continue the process the board laid plans for a $2,000,000 long-term beautification program to be financed from parking fees.

As the new Roundup Centre was going up the construction of a new operations center for the food services department was built at the corner of Fourteenth Avenue and Fourth Street. The building recognized the increasing importance of food and beverage service to the profit and loss statement. From $243,000 profit on sales of $3,122,000 in 1978, food services net income doubled and redoubled until in 1982 net income was $1,187,000 on sales of $5,956,000.

That profit was achieved, moreover, during a year in which the Calgary boom had collapsed. Interest rates soared to historic peaks and the Calgary Exhibition and Stampede was caught like everybody else. In 1978 it paid out less than $1,000,000 interest on its current and long-term debt. In 1982 the interest charges amounted to $3,476,000 and the company wound up the year with a whopping $2,137,000 loss on its operation despite a record gross income of $38,384,000. Such a loss naturally triggered a vigorous drive for economy and retrenchment and the following year the company got back into the black with a net income of $1,669,000.

The figures that get bandied about in the annual reports of the Calgary Exhibition and Stampede—$45,874,824 gross revenue for 1984, net operating income of $4,741,889, a net income overall of $377,931, Stampede attendance of 963,660 and gross attendance at the grounds of 3,960,000—chronicle the century of growth of a unique Canadian institution.

Another set of figures might also be used to highlight the growth of the Calgary Exhibition and Stampede. They are the two hundred and fifty employees who now constitute the permanent staff, compared with the half dozen who were needed when the Stampede was welded permanently to the Exhibition in 1923. But the best numbers of all to illustrate the growth of the organization are the ballpark numbers of two thousand volunteers that serve on the fifty-seven committees that are the heart and soul of the organization.

The preface to the annual reports for some years has begun with this sentence: "The Calgary Exhibition & Stampede is a non-profit organization which leases Stampede Park from the City of Calgary for the purpose of conducting the annual Calgary Exhibition & Stampede and its related operations." The emphasis in that sentence should be on the last three words—"its related operations." As the operations in Stampede Park were roaring through to the organization's centennial, those "related operations" were attracting three million people a year to more than three hundred separate events on the grounds.

Nor was the end of growth anywhere in sight! Contemplating the future, the Stampede might borrow the reply of Jerry Potts, the frontiersman guide of the North West Mounted Police, who, when asked, "What is beyond yonder mountain?" replied, "N'other Mountain!"

The Stampede's ghost of Jerry Potts would reply, "N'other Centennial!"

And what a centennial it will be, for the first giant stride toward that far-off event will be the 1988 Winter Olympics in the Saddledome in Stampede Park. That will be the climax of a herculean effort of an army of Calgarians. But it will be more than a climax, it will be a springboard into an infinitely greater future the second time 'round.

Appendixes

Year	City Population	Attendance
1884	506	
1886	2,000	500
1891	3,876	
1900		2,500
1901	4,091	
1904		6,322
1906	11,967	
1908	25,000	100,051
1909		55,375
1910		77,804
1911	43,704	91,097
1912		99,447
1913		104,529
1914		89,386
1915		81,828
1916	56,514	103,433
1917		110,028
1918		115,665
1919		127,248
1920		103,433
1921	63,305	96,120
1922		97,732
1923		137,838
1924		167,279
1925		178,668
1926	65,291	197,471
1927		210,879
1928		243,985
1929		258,469
1930		202,626
1931	81,636	198,118
1932		174,676
1933		188,436
1934		214,578
1935		222,808
1936	83,407	213,450
1937	85,726	220,554
1938		223,425
1939		240,035
1940		244,849
1941	87,267	267,420
1942		234,281
1943		265,852
1944	97,241	285,458
1945		294,101
1946		339,748
1947		334,464
1948	104,718	376,983
1949		407,954
1950		373,135
1951	129,060	408,267
1952		433,140
1953		451,837
1954		482,281
1955		520,794
1956	179,711	521,271
1957		538,375
1958	206,831	549,336
1959	218,418	591,715
1960	235,428	527,933
1961	241,675	514,857
1962	269,068	585,667
1963	276,975	572,246
1964	294,924	573,560
1965	311,116	559,764
1966	323,289	654,120
1967	335,806	798,575
1968	354,856	853,620
1969	369,025	803,764
1970	385,436	769,344
1971	398,034	895,097
1972	412,777	908,035
1973	424,787	993,777
1974	433,389	973,538
1975	453,812	878,644
1976	470,043	1,015,682
1977	487,569	1,069,830
1978	505,637	1,023,804
1979	530,816	983,096
1980	560,618	993,364
1981	592,743	1,063,289
1982	623,133	992,133
1983	620,692	941,040
1984	—	963,660

Calgary Spring Bull Sale

Year	# Sold	Amount
1901	64	$ 5,451
1911	86	8,362
1921	478	74,962
1931	570	98,410
1941	670	158,835
1951	729	816,375
1961	852	528,210
1971	537	551,055
1981	607	2,692,675

Directors of the Calgary Exhibition and Stampede since 1912

Abercrombie, V. W.
Adams, C. W.
Adams, E. D.

Bailey, Alex G.
Bailey, Eleanor
Baker, A. T.
Baker, C. M.
Barker, N. Stewart
Batchelor, Dudley E.
Bell, G. Max
Black, D. E.
Blackburn, L. C.

Boake, M. A.
Bowlen, J. J.
Brown, Ian S.
Brown, Jack
Brown, M. L.
Brown, O. E.
Burns, P.

Cahill, J. W.
Cameron, Holland
Caniff, A.
Carlyle, T. M.
Christie, N. J.

Chritchley, E. T.
Church, George
Church, Dr. R. B.
Collicutt, Frank
Copithorne, Marshall
Copithorne, W. H.
Crawford, George L.
Crawford-Frost, W. A.
Cross, A. E.
Cross, Clifton C.
Cross, Donald
Cross, J. B.

D'Arcy, J. F.
Davidson, J. W.
Dean, Basil
Dewey, E. J.
Dinning, Bob
Dinning, R. J.
Douglas, C. W.
Dutton, Mervyn

Edworthy, George
Egbert, W. G. N.

Finn, F. C.

Fowler, W. G.
Fox, Gordon

Gant, W. M.
Graves, W. Roy
Gray, James K.
Gregg, H. T. R.
Grogan, Jack A.

Hanson, M. L.
Harvie, Neil S.
Hays, Harry W.
Hays, Dr. Thos. E.

Henker, Harold
Herbert, G. F.
Hill, George
Holman, J. L.
Hook, Watson
Hornibrook, T. A.
Hutton, G. H.

Irwin, Ian

Jenkins, Ron
Johnston, Fred

Kennedy, Charles

Laidlaw, R. W. A.
Lane, George
Langford, Harry G.

Laycock, Jos. H.
Laycock, Thos.
Lepper, F. H.
Lougheed, E. Peter
Love, H. G.

Macarthur, W. R.
McBeth, F.
McCulloch, John
McDaniel, R. R.
MacDonald, A. Howard
McGuire, A. H.
MacInnes, Richard B.
McKillop, Archie
McKinnon, Ed
McKinnon, D. Keith
McKinnon, Fred

McKinnon, J. Angus
McVean, Bruce
Main, Dale S.
Manning, F. Clar
Marker, Dr. C. P.
Matthews, D. C.
Matthews, R. C.
Minnes, Patsi
Moore, W. K.
Moyer, J. W.

Nesbitt, Jack

O'Connor, Ed
O'Connor, Graham

Pallesen, P.
Parslow, I. V.

Peacock, Jack
Pearce, Gordon
Phillips, Ross
Poffenroth, R. W.
Porter, M. M.

Roberts, Ed R.
Robertson, W. E.
Rock, P. J.
Ross, D. A.
Rutherford, Dr. J. G.
Ruttle, I. G.

Smart, James
Smith, P. N.

Taprell, C. D.
Taylor, Bert E.

Tennis, Ward
Thornton, Harold
Turner, John

VanWart, I. S. G.

Walker, Col. James
Ward, R. W.
Webster, G. H.
Wilson, John Jr.
Wolley-Dod, A. G.
Wright, Bryce
Wright, Dr. Howard P.

Young, D. J.
Young, R. A. M.
Yule, J. Charles

Opened & Closed Stampede

	Opened	Closed
1929	The Hon. J. D. McGregor, Manitoba	Grant Hall
1930	The Hon. J. E. Brownlee	
1931	The Hon. W. L. Walsh	
1932	Viscount Rothermere	Brig. Gen. Allison
1933	The Hon. H. Guthrie, Min. of Justice	Senator P. Burns
1934	The Rt. Hon. R. B. Bennett	
1935	Maj. Gen. Sir Jas. H. MacBrien,	Maj. Gen. Sir Jas. H. MacBrien,
1936	The Hon. W. L. Walsh	
1937	The Hon. J. G. Gardiner	His Excel. Baron Tweedsmuir
1938	Brig. G. R. Pearkes	Hon. Alistair Buchan
1939	Hon. D. B. Mullen	W. M. Neal
1940	His Worship Mayor Andrew Davison	W. Switzler, H. L. Anderson
1941	The Hon. J. Bracken	Elwood A. Hughes
1942	Ordinary Seaman Instructor T. Campbell/Private George Clements/LAC Ev. Bunnell/Private Verlyn Tollison, U.S. Army	
1943	Air Vice Marshal G. R. Howsam	His Worship Mayor Andrew Davison
1944	R. W. Ward	Brigadier Edward S. Burke-Gaffney
1945	E. L. Richardson	His Excel. Viscount Bennett
1946		N. J. Christie
1947	The Hon. Ernest C. Manning	Jack Oakie
1948	A. L. Smith	C. M. Baker
1949	His Worship Mayor H. C. McCallum	Ambassador L. Steinhardt
1950	The Rt. Hon. Louis St. Laurent	His Excel. Viscount Alexander
1951	Frank Collicutt	John Fisher
1952	Lord Lovat	Guy Weadick
1953	N. J. Christie	The Rt. Hon. Louis St. Laurent
1954	The Hon. Ernest C. Manning	The Hon. J. J. Bowlen
1955	Commissioner L. H. Nicholson	Norman Luxton & Charles Beil
1956	His Excel. Vincent Massey	Clem Gardner
1957	N. R. Crump	The Rt. Hon. John Diefenbaker
1958	The Hon. D. S. Harkness	The Hon. Ernest C. Manning
1959	The Hon. J. A. D. McCurdy	The Hon. D. S. Harkness

	Opened		Closed
1960	The Rt. Hon. John Diefenbaker		General Sir Neil Ritchie
1961	Hon. George Hees		Mr. Justice M. M. Porter and Charles Beil
1962	Major Gen. J. M. Rockingham		His Worship Mayor Harry Hays
1963	The Hon. J. Percy Page		Gordon McGregor
1964	The Rt. Hon. Lester B. Pearson		Herman Linder
1965	Walt Disney		Maurice E. Hartnett
1966	U.S. Senator Robert F. Kennedy		Commissioner G. B. McClellan, RCMP
1967	Earl Mountbatten of Burma		Eric L. Harvie, Q.C.
1968	HRH The Duke of Kent		His Worship Mayor Jack Leslie
1969	His Excel. Roland Michener		D. E. Black
1970	His Worship Mayor Jean Drapeau		His Worship Mayor R. Sykes & Ed O'Connor
1971	Bobby Orr		Freckles Brown & Ed O'Connor
1972	The Hon. Peter Lougheed		The Hon. H. A. Olson
1973	Her Majesty Queen Elizabeth II		The Hon. C. Merv Leitch
1974	The Hon. Dr. J. W. Grant MacEwan		The Hon. Peter Lougheed
1975	Bobby Hull		Mrs. Mary Dover
1976	Steven M. Ford		7 Chiefs of Treaty 7
1977	HRH the Prince of Wales		Admiral R. H. Falls
1978	The Rt. Hon. Pierre Trudeau		The Rt. Hon. Pierre Trudeau
1979	Ken Read		Ken Read
1980	The Hon. Peter Lougheed		The Hon. Frank Lynch-Staunton
1981	His Excel. Edward Schreyer		Steve Podborsky
1982	Herman Linder		Warren Cooper
1983	Mickey & Minnie Mouse		Lanny McDonald
1984	Dr. Sally Ride		His Worship Mayor Ralph Klein

Parade Marshals

1956	His Worship Mayor Hiram McCallum, Toronto	1974	C. H. "Punch" Dickins/Sir Douglas Bader, V. C./Capt. Eugene Cernan, USN, NASA Astronaut
1957	His Worship Mayor Wilfred Hamel, Quebec City	1975	The Hon. Peter Lougheed
1958	His Worship Mayor Fred Hume, Vancouver	1976	Steven M. Ford
1959	Bing Crosby	1977	HRH the Prince of Wales/Commissioner M. Nadon, RCMP/7 Treaty 7 Indian Chiefs
1960	Phil Harris		
1961	H. E. Senora Lopez Mateos	1978	The Rt. Hon. Pierre Trudeau
1962	Commissioner C. W. Harvison, RCMP	1979	Ken Read/The Hon. Ralph Steinhauer/Wilf Carter
1963	Bob Hope		
1964	The Rt. Hon. Lester B. Pearson	1980	The Hon. Peter Lougheed/Ken Taylor
1965	Walt Disney	1981	His Excellency Edward Schreyer
1966	Red Adair	1982	Larry Mahan/Joe Alexander/Tom Bews/ Tom Erickson/Tommy Dorchester
1967	Nancy Greene		
1968	Bill Henry	1983	Mickey Mouse & Minnie Mouse
1969	Ron Northcott & Rink	1984	Wilf Carter/Gaetan Boucher
1970	Arthur Godfrey		
1971	The Rt. Hon. Pierre Trudeau		
1972	Chief Dan George		
1973	Commissioner W. L. Higgitt, RCMP		

Stampede Queen and Princesses

1946	Patsy Rodgers		Karen Downey	1967	Patsy Allan		Carol Ovans
1947	Doreen Richardson		Kay Larsen		Candace Smith	1977	Gillian Newman
	Eva Brewster	1958	Jennie Chow		Bonnie MacGregor		Sylvia Wittmoser
1948	Gloria Klaver		Beverley-Ann Haeh	1968	Diane Leach		Brenda Orr
	Marg Forsgren		Isabella Hamilton		Heather Lawrence	1978	Dawne VanWart
	Shirley Kemp	1959	Julie Akkerman		Arlene Weidner		Judy Shaw
1949	Merle Stier		Doreen Wynne	1969	Carol Burns		Patti Stephens
	Inez Melby		Margaret Powell		Patty Johnston	1979	Pam Jonassen
	Marion Birchall	1960	Margot Turney		Winnifred Reid		Shauna Harrington
1950	Eileen Beckner		Judy Taylor	1970	Vicky Hayden		Brenda Warden
	Gussie MacDonald		Gail Leonard		Lynn Boake	1980	Jodi Merriman
	Ann Dutchak	1961	Marie Sharpe		Cheryl Going		Dawn Pringle
1951	Marion McMahon		Lynn Puckett	1971	Leslie MacDonald		Audrey Collins
	June Dewhirst		Sharon Taylor		Wendy Copithorne	1981	Cathy Robinson
	Shirley Clarke	1962	Donna Thomson		Shirley Inkster		Diane Hamilton
1952	Sherry Moore		Linda Rennels	1972	Patti Girling		Barb Penner
	Donna Christie		Fran Reeder		Diane Wallace	1982	Michelle Williamson
	Helen Smith	1963	Frances Swann		Dawn McLean		Penny Watt
1953	Edith Edge		Beryl Edge	1973	Suzanne Randall		Jenny Baillod
1954	Evelyn Eaglespeaker		Dixie Girletz		Joan Horne	1983	Shannon Leinweber
	Peggy Fisher	1964	Sharon Patterson		Betty Knight		Marlie Milne
	Kay Dench		Gail Henry	1974	Happy Barlow		Sharon Dacen
1955	Mary Ellen Jones		Gwenda Marshall		Karen Kraft	1984	Pat Brown
	Joan Johnson	1965	Donna Israelson		Sis Thacker		Michelle Fussell
	Elaine Kent		Frances Chamberlain	1975	Barbie Howard		Monica Perchaluk
1956	Shirley Willock		Mary MacDonald		Chris Wigle		
	Carolyn Scheoppe	1966	Betty Wright		Stacy Kirk		
	Kay Marshall		Lorraine McLean	1976	Cindy Moores		
1957	Marquitta Elton		Anne Neilson		Wynne Anderson		

Stampede Rodeo Champions & Trophy Winners

Year	All Around North American	All Around Cowboy	Saddle Bronc
1912		Clem Gardner	Tom Three Persons
1919			Yakima Canutt
1923			Pete Vandermeer
1924		Pete La Grande	Pete La Grande
1925			Al Falconer
1926			Mike Stuart
1927			Pete Knight
1928	Paddy Ryan	Lee Ferris	Slim Watrin
1929		Lee Ferris	Earl Thode
1930	Paddy Ryan	Frank Sharp	Chuck Wilson
1931	Eddie Woods	Herman Linder	Gene Ross
1932	Herman Linder	Herman Linder	Pete Knight
1933	Eddie Woods	Herman Linder	Pete Knight
1934	Herman Linder	Herman Linder	Stub Bartlemay
1935	Herman Linder	Herman Linder	Turk Greenough
1936	Herman Linder	Herman Linder	Carl Thode
1937	Don Thomson	Don Thomson	John Hordan
1938	Herman Linder	Herman Linder	Earl Thode
1939	Clark Lund	Clark Lund	Guy Cash

Year			
1940	Jack Wade	A. K. Lund	Nick Knight
1941	Frank McDonald	Frank McDonald	Jerry Ambler
1942	Arnold Montgomery	J. Robinson	Doff Aber
1943	Arnold Montgomery	Wally Lindstrom	Turk Greenough
1944	Bill Linderman	Wally Lindstrom	Bill Linderman
1945	Bill Linderman	J. Robinson	Bill Linderman
1946	Bill Linderman	Frank Duce	Jerry Ambler
1947	Bill Linderman	Frank Duce	Jim Like
1948	Bill Linderman	Ken Brower	Bill Linderman
1949	Eddy Akridge	Reg Kesler	Casey Tibbs
1950	Gerald Roberts	Reg Kesler	Casey Tibbs
1951	Bill Linderman	Harold Mandeville	Bill Linderman
1952	Wilf Girletz	Wilf Girletz	Frank Duce
1953	Del Haverty	Gordon Earl	Deb Copenhaver
1954	Gordon Earl	Gordon Earl	Marty Wood
1955	Casey Tibbs	Wilf Girletz	Deb Copenhaver
1956	Keith Hyland	Keith Hyland	Bob Robinson
1957	Keith Hyland	Keith Hyland	Marty Wood
1958	Guy Weeks	Wilf Girletz	Deb Copenhaver
1959	Del Haverty	Wilf Girletz	Winston Bruce

Year			
1960	George Myren	George Myren	Jim Tescher
1961	Guy Weeks	George Myren	Marty Wood
1962	Guy Weeks	George Myren	Leo Brown
1963	Mac Griffith	Kenny McLean	Ronnie Raymond
1964	Kenny McLean	Kenny McLean	Marty Wood
1965	Kenny McLean	Kenny McLean	Marty Wood
1966	Jim Houston	Doug Flanigan	Bob Gottfriedson
1967	Tom Bews	Tom Bews	Chuck Swanson
1968	Jim Houston	Kenny McLean	Kenny McLean
1969	Gid Garstad	Gid Garstad	Jim Smith
1970	Gid Garstad	Gid Garstad	Jerry Sinclair

Year	All Around Championship	Saddle Bronc
1971	Benny Reynolds	Tom Tate
1972	Phil Lyne	Darryl Kong
1973	Dale Rose	Jim Smith
1974	Larry Mahan	Melvin Coleman
1975	Larry Ferguson	Bobby Berger
1976	Tom Ferguson	Joe Marvel
1977	Jack Hannum	Joe Marvel & David Bothum
1978	Roy Cooper	Wilf Hyland
1979	Gary Zilverberg	Andy Copeland
1980	Gerald Bruhn	Gerald Bruhn
1981	Harley Hook	Butch Knowles & Gary Bruhn (NW rodeo team)
1982	Robert Hoff	Bobby Brown & Mel Hyland
1983	John Smith	Brad Gjermundson & Butch Knowles
1984	Greg Schlosser	Brad Gjermundson & Bud Monroe

Year	Bareback Bronc	Novice Saddle Rider	Calf Roping
1912	Jim Massey		
1919	Jesse Stahl		
1923	Kenneth Cooper		Eddie Bowlen
1924	D. McDonald		Ray Knight
1925	Norman Edge		Mike Stuart
1926	Harry Knight	Harry Knight	Ray Knight
1927	Jack Hill	Pete Knight	Pete Bruisehead
1928	Norman Edge	Leo Watrin	Eddie Bowlen
1929	Herman Linder	Herman Linder	Floyd Peters
1930	Lee Ferris	Pete Knight	Floyd Peters
1931	Lee Ferris	Slim Watrin	K. H. Galbraith
1932	Smoky Snyder	Harry Knight	Pat Burton
1933	Nate Waldrun	Pete Knight	Pat Burton
1934	Herman Linder	Herman Linder	A. M. Burton
1935	Don Thomson	Harley Walsh	Pat Burton
1936	Herman Linder	Harley Walsh	Warner Linder
1937	Muff Doan	Jerry Ambler	Pat Burton
1938	Urban Doan	Herman Linder	Hugh Connell
1939	Chet McCarty	Sykes Robinson	Al Galarneau
1940	Paul Carney	Harley Walsh	Pat Burton

Year	Bareback Bronc	Novice Saddle Rider	Calf Roping
1941	Urban Doan	Wally Lindstrom	Bill Mounkes
1942	Jack Wade	Urban Doan	Jack Morton
1943	Urban Doan	Urban Doan	Floyd Peters
1944	Mitch Owens	Carl Olsen	Andy Gamlin
1945	Gerald Roberts	Frank Duce	Floyd Peters
1946	Jimmy Schumaker	Frank Duce	Al Galarneau
1947	Jimmy Schumaker	Bob Lauder	Geo Leask
1948	Ken Brower	Jim Turner	F. C. Stover
1949	Gene Rambo	Wilf Girletz	Jimmie Cooper
1950	Casey Tibbs	Lem Horner	Rudy Doucette
1951	Bill Linderman	Bill Johnson	Jim Stavely
1952	Jim Shoulders	Bob Chalmers	F. C. Stover
1953	Del Haverty	Keith Hyland	F. C. Stover
1954	Buck Rutherford	Alfred Owens	Cliff Vandergrift
1955	Gene Gunderson	Jack Hooker	Byron Wolford
1956	Alf Owen	Ray Vanderiett	Byron Wolford
1957	Don Wilson	Roy Robinson	Sonny Hendrick
1958	John Hawkins	Garth Maxwell	Dean Oliver
1959	Del Haverty	Bob Gottfriedsen	Dale Smith
1960	Jack Buschbaum	Peter Bruisehead	Dale Smith
1961	George Myren	Wayne Vold	Vernon Kerns
1962	Jim Roeser	Shawn Davis	Mel Potter
1963	Buddy Peake	Ivan Daines	Dale Smith
1964	Doug Flanigan	Jack Phipps	Dean Oliver
1965	Jim Clifford	Ivan Daines	Lee Ferris
1966	Harry Tompkins	Mel Hyland	Richard Stowers
1967	Jim Mihalek	John Picray	Lee Cockrell
1968	Clyde Vamvoras	Ed Biegler	Lorne Wells
1969	Larry Mahan	Oliver Lewis	Dean Oliver
1970	Paul Mayo	Rocky Hubley	Warren Wuthier
1971	Clyde Vamvoras	Bart Brower	Tooter Waites
1972	Joe Alexander	Tom Robertson	Ronny Sewalt
1973	Ace Berry	Charlie Simmons	Tom Ferguson
1974	Larry Mahan	Clinton Morin	Gary Ledford
1975	Jim Dix	Kirk Thomson	Barry Burk
1976	Royce Smith	Lee Coleman	Dean Oliver
1977	Mickey Young	Lee Coleman	Jack Hannum
1978	Chick Elms	Duane Daines	Roy Cooper
1979	Rod Sinclair	Tim Kelly	Scott Clements
1980	Kevin Jefferies	Keith Stewart	Danny Cross
1981	Jim Dunn & Pat Price (NW rodeo team)	Guy Shapka	Roy Cooper & Sparky Trotter (BC rodeo team)
1982	J. C. Trujillo & Jimmy Cleveland	Marty Kelliher	Roy Cooper & Barry Burk
1983	Jim Dunn & Steve Dunham	Allan McKenzie	Chris Lybbert & Roger Gunsch
1984	Steve Dunham & Larry Peabody	Mark Leggette	Greg Cassidy & Roy Cooper

Year	Brahma Bull Riding	Chuckwagon Race Driver/Sponsor	Steer Decorating
1923	C. Patterson	Bill Somers/ Dan Riley	
1924	V. McDonald	Bagley/ Tom Lauder	

Year	Brahma Bull Riding	Chuckwagon Race Driver/Sponsor	Steer Decorating
1925	Norman Edge	Collins/Jim Ross	
1926	Tom McCoy	Dick Cosgrave	
1927	Norman Edge	Tom Lauder	Paddy Ryan
1928	Lee Ferris	Tom Lauder	Bob Crosby
1929	Frank Sharp	Jim Ross	Everett Bowman
1930	Eddie Woods	Dick Cosgrave	John Bowman
1931	Smoky Snyder	Clem Gardner	Oral Zumwalt
1932	Smoky Snyder	Jim Ross	Ralph Stanton
1933	Frank Sharp	Dick Cosgrave	Frank McDonald
1934	Herman Linder	Sam Johnson	Chick Hannon
1935	Herman Linder	Dick Cosgrave	Warner Linder
1936	Herman Linder	Dick Cosgrave	Warner Linder
1937	Don Thomson	Dick Cosgrave	A. K. Lund
1938	Herman Linder	Dick Cosgrave	Warner Linder
1939	Urban Doan	Sam Johnson	Ray Mavity
1940	Jack Wade	Dick Cosgrave	Jack Wade
1941	Jerry Ambler	Chas Lundseth	Frank McDonald
1942	Jerry Ambler	Dick Cosgrave	Jimmy Wells
1943	Jerry Ambler	Dick Cosgrave	Jimmy Robertson
1944	Muff Doan	Theo Thage	Pud Adair
1945	Jimmy Schumaker	Alvin Hilker	Floyd Peters
1946	Johnny Tubbs	Ron Glass/John Phelan	Tom Duce
1947	R. Thompson	Ron Glass/John Phelan	Scotty Bagnell
1948	Jim Shoulders	Johnny Swaine	Elliott Calhoun
1949	Buck Rutherford	Ron Glass/Johnny Phelan	Everett Vold
1950	Jim Shoulders	Bob Heberling	Everett Vold
1951	Jim Shoulders	Hank Willard/Nelson	Tom Duce
1952	Jim Shoulders	Hank Willard/Commodore Allen	Jim Jones
1953	Gordon Earl	Hank Willard/Commodore Allen	Harry Dodging Horse
1954	Gordon Earl	Hank Willard/Commodore Allen	Francis Many-wounds
1955	Buck Boyce	Hank Willard	Stan Walker
1956	Dick Nash	Lloyd Nelson	Bud Butterfield
1957	Bruce Coker	Dale Flett/Peter Bawden	Harold Mandeville
1958	Gid Garstad	Bill Greenwood/Merle Anderson	Bud Van Cleave
1959	Jim Shoulders	Hally Walgenbach/Peter Bawden	Bud Butterfield
1960	Ed Letourneau	Hally Walgenbach/O. Burkinshaw	Stan Walker
1961	Bob Shepherd	Hally Walgenbach/O. Burkinshaw Dale Flett/Peter Bawden	C. R. Jones

Year	Brahma Bull Riding	Chuckwagon Race Driver/Sponsor	Steer Decorating
1962	Bill Hand	Dale Flett/Peter Bawden	Bud Butterfield
1963	Mac Griffith	Dale Flett/Peter Bawden	Bud Butterfield
1964	Joe Green	Hally Walgenbach/Pratt & McKay	Stan Walker & Alex Laye
1965	Gid Garstad	Bill Greenwood/Janko Brothers	Arnold Haraga
1966	Gid Garstad	Bill Greenwood/Siegert Nielson	Stan Walker

Year	Brahma Bull Riding	Chuckwagon Race Driver/Sponsor	Steer Wrestling
1967	Larry Condon	Bob Cosgrave/Flett Brothers	Roy Duvall
1968	Tony Haberer	Garry Dorchester/Denham Brothers	Mark Schricker
1969	Gary Leffew	Bob Cosgrave/John Irwin	Dave Penner
1970	Jack Ward	Tom Dorchester/Jack Scheckter	Ed Galemba
1971	Bill Nelson	Tom Dorchester/Stewart Ranch	Billy Hale
1972	Phil Lyne	Ralph Vigen/R. J. Keen	Bob Marshall
1973	Leo Brown	Slim Helme	Harley May
1974	Brian Claypool	Kelly Sutherland/Norman Nilsen	Tom Ferguson
1975	Leander Frey	Kelly Sutherland/Norman Nilsen	Tom Ferguson
1976	Brian Claypool	Ralph Vigen/Northern Metallic Sales	Larry Dawson
1977	Sandy Kirby	Kelly Sutherland/Archie Hackwell	Fred Larsen
1978	Joe Dodds	Kelly Sutherland/Maclin Ford	Fred Hirschy
1979	Greg Pennington	Buddy Bensmiller/Lloydminster Spill	Dave Hofer
1980	Colin Murnion	Herman Flad/Comanche Drilling	Bill Hammond
1981	Lee Newman & Lavar Winebarger	Bruce Craige/Century 21 Real Estate	Harley Hook & Sid Britt
1982	Dale Johansen	Dave Lewis/Panee Memorial Agriplex	Ken Guenthner & Greg Butterfield
1983	Wacey Cathey & John Smith	Tom Glass/Gulf Oil	Sole Smith & Lee Phillips
1984	Dale Johansen & David Urick	Dallas Dorchester/J & L Supply Ltd.	Tom Switzer

Year	Wild Cow Milking	Wild Horse Race
1923		Neil Campbell
1924	E. Burton	Frank Hodgkins
1925	Jack Brown	Frank Hodgkins

Year	Wild Cow Milking	Wild Horse Race
1926	Bert Long	
1927	Richard Merchant	Frank Hodgkins
1928	King Bearspaw	Hugie Long
1929	Irby Mundy	Norman Edge
1930	W. J. Helmer	Archie Miller
1931	W. J. Gray	Geo McIntosh
1932	Johnny Left Hand	
1933	Irby Mundy	
1934	Roy Matthews	
1935	Bob Crosby	
1936	Clark Lund	
1937	Ernest Hall	
1938	Irby Mundy	
1939	Chet Baldwin	
1940	Cliff Vandergrift	
1941	Fred Burton	
1942	A. Galarneau	Urban Doan
1943	Cliff Vandergrift	Chet Baldwin
1944	Johnny Left Hand	Ken Leadley
1945	Cliff Vandergrift	John Spotted Eagle
1946	Don Leask	Cliff Vandergrift
1947	Bill McLean	Cliff Vandergrift
1948	F. C. Stover	John Spotted Eagle
1949	Fred Galarneau	Cliff Vandergrift
1950	Don Leask	Bill Graham
1951	Mac Leask	Cliff Vandergrift
1952	Mac Leask	Bill Graham
1953	George Leask	Bill Graham
1954	George Leask	Chip Nunamker
1955	George Leask	Cliff Vandergrift
1956	Herb Christie	Don McLeod
1957	Reg Kesler	Orville Strandquist
1958	Orville Strandquist	Cliff Vandergrift
1959	Reg Kesler	Cliff Vandergrift
1960	Cliff Vandergrift	Len Chartier
1961	Alex Laye	Roy Groves
1962	Reg Kesler	Bill Graham
1963	Gilbert Bintz	Orville Strandquist
1964	Kenny McLean	Jim Clifford
1965	Wilf Girletz	Cliff Vandergrift
1966	Wilf Girletz	Greg Kesler
1967	Ed Cochlan	Greg Kesler
1968	Clark Schlosser	Ernie Dorin
1969	Lorne Wells	Ernie Dorin
1970	Allan Currier	Ernie Dorin
1971	Ed Cochlan	Don Copithorne
1972	Pat McHugh	Don Copithorne
1973	Lorne Wells	Ernie Dorin
1974	Lorne Wells	Don Copithorne
1975	Lorne Wells	Don Copithorne
1976	Pat McHugh	Ernie Dorin
1977	Lorne Wells	Roy Groves
1978	Alex Laye	Dave Shields
1979	Kelly Rowsell	Don Copithorne
1980	Chuck Swanson	Roy Groves
1981	Bill Nugent	Trevor Helmig
1982	Allan Currier	Glen Helmig

Year	Wild Cow Milking	Wild Horse Race
1983	Allan Currier	Don Copithorne
1984	Keith Smith	Don Copithorne

Year	Novice Bareback Riding
1977	Robin Burwash
1978	Wayne Fullerton
1979	Dale Blagen
1980	Rod Bevans
1981	Clint Corey
1982	Rod Bevans
1983	Rod Bevans
1984	Shawn Orr

Year	Wild Steer Riding	Year	
1924	C. Brunner	1965	Greg Butterfield & Buddy Hamilton
1925	W. Goodrich	1966	Doug Vold
1926	Jas Boyle	1967	Mason Cockx & Brian Claypool
1927	Joe Fox		
1928	Bill Bagley	1968	Kevin Fox
1929	Joe Fox	1969	Dale Greenwood
1930	Paddy Cayan	1970	Cam Hamilton
1931	Gerald Ambler	1971	Buddy Currie
1932	Joe Gray	1972	Glen Freeborn
1933	Duncan Cragg	1973	Marty Lyle
1934	L. C. Cawsey	1974	Ryan Smith
1935	Bobby Swain	1975	Tyler Miller
1936	Joe Kootenay	1976	Ty Northcott
1937	Archie Preston	1977	Jay Shockey
1938	Kenneth McLean	1978	Bruce Kostelansky
1939	Earl Mayfield	1979	Jerry Manvel
1940	Glen Lee	1980	Eddie Fast
1941	George Aldoff	1981	John Alstott
1942	Lyle Doan	1982	Shawn Harder
1943	Thomas Jerry	1983	Rod Hay
1944	Horace Holloway	1984	Frank Herbert
1945	Bob Duce		
1946	Red Mulgrew		
1947	Bob McKay		
1948	Harry Dodging Horse		
1949	Thos Lauder		
1950	Cody Morris		
1951	Charles Cassidy		
1952	James Grey		
1953	Tommy Yellow Sun		
1954	Bill Stuckley		
1955	Jerry Weiss		
1956	Keith Powell		
1957	Frankie Cockx		
1958	Wayne Vold		
1959	Ivan Daines		
1960	Ivan Daines		
1961	Ivan Daines		
1962	Franklin Daines		
1963	John Dodds		
1964	Brian Anderson		

Index